MISSIONARY INTERESTS

MISSIONARY INTERESTS

PROTESTANT AND MORMON MISSIONS IN THE NINETEENTH AND TWENTIETH CENTURIES

Edited by David Golding and Christopher Cannon Jones

WITH A FOREWORD BY LAURIE F. MAFFLY-KIPP

CORNELL UNIVERSITY PRESS

Ithaca and London

Publication of this book was made possible by generous grants from the Church History Department of the Church of Jesus Christ of Latter-day Saints and the Neal A. Maxwell Institute for Religious Scholarship at Brigham Young University.

Copyright © 2024 by Cornell University

All rights reserved. Except for brief quotations in a review, this book, or parts thereof, must not be reproduced in any form without permission in writing from the publisher. For information, address Cornell University Press, Sage House, 512 East State Street, Ithaca, New York 14850. Visit our website at cornellpress.cornell.edu.

First published 2024 by Cornell University Press

Library of Congress Cataloging-in-Publication Data

Names: Golding, David, 1982– editor. | Jones, Christopher C., 1983– editor. | Maffly-Kipp, Laurie F., 1960– writer of foreword.
Title: Missionary interests : Protestant and Mormon missions in the nineteenth and twentieth centuries / edited by David Golding and Christopher Cannon Jones, with a foreword by Laurie F. Maffly-Kipp.
Description: Ithaca [New York] : Cornell University Press, 2024. | Includes bibliographical references and index.
Identifiers: LCCN 2023039443 (print) | LCCN 2023039444 (ebook) | ISBN 9781501774423 (hardcover) | ISBN 9781501774430 (paperback) | ISBN 9781501774454 (epub) | ISBN 9781501774447 (pdf)
Subjects: LCSH: Protestants—Missions—History—19th century. | Protestants—Missions—History—20th century. | Latter Day Saints—Missions—History—19th century. | Latter Day Saints—Missions—History—20th century. | Missionaries—History—19th century. | Missionaries—History—20th century. | Latter Day Saint missionaries—History—19th century. | Latter Day Saint missionaries—History—20th century.
Classification: LCC BV2400 .M374 2024 (print) | LCC BV2400 (ebook) | DDC 207/.20909034—dc23/eng/20230908
LC record available at https://lccn.loc.gov/2023039443
LC ebook record available at https://lccn.loc.gov/2023039444

Contents

Foreword LAURIE F. MAFFLY-KIPP   vii

A Note on Terms   xi

Introduction CHRISTOPHER CANNON JONES AND DAVID GOLDING   1

1. Heathen Landscapes: Of Souls and Soils KATHRYN GIN LUM   8

2. Before "Woman's Work for Woman": Protestant Missionary Applications and Gender EMILY CONROY-KRUTZ   17

3. Humanitarian Encounter in Late Ottoman Turkey: State, American Protestant Missions, and the *Christian Herald* Armenian Relief Fund DEVRİM ÜMİT   34

4. Dueling Orientalisms: The Scottish Imagination in the Mormon Missionary Mind TAUNALYN FORD   45

5. Shoshone Worlds, Bannock Zions: Protestant and Latter-day Saint Missionary Work among the Shoshone and Bannock AMANDA HENDRIX-KOMOTO   53

6. Traveling Elders: The Latter-day Saint Gaze on Africa in the Early Twentieth Century JEFFREY G. CANNON   65

7. Earthquakes, Mudslides, and Hurricanes: Natural Disasters and Humanitarian Aid in Evangelical Missionary Strategy LAUREN F. TUREK   94

8. Inventing Rupture in India and America: Adivāsi Converts, Hindu Nationalists, and American RLDS Missionaries, 1966–1996 DAVID J. HOWLETT   105

9. Technological Christianity: Transferring Processes, Forms, and Organizational Tools within Global Missionary Encounters MELISSA WEI-TSING INOUYE   123

10. Missing Missiology: Latter-day Saint Missionary Pragmatism and the Search for Scholarship DAVID GOLDING   141

11. American Missionaries and the Struggle for Control of Christianity's Symbolic Capital DAVID A. HOLLINGER   152

Acknowledgments   167

Notes   169

Index   209

About the Authors   213

Foreword

Laurie F. Maffly-Kipp

Who cannot be fascinated by missionaries, those souls willing to renounce everything they have known in life for the sake of an ideal? Their work seems to me the most purely utopian of ventures. Incidentally (and this is something I only became aware of after beginning my own studies), I have a distant relation whose claim to fame resulted from the audacious decision to volunteer as the first Presbyterian missionary from Canada (Nova Scotia) to the New Hebrides (now Vanuatu) in the 1840s. In 1848 the Reverend John Geddie, a Scottish immigrant and minister on Prince Edward Island, packed up his wife and two young children and moved over fifteen thousand miles to eastern Melanesia. He lived there until the end of his life some two decades later, with his chief claim to fame being that he was the first representative of the London Missionary Society in that area not to be eaten by the locals. When asked what motivated him, he answered, "The love of Christ sustains us and constrains us. My heart pants to tell this miserable people the wonders of redeeming love."[1]

That response speaks volumes about the world of Christian missions, with its mix of ardent idealism, its power to motivate intensely risky action, and its simultaneous "love" for—yet derision of—the current state of the unconverted. His words are confounding, enraging, and potentially deadly all at the same time, not unlike the characteristics of Nathan Price, Barbara Kingsolver's Baptist minister in her novel *The Poisonwood Bible*, who seems constantly perched on a knife's edge between a purified faith and utter insanity. Missionaries like Geddie and Price are driven by ideals and ego, fueled by a fervor that is hard for most of us to imagine.

But it is a mistake to focus exclusively on the zealous certainty and to forget that Christian missions are, by definition, experimental. The New Testament injunction from Jesus Christ to "go and make disciples of all nations" contains little more than the advice to baptize and teach the faith to newcomers. How this happened, and when and where it should happen to particular groups of people, was never explicitly stated. Nor are the desired results of this experiment detailed in the message. This fuzziness leaves plenty of room for interpretation and improvisation—not to mention argument—over the task at hand. What exactly is a Christian mission? And which (or whose) interests are we talking about?

In chronicling the historical laboratory of the missionary experiment, the various groups of Christians that emerged from the aftermath of the early Christian era tended to stick together. Later, Catholics, then Protestants, and finally Mormons picked up the mantle of evangelization and proceeded in distinct ways, with their means determined by differing ecclesiastical organizational models and definitions of what constituted membership in the Christian community. They parted ways over the most fundamental questions: Who is authorized to baptize, or initiate, new members? What are the practical requirements of membership? Where should these missions begin? Finally, what are we trying to produce, at the end of the day? Or is it enough that we are performing the work and leaving the results to providence?

For centuries, these investigations have been carried on with little comparative examination. Why consult with one's rivals if one believes them to be wrong in the first place? The animosity between Catholics and Protestants, later joined by members of the Church of Jesus Christ of Latter-day Saints and other Mormons, left little incentive for historians within these traditions to compare tactics (although, on the ground, many missionaries were clearly looking over their shoulders and borrowing strategies from their competitors). As the study of religion became more explicitly comparative in the late twentieth century, and as other historians grew aware of the importance of evangelistic activity to the construction of nations, races, and empires, this situation began to turn. In the 1970s and 1980s, scholars of Native American and African American history, including James Axtell, Francis Paul Prucha, and Albert G. Raboteau, highlighted the comparative strategies of Catholics and Protestants in their missionary endeavors.[2]

Mormon missionaries generally have been left out of this titanic ecclesiastical battle in the scholarship on Christian missions. Although they were relative newcomers to the evangelistic scene in the 1830s, followers of Joseph Smith Jr. jumped into the missionary enterprise almost immediately. But the general scorn they faced from other Christians, along with their relatively small numbers and (initially) meager means of support, meant their efforts were not treated in any serious way by those outside their own tradition. After World War II Mormons had gained considerable cultural and financial capital in the United States, but their oblique relationship to imperial projects rendered them anomalous in the missionary context. Scholars of nationalism couldn't characterize them in a way that fit neatly into studies of empire, and their distinctive headquarters in the American West meant that their interactions with Indigenous peoples and African Americans took a unique path (one no less fraught, of course), making direct comparison difficult.

All these factors are what make this book so pathbreaking. It is precisely in the comparison of various methods, goals, and means that the full scope of the Christian missionary experiment comes into sharper focus. The German philologist Max Müller famously noted, with respect to religious traditions, that "he who knows one, knows none"—so, too, with missions. When we place Mormon, Protestant, and Catholic missions alongside one another, we see all of them in greater relief. We glimpse the differences in values, practices, institutions, technologies, and cosmologies that are otherwise implicit and assumed.

The simplest example of the vantage offered by comparison can be found in the contrast over who is authorized to conduct missions and in what capacities they are allowed to work. The chapters in this book highlight the debates over these considerations: Can women be missionaries? If so, where, and who gets to decide? Can new converts themselves serve as missionaries? If so, at what stage of their spiritual development? Perhaps most significantly in our time, as several of the chapters pointedly explain, we are faced with the issue of whether newly converted peoples (e.g., those from Africa or South America) can evangelize among the unconverted in the United States or Europe, those original "cradles" of Christian tradition. If not, what does this say about assumptions regarding race and nation?

One can see how quickly comparison explodes any easy assumptions about missions, conversion, and even the nature of Christianity itself. These insights are important as historical statements, yes. But they are also important because they afford glimpses into the tenuous nature of the missionary experiment, a venture always in flux. As with all experiments, the scientists of Christian missions confronted frequent failure, missed and novel opportunities, and unanticipated consequences: the Shoshone who used Mormon temple construction to honor their massacred relatives; the young German who relied on Latter-day Saint technologies to resist the Nazis; the natural disasters that open new doors for evangelical outreach; and the social ruptures that lead, ironically, to fundamental changes in the cultures of the missionaries themselves. So, too, missions have brought out less than noble sentiments, as evangelicals have had to determine who is "deserving" of their calling or their message. Why white and not Black South Africans? Why men and not women? Why Ottoman Christians, not Muslims—and only those who were not Catholic?

This collection reflects an important starting point in that comparative scholarly labor, one that provokes those fundamental questions at the heart of the Christian missionary enterprise. While no single volume could encompass all the missionary experiments that deserve exploration, this book takes the first steps toward the juxtaposition of Protestant and Mormon labors in the nineteenth and twentieth centuries, a period when these traditions vied for converts from Africa to India to the Pacific. It may prompt intense discussions about whether their missionary endeavors were more alike than different and how their contests were engaged in specific political and social contexts. At the very least, the reader cannot fail to recognize that the stakes of these battles were about the foundations of Christianity itself.

One might well ask, of course, whether it isn't more instructive to explore the millions of Mormons within the United States, or the many Protestant denominations there. Why not aim for the demographic or institutional center? Wouldn't those experiences tell us more about these religious traditions than the study of some lone outpost in eastern Turkey or Washakie, Utah? The chapters in this book help to demonstrate that a tradition is put to its test at its geographical, ideological, and confessional peripheries. As the missionaries often lamented to their sponsors, "You don't understand what it is like here 'on the ground.'" It is there that values are tested, that experiments are conducted, and that idealism runs up against pragmatism. Missions are, indeed, a Christian laboratory, one well worth investigating.

In another context, Julie Byrne has argued for the importance of studying separatist Catholics, those relatively tiny groups that declared independence from the mammoth Roman Catholic tradition: "It is 'other Catholicism' because it is institutionally separate from bigger churches. But it is also 'other' because it harbors and tests that which is elsewhere disallowed. . . . It is Catholicism's research lab. It is Catholicism's arts incubator. It is Catholicism's black sheep. In short, it is part of how modern Catholicism works. Through independents, then, one can see better the thoughts and unthinkables, centers and peripheries, flows and fault lines of Catholicism and American religion."[3] So, too, we can analyze through these case studies the scientists of missions at the heart of Christian life: those workers who had to act on—and often improvise—their faith "on the ground."

A Note on Terms

A technical nuance exists for the terms "Mormon," "Latter-day Saint," and "Latter Day Saint" that has implications for the chapters that follow. These terms apply to different groups and churches despite very often being used coterminously by the general public and in previous scholarship. (The appearance of both a hyphenated "Latter-day" and an unhyphenated "Latter Day" is not a typographical slip.) We use "Latter-day Saint" to refer to people or institutions associated with the Church of Jesus Christ of Latter-day Saints headquartered in Salt Lake City, Utah, the largest institution within the broader Mormon movement and what the general public often takes to represent the "Mormon Church." We use "Latter Day Saint" (without the hyphen) to refer to people or institutions associated with churches and movements beyond the church based in Salt Lake City that also trace a heritage to Joseph Smith's earliest New York congregation. "Mormon" refers to the religious movement and culture that encompasses active adherents, lapsed members, regions, and communities associated with the broader Mormon cultural setting. The initialism "LDS" is short for "Latter-day Saint"; "RLDS" refers to the Reorganized Church of Jesus Christ of Latter Day Saints headquartered in Independence, Missouri, which in 2001 was renamed Community of Christ.

Introduction

Christopher Cannon Jones and David Golding

On January 12, 1853, two American missionaries met one another for the first time in a place far from home. Julius Beardslee and Aaron Farr shared much in common, though neither perhaps immediately realized it when their paths crossed in the streets of Kingston, Jamaica. The pair were born less than a year apart in New England. Each was raised in a devout Congregational home, and each felt a call at a young age to preach the gospel. Beardslee and Farr, furthermore, came to Jamaica with similar goals. As Beardslee put it in a letter to a friend before departing for the West Indies, he planned to "carry forward the work of the Lord" there, amid the "workings of Emancipation[,] Moral Condition, and wants" of the island's formerly enslaved population. Farr likewise looked forward to "Promulgat[ing] the Gospel of Jesus Christ to the inhabitants" of Jamaica, whom he described as "once bond, now free, Licentious [and] uncouthed."[1] For both missionaries, their missions to Jamaica were civilizing efforts.

In spite of their shared aims, Farr and Beardslee remained far apart in several respects. Beardslee was, at the time of their meeting, the far more experienced missionary, having first arrived in Jamaica fourteen years earlier. He spent most of his time in Jamaica connected to the American Missionary Association, an interdenominational Protestant organization composed primarily of Congregationalists and Presbyterians. Farr, by contrast, had arrived in the West Indies just a day before he met Beardslee as part of the first group of missionaries sent to the island by the Church of Jesus Christ of Latter-day Saints. Aaron Farr's diary that day describes their encounter: "Spent the day in Study and visiting a Local Minister by the name of Beardsley[, who] Said he should Preach in the Evening." After Beardslee invited the Mormon elders to hear his sermon, Farr "asked him if there would be any objections to the An[n]oun[ce]ment" of their own meeting the following night. Beardslee agreed, and that night, following his preaching, he invited Aaron Farr, Darwin Richardson, and Alfred Lambson to introduce themselves and make the announcement.[2]

This instance of cooperation later gave way to suspicion, rivalry, and occasional hostility between Latter-day Saint and Protestant preachers on the island. Less than two weeks later, Farr met another "American Missionary from Newyork" who would "not so much [as] talk with us." The missionary—a "Rev. Dr. Ware"—had recently heard "an expose" of the Mormons' "doctrine" and "said he had a verry poor opinion of us." Only when Farr and his companion told him they were near starving did he agree to feed them ("he said he would feed a hungry thief so his good lady got us a lunch") before sending the elders on their way. When the Latter-day Saint missionaries left Jamaica in early February, they blamed their general lack of success there on, among other things, the "wicked influence" of "Reveren[d]s [and] Priests."[3] Similar scenes of contest and conflict between Protestant and Mormon missionaries played out across the globe in the nineteenth and twentieth centuries.

In August 1852, Brigham Young, president of the Church of Jesus Christ of Latter-day Saints, called more than one hundred men as missionaries, sending them "to the four quarters of the globe." The majority of those called were sent to strongholds and scattered outposts of the British Empire.[4] In each area—Jamaica, Africa's Cape of Good Hope, Australia, India, and Hong Kong, to name just a few—Latter-day Saints were preceded by Protestants from not only England but also the United States.[5] In the early nineteenth century, as American Protestantism's foreign missionary movement emerged, representatives from US missionary organizations collaborated with their British counterparts to try to convert the world.[6] Due to Mormonism's own success in attracting white Protestants in both the British Isles and the United States, the Church of Jesus Christ of Latter-day Saints identified those far-flung regions of the British Empire as prime spots to extend their own reach in spreading their unique gospel telling of restored prophetic authority, new revelation and scripture, and the imminent second coming of Jesus Christ.[7]

The competition for converts continued throughout the nineteenth century and intensified in the twentieth as Latter-day Saints expanded their global reach and established a more permanent presence in the mission field. Protestants, meanwhile, divided into rival camps, as mainline (or *ecumenical*) denominations began to question traditional modes of missionary work, and evangelicals attempted to reinvigorate the missionary enterprise their more liberal counterparts left behind.[8] Beginning in the 1960s and 1970s, those same evangelicals began to seriously wrestle with the imperial aspects of their missionary efforts around the globe and worked to empower local Protestant churches toward a missiology based on partnership instead of paternalism.[9] While Mormons remained shut out of these internal Protestant debates, they confronted some of the same challenges concurrently. After Latter-day Saint leaders began discouraging the migration of new converts to the North American West at the turn of the twentieth century, the church experienced unprecedented growth in new regions. That growth accelerated in the wake of World War II, causing church leaders to confront the need to train local leadership to work with, instead of under, American missionaries.[10]

In spite of their theological and ecclesiastical differences, Mormon and Protestant missionaries from the United States shared much in common. From the perspective of those they tried to convert, the different groups of missionaries often represented the same Western imperialist project, seeking not only to Christianize but also civilize prospective converts. Despite their proximity to (and ongoing rivalry with) one another, and the broader commonalities that occasionally linked them to each other, the missionaries' experiences have largely remained isolated in scholarly research on the subject.

This book aims to correct that oversight. It brings together in a single volume some of the most exciting work currently being done by historians of Christian mission. These chapters grew out of a symposium held in Salt Lake City, Utah, in November 2019. The idea for that symposium originated just a year earlier, over lunch in Saint Louis, Missouri. That lunch included both editors of this book, as well as Spencer McBride (Church History Library), Emily Conroy-Krutz (Michigan State University), and Brian Franklin (Southern Methodist University). As we discussed our respective research, we realized that although each of us focused on a different group of missionaries—some mainline Protestant, some evangelical, and others Mormon—there was considerable geographic and thematic overlap in our projects. The conversation soon shifted to several other scholars' research, and we began imagining the possibilities of bringing a group of historians together to present their work, respond to that of others, and see what emerged. With the generous support of the Church History Department of the Church of Jesus Christ of Latter-day Saints and the Neal A. Maxwell Institute for Religious Scholarship at Brigham Young University, those plans became a reality in 2019, when a dozen invited scholars convened in the Church History Library in Salt Lake City to workshop precirculated papers to one another and other participants from the local academic community. Those papers—expanded and revised based on the conversations that ensued that day—are presented here. This is the first book to compare and contrast Protestant and Mormon missions across time and space. We hope it will provide a starting point for future work exploring the two groups' entangled histories.

The emergence of Mormonism coincided with an early surge in missionary activity among North American Protestants. Protestant "home missionaries" in the 1830s and 1840s United States tracked Mormon missionary movements throughout the country and mounted several campaigns to intercept potential converts.[11] Mormons launched their first overseas missions to Britain in the 1830s just as missionaries of the London Missionary Society reached Samoa. By the 1840s, Mormon missionaries had also begun work in the Pacific Islands and started making plans to venture even farther abroad.[12] Encounters between these missionary cohorts multiplied into the twentieth century but started to diverge when both introduced major transformations to their mission strategies. Efforts to "modernize" missions encouraged mainline Protestants toward but discouraged Mormons from greater ecumenism. As missiology increased in institutional support, Latter-day Saints remained unaware and apparently uninterested, continuing their global mission program from a centralized bureaucracy, though one forced to confront many of the same questions and challenges as their Protestant counterparts.[1]

The chapters in this volume explore those entangled histories in a variety of ways. The book's foreword by Laurie F. Maffly-Kipp, whose distinguished career has included work on both Protestant and Mormon missions, looks at the historiographical stakes of the project. The New Testament commission to "go and make disciples of all nations" left the task widely open to interpretation, setting up a missionary experiment Christians of all kinds could undertake—with or without stereotypical zeal. Maffly-Kipp notices how comparative analyses of the "Christian laboratory" evident in missions, like those represented in this book, bring greater focus to fundamental questions of world Christianity and the histories surrounding Christian and interreligious experience.

The chapters that follow are arranged in broadly chronological order, beginning in the early nineteenth century and progressing to the turn of the twenty-first century. Some address Protestant or Mormon missions and missionaries only; others bring the respective experiences of both groups into comparative perspective, or note momentary connections, cooperation, or competition between the two. While each chapter was written individually, some speak to others in particular ways, a result of both common interests and the dialogue that occurred between participants at the November 2019 conference. Throughout, certain key themes emerge, and we hope readers will discover connections between the various chapters and the respective histories they describe.

Kathryn Gin Lum's opening chapter on the conception of the "heathen world" in the minds of early American missionaries sets the stage for much of what follows. In spite of the very real differences between the various regions of the globe to which missionaries went, they collapsed them into a single wilderness that could only be tamed by the Christian conversion of its inhabitants. Additional chapters throughout the book build on this framework. In chapter 4, Taunalyn Ford argues that both Protestant and Mormon missions in mid-nineteenth-century India were inflected with a decidedly Scottish orientalist gaze, thanks to the early leadership and influence of missionaries like John Murray Mitchell (Church of Scotland) and Hugh Findlay (Latter-day Saint). By contrast, chapter 6 by Jeffrey G. Cannon explores how Latter-day Saint missionaries in early twentieth-century Africa used photography to reify the continent's inhabitants as exotic Others in need of both Christian conversion and Western civilization.

Cannon's focus on the technologies of missions is extended further in Melissa Wei-Tsing Inouye's discussion in chapter 9 of "cultural technologies," those techniques used by missionaries to facilitate relationships with converts and organization in their missions. Comparing the efforts of missionaries from the London Missionary Society, the True Jesus Church, and the Church of Jesus Christ of Latter-day Saints, Inouye notes the portability of each group's religious rites and organizational structures as they were transported to new regions and divergent peoples around the globe.

In much the same way that the missionaries in Africa analyzed by Cannon used photography and those compared by Inouye utilized church structure, schools, and language reform in their efforts to connect with and organize the people they encountered and converted, other missionaries saw humanitarian aid as a way to do so. In chapter 3, Devrim Ümit examines the Eastern Turkey Mission of the American Board of Commissioners for Foreign Missions (ABCFM) from 1876 to 1909, as American missionaries sought to expand the reach of the post–US Civil War "benevolent empire" at the same time that Ottoman Turkey was struggling to maintain its standing as a Muslim empire. In chapter 7, Lauren F. Turek takes readers from the nineteenth-century Middle East to late twentieth-century Latin America, considering how evangelical and Pentecostal American missionaries mobilized to provide aid to earthquake-ravaged Colombia, seeing in disaster aid an avenue to proselytize Colombians.

Emily Conroy-Krutz and Amanda Hendrix-Komoto, meanwhile, highlight the role women and families—as both an ideal and a lived reality—played in missionary work. In chapter 2, Conroy-Krutz analyzes women's applications to the ABCFM, highlighting the central role women played in Protestant missions and the meanings those women found in their efforts. In chapter 5, Hendrix-Komoto, in turn, examines the competing efforts of Protestant and Mormon missionaries to convert the Northwestern Shoshone in the American West, comparing the groups' respective approaches to marriage and other sacraments in appealing to their Indigenous audiences.

In chapter 8, David J. Howlett complicates narratives of both Protestant and Mormon missionaries by examining the Reorganized Church of Jesus Christ of Latter Day Saints (RLDS) mission in India. RLDS missionaries shared parts of their history with Latter-day Saints but had, by the mid-twentieth century, begun a move toward ecumenical Protestant Christianity, a process on display in their efforts to convert the Sora people in India. Howlett also offers important insight into the multiple meanings of conversion, the relationship of missionaries to the state, and the complicity (or lack thereof) of missionary agents in colonialism. In chapter 10, David Golding compares the development of Protestant missiology with the Latter-day Saint lack thereof and notices a difference of pragmatism in seeking proselytes. Their divergence over mission theory meant the groups could proselytize in parallel (sometimes in competition) yet remain mostly indifferent to each other's motives. This trend has only recently been interrupted by Protestant and Mormon scholars working in missiology taking new interest in each other's projects.

The book concludes in chapter 11 with David A. Hollinger's analysis of American missionaries and their presence within broader cultural trends in Christianity at large. Efforts to spread the Christian gospel beyond the North Atlantic West sharpened rhetorics and notions of the nature of Christianity itself and the worldly projects carried out in the name of that faith. Divisions within global Protestantism reflected a setting less monolithic than often supposed by historians of missions and missionaries—an array of enterprises intent on fulfilling the Great Commission yet too diverse to direct much attention to Mormon missionary interests.

Within Mormon studies, the subject of missions has frequently elicited frustrations of a couple of varieties—that those studies within the field tend to keep a parochial focus and that well-established fields of history and missiology tend to overlook (or at times exclude) Mormon actors and episodes. Within broader historiographical subject areas in which Protestant missions appear, studies have frequently interrogated the absence of key actors, such as women, Black and Indigenous peoples, and working-class participants. All together, the chapters here offer a launch point for further integration and synthesis across a more diverse missionary laboratory. Whether from a Mormon or Protestant context, historians can proceed with awareness of the uneven development of mission identities, strategies, and activities, and scholars can fine-tune their attention to shared and divergent avenues of missionary engagement. Missionaries within liminal spaces of the proselytizer and the proselytized, the feminine and the masculine, the colonizer and the colonized, or the racially privileged and the racially subordinated present sources of interruption and sites of encounter relevant to broad lines of historiography.

Aaron Farr's mission to Jamaica was short-lived. On February 10, less than a month after his arrival on the island, he and the other Latter-day Saint elders boarded the steam ship *Ohio* and set sail for New York City. The missionaries had made just four converts in Jamaica, confronting in Kingston and Spanish Town uncooperative civil authorities, hostile mobs, and a populace "verry ignorant of Christianity[,] sivility[,] and . . . humanity." In a letter written to Church President Brigham Young providing an account of the mission, Farr singled out the hostility of "Rev[e]ren[d]s, Priests, Doctors, and Editors" for its failure. Whenever the missionaries found interested Jamaicans "willing [to] come out and investigate the Principles of the Gospel," he explained, Protestant missionaries would become "greatly Excited" and work harder to convince their congregants to "close their Eyes and Ears to the truth."[13] While Protestants like Julius Beardslee would surely have disputed that they were keeping people *from* the truth, the budding sense of competition and rivalry was real.

Conflict between Protestant and Mormon missionaries continued throughout the nineteenth century wherever the two came into contact, especially as Latter-day Saints began making significant inroads in regions in both the United States and abroad.[14] And over the course of the twentieth century, as Latter-day Saints attracted more and more converts in Asia, Europe, Latin America, and even the evangelical stronghold of the American South, evangelical Protestants responded with increasing alarm, warning their members of the Mormon threat and attempting to counter pro-Mormon messaging.[15]

The competition between the two groups, however, should not overshadow what they shared in common. Both evangelicals and Mormons, for example, shunned ecumenical efforts that threatened to undermine their respective messages. Both utilized many of the same methods, tools, and technologies in their missionary work. And both sometimes struggled to differentiate—both internally and from the perspective of those they encountered at home and abroad—between their message and the politics of American imperialism.

CHAPTER 1

Heathen Landscapes
Of Souls and Soils

Kathryn Gin Lum

On an early spring evening in 1834, lawyer and reformer Thomas Smith Grimké, brother of Angelina and Sarah, regaled a Charleston audience with an "Address on the Power and Value of the Sunday School System in Evangelizing Heathen and Re-constructing Christian Communitys." Grimké opened with a lengthy hypothetical scene. Imagine a remote island, he said. Mountains undulate against the open sky, and waterfalls cascade gently to valleys below. The island is lush and beautiful, untouched by the hand of "civilization," and inhabited by "a race, at once artless in manners, kind in their affections, and obedient to the dictates of natural justice."[1]

But then a merchant ship appears. Finding that the inhabitants have little of value, and the island no gold or silver for the taking, it quickly departs. Next comes a ship of scientists and then a battleship, neither of which sees anything of interest.[2] Finally, a humble missionary bark emerges over the horizon. Before stepping off, the missionaries "entrea[t] with many tears of faith and hope, that the heathen island before them might 'rejoice and blossom as the rose,' and 'the wilderness and solitary place might be glad' through their labors."[3]

Where the previous vessels saw the island and its inhabitants as destitute and uninteresting, it is Grimké's missionaries who see real value in the island's soil and souls. They read wilderness as the quintessential mark identifying the island as "heathen," hearkening back to the term's roots as "heath, barren, uncultivated"⁴ and signaling a field ripe for their intervention. Despite the island's natural lushness, and its people's seeming innocence, Grimké's missionaries believe that it requires a different kind of blossoming.

This opening scene may be fictitious, but nineteenth-century American Protestant missionaries and their supporters frequently referenced the same scriptural passages about heathen wildernesses blossoming and rejoicing. The passages come from Isaiah 35, signaling the coming of the Glory of Zion: "The desert shall rejoice, and blossom as the rose. . . . And the parched ground shall become a pool, and the thirsty land springs of water."⁵ The preceding chapter of Isaiah also comes up frequently in missionary texts; it explains why wildernesses are such in the first place—because of the anger of the Lord against unbelieving inhabitants: "And the streams thereof shall be turned into pitch, and the dust thereof into brimstone. . . . And thorns shall come up . . . and it shall be an habitation of dragons, *and* a court for owls."⁶ Seeing "heathen" lands through the interpretive lens of both Isaiah 34 and 35, missionaries understood them to be wild and overgrown because of the sin of their inhabitants, no matter how lush and verdant they might actually be. With such a view of heathen lands, they could believe in their own presence as heralding the "blossoming" of the "rose" and the rejoicing of the "wilderness."

In this brief chapter, I want to explore how this imagined, blanket conception of the "heathen world" as moral and literal wilderness made such by unbelievers coincided with growing awareness of the visible and climatic differences between far-flung parts of the world and its people. I ultimately want to suggest that, although most American Protestants recognized and made much of the differences between taro patches and savannas, "rude" huts and densely packed cities, they nevertheless subsumed them under the imagined rubric of untamed wilderness rendered such by the intransigence of the "heathens" who dwelled there. No matter how verdant or arid, they believed that all heathen landscapes shared the same characteristics and needed the same kinds of intervention. Just as Isaiah 34 explained the desolations of the land as a result of the Lord's anger against unbelieving nations, so Americans explained the unproductiveness of untamed "heathen" geographies as a result of the incorrect religious orientation of their inhabitants.⁷ They also brought to the soil an intensely Protestant understanding of the changes that could be wrought by conversion. The change of heart, they believed, would redeem not only converts' eternal souls but also the soils on which they lived.

In *The Christian Imagination: Theology and the Origins of Race*, Willie James Jennings explains that "land and body are connected at the intersection of European imagination and expansion."⁸ Land and body are also intimately connected at the intersection of non-Christian views of the world and humans' place within it.[9] Christian colonization provoked a violent rupture in which, as Jennings writes, "the earth, the ground, spaces, and places [were] removed as living organizers of identity and as facilitators of identity."[10] Jennings explains how the Christian imagination divorced itself from the land. By claiming to replace Jews as God's chosen people, Christians uprooted themselves not only from a particular ethnic identity but also from a particular relationship to the land of Israel. While Israel continued to loom large in the Christian imagination, the literal, physical space of Israel was no longer the basis of Christian identity as it was for Jews.

Christian European colonizers upheld the proper Christian as one who understood that the land was theirs to subdue, subdivide, and sell. A right view of the land as the creation of the one true God, given to men (gender-specific) as their burden to toil over and subdue, was supposed to produce a right attitude toward it: instead of idly plucking its fruits here and there and hunting its fish and game willy-nilly, people who knew the true God were to domesticate and regulate its productions and, in so doing, regulate their labor industriously. As Jennings puts it, "The new worlds were transformed into land—raw, untamed land. And the European vision saw these new lands as a system of potentialities, a mass of undeveloped, underdeveloped, unused, underutilized, misunderstood, not fully understood potentialities. Everything—from peoples and their bodies to plants and animals, from the ground and the sky—was subject to change, subjects for change, subjected to change. The significance of this transformation cannot be overstated. The earth itself was barred from being a constant signifier of identity."[11]

The papal bulls issued by Pope Alexander VI in 1493 and 1494 divided the lands discovered and to-be-discovered between Portugal and Spain by an imaginary line west of the Azores. The basis of the papal claim to these lands was that they were not inhabited by Christians and were therefore "barbarous nations" that needed to "be overthrown and brought to the faith itself."[12] This became known as the "doctrine of discovery," in which the heathenness of non-Christian people justified the takeover of their lands for the good of their bodies and souls, and for the good of the land itself.

Colonial accounts of the transformation of the American landscape drew from the same evocative passages in the book of Isaiah that Thomas Smith Grimké referenced in his 1834 sermon. The Corporation for Promoting the Gospel among the Heathen in New-England produced a boosterish account of their efforts in the 1652 *Strength out of Weakness; Or a Glorious Manifestation of the Further Progresse of the Gospel among the Indians in New-England*. Though the Native people had "wasted the remainder of Natures Riches to the utmost degeneracy that an Immortall rationall being is obnoxious unto," the corporation explained, the Lord had now "powred his Spirit on the seeds of the Heathen, & his blessing on their Off-spring." The result could be marked both on the lives of the heathen, and on the land itself: "In the Wildernesse are waters broken out, and streames in the Desert, the parched ground is become a Poole, and the thirsty Land—springs of water: in the Habitation of Dragons where each lay, there is grasse with Reeds and Rushes."[13] A letter reproduced later in the same volume, by John Endecott, provided specifics as to how Christianized American Indians were transforming the landscapes on which they lived, not only with productions of the soil but also the built environment. "To tell you of their industry and ingenuitie in building of an house after the *English* manner . . . , their being but one *English*-man a Carpentere to shew them, being but two dayes with them, is remarkeable." Trees had become raw material to fell and hew, creating more empty space for planting crops, mowing grass, and constructing further buildings. Endecott explained that the Indians had also built a fort and bridge and intended to build a water mill, further bringing the landscape under human control. Of course, Endecott and other English colonists failed to recognize that Native people had already wrought changes to the land, albeit with a much smaller environmental impact.[14]

In order to justify the often brutal methods earlier generations had exacted to extract compliance from Native souls and soils, later generations of colonists emphasized just how difficult a situation the early colonists had encountered. In his 1721 *India Christiana*, Cotton Mather described, disapprovingly, the Native people's supposed refusal to be awed by Euro-American ways. "Tho' they saw a People Arrive among them . . . who had *Houses full of Good Things*, vastly out-shining their squalid and dark *Wigwams*; And they saw this People Replenishing their *Fields*, with *Trees* and with *Grains*, and useful *Animals*, which until now they had been wholly Strangers to; yet they did not seem touch'd in the least, with any *Ambition* to come at such Desireable Circumstances, or with any *Curiosity* to enquire after the *Religion* that was attended with them," Mather marveled. For Mather, it was their *"Religion"* that explained the colonists' houses, fields, and beasts of burden. Lacking that, the Native people turned into even less "useful *Animals*" than the domesticated beasts of the colonists: "To *Humanize* these Miserable *Animals*, and in any measure to *Cicurate* [tame] them & *Civilize* them, were a work of no little Difficulty."[15]

But learning the attitudes toward land that Christian Europeans brought to bear ultimately did not guarantee to Native people the right to divide and sell it to private citizens. In the landmark 1823 Supreme Court case, *Johnson & Graham's Lessee v. M'Intosh*, Chief Justice John Marshall, writing on behalf of a unanimous court, maintained that Native people could only sell their land to the federal government. They could not engage in private transactions because they did not have real ownership of the land. The court based this decision on the doctrine of discovery, which Marshall said was "confined to countries 'then unknown to all Christian people.'" It was on this basis that the first English explorers had "assert[ed] a right to take possession notwithstanding the occupancy of the natives, who were heathens, and at the same time admitting the prior title of any Christian people who may have made a previous discovery."[16] Marshall claimed that "the charter granted to Sir Humphrey Gilbert in 1578 authorizes him to discover and take possession of such remote, heathen, and barbarous lands as were not actually possessed by any Christian prince or people. This charter was afterward renewed to Sir Walter Raleigh in nearly the same terms."[17] And now the federal government alone, as the lasting representative of these first Christian English discoverers, could claim the right to possess the land; they allowed Native people to live on it and to transfer their lands to the government but not to dispense with it as or to whom they pleased.

As scholar Steven Newcomb has shown, the doctrine of discovery and Marshall's reference to Indians as heathens did not simply constitute a throwaway statement about the past but rather a continued justification for the present and future. "Legal thinking," writes Newcomb, "is a product of the human imagination."[18] The imagination of Native people as incapable heathens, and of colonists as not only Christians but God's New Israel, rendered Native lands subject to takeover, just as the heathenness and idolatry of the Canaanites justified the Israelites' violence against them and their lands. And it continued to inform the view of Native lands and landscapes—along with their souls—as uncultivated, barren, and in need of Christian intervention.

Such attitudes toward Native peoples and the lands and landscapes on which they dwelled also informed Euro-American approaches to other regions of the world. With the Revolution in the rearview mirror, Americans set their sights on the globe and not just on the interior of the continent.[19] Even if many of the regions to which they turned had already been "discovered" and were understood to be under the governance of other bodies, the imaginative legacy of the doctrine of discovery nevertheless emboldened them to see in overseas landscapes evidence of how heathenism had rendered them wild and barren, as well as potential for what they might become under the Christian oversight of peoples of European origin.

This emboldened vision manifested both in broad geographic surveys of the "known world" and in specific reports and descriptions of particular places.[20] For the purposes of this short chapter, I will focus on the broad geographic imagination of Jedidiah Morse. In the chapter of my larger book project that this comes from, *Heathen: Religion and Race in American History*, I also look at case studies from Hawai'i, South Africa, India, and China.

Congregationalist minister Morse's bestselling *American Universal Geography* shaped the worldviews of generations of American schoolchildren and adult readers.[21] In this volume, Morse surveyed the histories, natural productions, and religions of the "known world," drawing from travelers' and historians' accounts. Since America was "yet in its infancy,"[22] he averred, Europe was the standard of development against which all else could be measured. Morse described it as the "smallest, but most important grand division of the earth." Despite its small size, he wrote, Europe's "nations have the skill of making the best use of their natural productions." Morse explained that "wherever the christian faith has penetrated, learning, industry and civilization have followed."[23] Viewing Christianity as the main source of Europe's strength and prosperity suggested that any other part of the world could partake of the same if Christianized.

That said, Morse also drew on climatic theories to explain how the natural landscape of Europe had supposedly produced a world-conquering people. God had not blessed Europeans with fertile soil, balmy weather, and compliant beasts. To the contrary, said Morse, "the greatest part of Europe is under the influence of a climate, which being tempered with a moderate degree of cold, forms a race of men strong, bold, active and ingenious," forced "by necessity to make the best they can of the smaller share of vegetable and animal treasures, which their soil produces." In other words, what set Europeans apart was their ability to make the land blossom through innovation borne of God-given necessity and encouragement.[24]

According to Morse, the same could not be said of other parts of the world. "Asia and Africa have immense deserts, such as are no where to be found in Europe"; these arid expanses were partly the result of "natural and insuperable disadvantages of situation" but were also due to "want of industry, which is at once the cause and effect of desolation."[25] Morse admitted that some regions were not actually deserts; Asia, he said, was "superior" to "Europe and Africa" in "the serenity of its air, the fertility of its soil, the deliciousness of its fruits, [and] the fragrancy and balsamick qualities of its plants." Asia's built landscapes and mature agricultural systems also revealed the longevity of its civilizations.

And yet, for all that the landscapes of Asia could *appear* well designed, verdant, and abundant, Morse claimed that "it affords but a scanty supply for its numerous millions. Creatures which die with disease, and even the vermin, which swarm over their own bodies, afford them a repast. . . . They are Pagans; every person, from the meanest peasant to the monarch himself, has an altar and *deity* of his own."[26] The idea that "Pagan Asiatics" could not feed their swelling populations, except with the diseased carcasses of similarly malnourished animals and the rats that fed on them, would be repeated when Chinese migrants began arriving in America in the second half of the century.

Morse devoted less attention to the landscapes of Africa, noting instead that the Africans "themselves," rather than anything they cultivated or produced, "constitute the principal article of exportation." He described the Christians and "Mahometans" of Africa as no better than heathens; the former "do not deserve the Christian name" and the latter were shrouded in "darkness and delusion."[27] To Morse, Africa remained to be explored, cultivated, and made productive.

We might conclude, from this brief sketch, that Morse's understanding of the world, and that which he presented to his readers, moved in a hierarchical direction. He classified people and their landscapes according to a civilizational ladder, with Europeans at the top, Asians somewhere in between, and Africans at the bottom. Morse's work reflected the popularity of the four stages theory of development formulated by Adam Smith and others in the mid-eighteenth century, which divided the world's known peoples into hunter-gatherers, shepherds, agricultural societies, and commercial societies.[28] As one scholar has put it, Morse's work and other popular antebellum geographies "are not *complexly* racist"; they show "how the white majority and its idealogues saw and felt about racial hierarchies" and "br[ought] to the classroom a new mode of its transference."[29]

But even while Morse made much of apparent civilizational differences between regions and peoples, his work was not just "simply" racist. "Racist" is not a simple term and does not solely imply the hierarchical thinking that would become characteristic of scientific racism, in which different peoples were ranked according to supposedly innate phenotypical and intellectual characteristics. Morse explained different societies' placement on civilizational ladders as a result of a complex of factors, not all innate, including religious orientation, climate, and soil composition.

Furthermore, I want to suggest that Morse's body of work did not only project a hierarchically arranged and racially differentiated world but also perpetuated an older—but still influential—view of the world's non-Christian landscapes and peoples as one and the same in their heathenness. Some scholars have suggested that this older view was a hallmark of a religious and not yet racial way of looking at the world, since it allowed potential for change—for heathens to become Christians and for their thorny "wildernesses" to "blossom as the rose."[30] But if we understand race as, to use Sylvester Johnson's words, "a colonial process that has constituted 'Europeanness and non-Europeanness' through material, discursive, and noncorporeal domains," then we might actually see how this binary view of the world was—and continues to be—simultaneously a religious *and* racial project. Race, understood as a *"governing* formation . . . that has structured the *political rule* of Europeans over non-Europeans"—again to quote Johnson—has operated to render non-European people and their lands as perpetually in need of oversight, no matter how supposedly "advanced" they might seem on a civilizational ladder of development.[31]

Of course, missionaries did, out of necessity, recognize and draw distinctions between regions and peoples to determine where to most effectively direct limited funds and volunteers. As Emily Conroy-Krutz has pointed out in her book *Christian Imperialism: Converting the World in the Early American Republic*, antebellum American missionaries created "hierarchies of heathenism." They thought that their work would meet with more success if they started with heathens in the middle—those who were neither so "developed" as to consider themselves superior to would-be evangelists nor so "undeveloped" as to require too much remedial intervention.[32]

But while hierarchical evaluation might make sense pragmatically, Jedidiah Morse and likeminded antebellum Americans ultimately marked little difference between the ontological status and eternal outcome of all non-Christian people: no matter how apparently "civilized" or not, as "heathens" they were unregenerate sinners and bound for hell unless and until they were saved for Christ. And, just as in Grimké's opening scene about the hypothetical island, no matter how lush or verdant a "heathen" landscape might seem, it still needed the assistance of Christians to make it truly bloom as God (and His colonizers) desired.

In a September 1821 sermon given at the annual meeting of the American Board of Commissioners for Foreign Missions, Morse made this overriding perspective on the "heathen world" clear. "The heathen nations, and those now buried in the darkness and delusion of Mahometanism, are a very large proportion of the inhabitants on our globe," he lamented.[33] "The world, since the fall of man, has been, and is still, principally under the immediate dominion of Satan."[34] The verse Morse chose for his sermon text, Psalm 2:8, was another favorite of missionaries and their boosters. It promised Satan's eventual overthrow: "Ask of me, and I shall give thee the heathen for thine inheritance, and the uttermost parts of the earth for the possession." Morse claimed that the verse was a "prophesy concerning the Kingdom of CHRIST," which promised its eventual "exten[sion]" over the whole world."[35] He explained that inheriting the heathen and possessing their land went hand in hand and entailed Christ's "enjoying and delighting in them, as his purchase, his property . . . , bringing forth the fruits of righteousness to his praise, and rendering him the homage, service and gratitude due to him as their Lord."[36] The agricultural terminology—"fruits of righteousness"—was deliberate and signaled the blossoming of the "heathen world" once it was made Christ's (and his representatives') "property."[37]

Some objected, Morse noted, that "savages can never be tamed.... Educate them in the best manner you can, their original character will remain unaltered."[38] In other words, Morse was aware of the notion of hereditary heathenness, which some scholars say emerged in the seventeenth century, others in the eighteenth, solidifying by the nineteenth.[39] But he rejected it: "Will any one venture to say, that GOD cannot fulfil this promise to his Son? ... Yes, GOD *can* give the blessing of a new heart to a wild Indian, to a Hindoo, a Turk, a negro, a Hottentot, as easily as to the most enlightened, polished, and best educated, in civilized nations." And once their hearts were renewed, said Morse, this would "invariably produc[e] a new character, and always the same character."[40] For "GOD, we see is compassionately concerned for *all* men, without distinction of nations or character. None are sunk so low in ignorance and stupidity, as to be considered unworthy of his notice and compassionate care."[41]

Again, this kind of perspective is often seen as an older, gentler form of binary othering that virulent scientific racism would eventually overthrow. But it was neither necessarily gentle nor eventually overthrown. For in the idea that a "new heart" could undo all the trappings of "nations or character"—indeed, producing *"always the same character"* in converts—we can see the cultural violence and conformity that conversion was supposed to produce, entailing the wholesale transformation of bodies and lands in addition to souls. Different kinds of racial thinking coexisted and interacted, and we fail to capture the full range of othering in which Americans engaged if we assume that the one (hereditable, biological, hierarchical othering) overtook and eventually replaced the other (binary, religious changeability).

CHAPTER 2

Before "Woman's Work for Woman"
Protestant Missionary Applications and Gender

Emily Conroy-Krutz

For eight years, Ermina Nash had thought about "going to the heathen," but she had always assumed it could never be. She "saw no probability of ever attaining the object of [her] desires," and yet she continued to pray that "if it was the Lord's will, [she] might one day" become a missionary. If given the chance, she felt that she could "cheerfully endure any trial" with God's help, "and freely leave all [her] friends, and all the comforts of civilized life." As she wrote to Jeremiah Evarts in 1825, she turned to poetry to express the "motives and feelings" that compelled her to apply to serve the American Board of Commissioners for Foreign Missions (ABCFM):

> While I of their miseries hear,
> Oft with ardor do I cry,
> Burst ye chains that bind me here
> And let me thither fly.

Now, in 1825, she hoped that what had earlier seemed impossible might now be possible: that she could be of use to the mission movement at one of the fields of the ABCFM. She was willing to go to "any station" where she might be useful, which for the ABCFM at that time included missions in South Asia, the Sandwich Islands, and North America. She was twenty-four years old, healthy, and an experienced and pious teacher. And soon she would become an assistant missionary to the Choctaw. But before that could happen, she had spent the years from 1817 through 1825 thinking, praying, and wondering if a place would ever open for her.[1]

Nash was far from the only woman who spent years silently contemplating the possibilities—or lack thereof—for her participation in the mission movement. Throughout the papers of the ABCFM, we can find many other women anxiously considering and asking about policies on women in mission—letters that suggest the existence of even greater numbers of women who kept their questions to themselves. The years of silence that preceded an application are poignant reminders of the limitations on women's full participation in many aspects of American religious life in general and the foreign mission movement in particular in this period, even as the women themselves could feel a strong sense of calling to greater activity. Protestant women did have important work they could do in this project, and this correspondence reveals some of the ways that they claimed roles for themselves in the face of ambivalence. Women were among the most dedicated supporters of the Protestant mission movement, in spite of the limitations placed on their leadership.

The late nineteenth century has been the era to receive the most attention for women's work in foreign missions, not least because the paths to service were significantly less fraught than in these early decades. Women's mission boards were founded by most denominations in the years after the Civil War, providing many new opportunities for mission work, especially for single women. By the end of the century, (mostly, but not exclusively) white Protestant women would emphasize the unique service they could perform for the women of the non-Christian world with the catchphrase "woman's work for woman." Under this mantra, women were seen as having a particular role to play in the mission movement: they would serve the women of the world, helping to lift them up to the elevated status that women in the United States enjoyed, even as these missionary women could challenge the restrictions they faced within American society as well. With women's missionary boards endorsing this idea and sending out huge numbers of single women into the mission field, it was "woman's work for woman" that made women into the majority of American missionaries abroad from the turn of the century forward.

Yet the seeds of these ideas were present in the early nineteenth century as well, long before the postbellum women's mission boards were founded. In 1823, Jeremiah Evarts would celebrate women in missionary work for precisely this: working to "rescue multitudes of females from the oppression and denigration they are suffering, and to make them ornaments of Christian Society on earth, and heirs of immortality beyond the grave."[2] But at the same time, Evarts and his colleagues at the ABCFM were unsure about women—married or single—in mission work. These early decades are marked by ambivalence and questions—from both the mission boards and women themselves—about how and where they might serve this movement. And for at least 160 women in the years between 1819 and 1838, the results can be found in tentative letters exploring the possibility of whether or not they might be chosen as missionaries for the ABCFM to any of its stations around the world.

Scholars of women and missions have long noted the ways that women's place within the early American Protestant foreign mission movement was complex and ambiguous. Religious print culture celebrated women's missionary contributions even as most women were prevented from direct missionary service. The very few could be wives or assistants; the majority remained at home and took part in auxiliary societies. In this capacity, they raised funds for the missionary cause in general, supported individual missions and missionaries, read and shared news of the places where missionaries worked, and tried to inspire their fellow Protestants to embrace the mission cause. They were the backbone of the movement but not its leadership. Women who felt called to mission might marry into the field through what historian Dana Robert has called the "missionary conjugal network." These early missionary wives were understood to have a range of responsibilities, including the management of missionary households and enabling their husbands to be more effective missionaries. They might also teach in mission schools, facilitate prayer circles for female converts, and generally serve as examples of Christian womanhood for all who might observe them. The options for single women were much less clear. For all that women could do, the mission boards remained unsure about the propriety—and at times, the safety—of sending American women out into the "heathen world."[3]

This tension is fully consistent with American Protestant women's experience in the period in general. Across denominations, Protestant women in these decades were generally assumed to have a natural predilection for morality and spiritual matters. They made up the majority of church membership and could find some leadership roles through women's moral and social reform organizations or prayer groups, yet ordination to ministry was not an option in any denomination. In the same years that mission boards and interested women pondered the place of women in missions, American women could be found teaching Sunday schools, advocating for expanded educational opportunities, raising money for a wide range of causes, and more. Submissiveness to the will of God was a virtue all Protestants tried to embody. For women, that virtuous submission extended as well to the men in leadership positions within Protestant organizations. But it could not turn off the sense that God was calling them to do more. As they sought to reconcile these competing impulses, both the women and the mission boards created an early framework for understanding women's mission work. Sometimes, they found, the door could open—but only if women found the bravery to ask.

Gender and Protestant Mission Work

Missionary candidates, male and female alike, all displayed a certain amount of insecurity in their ability to serve. Congregational and Presbyterian piety demanded as much. Yet women's questions about whether they could serve were not only about searching themselves for signs of a true calling. They were also about whether missionary organizations had any place for them at all as women. Those few celebrated female missionaries were at once exemplary and extraordinary: represented in print culture as emblematic of the faith and dedication that all Christians should possess while also displaying that faith and dedication in circumstances seemingly unique and impossible for most Anglo-American Protestant women to replicate. Women like Harriet Newell would inspire generations of American Protestants, even as it was not always clear how to follow in her footsteps.[4]

That very first conversation in which a woman said out loud that she wanted to serve as a missionary, that she felt some sort of calling to go into the field to serve the heathen, was difficult precisely because in the early decades of the century it was a desire both obvious and seemingly impossible for any given individual. Could God really be calling her—*her*—to this glorious work? And if so, would a way ever be opened for her to do it? When female missionaries and missionary assistants were widely celebrated on both sides of the Atlantic for their participation in the world mission movement, ordinary individual women in the early nineteenth century could be inspired to emulation and some anxiety. Was there a place for them, too? Keeping those hopes hidden until a possibility seemed to present itself, sometimes for years, perhaps sometimes forever, women at home followed the mission movement and wondered where their place within it could be. When a way seemed finally possible, only then would they confess these desires and, if met with support, begin the process of putting themselves forward for missionary service.

The Potter family presents us with examples of some of the ways that gender worked in these letters. William Potter first applied to serve as a missionary in 1819, at the age of twenty-four. His application came to the ABCFM through an introduction from James Morris. Morris could attest to Potter's piety, intelligence, and discretion. Potter's own letter, which followed shortly after, spoke of the several years he had been considering missionary service. Like his female contemporaries, as we will see, he had spent some time discerning whether God was truly calling him to mission work. Unlike them, he was able to approach the ABCFM with some confidence once he had come to a decision. He spoke of his "duty" to serve as a missionary and was soon appointed to the Cherokee mission on the strength of his good character and experience in teaching and weaving. These skills would be useful in the mission schools, where young men and women were trained in the "arts of civilization."[5] In his second letter to the ABCFM, Potter introduced the idea of women accompanying him. Might he bring a "female companion" with him to the mission station? It soon became clear that Potter hoped for two women to accompany him: his wife and his sister.

Potter's discussion of his wife did not include much detail. He simply wrote that he hoped that he had "made a choice of one who is 'qualified for the service and truly dedicated to the missionary cause,'" echoing the ABCFM's advice as to what type of woman would make an ideal missionary wife. In contrast, his discussion of his sister was extensive and reveals many more details. His thirty-year-old sister, a pious and commonly educated woman with much experience caring for children, had been excited to learn that Potter was to serve as a missionary. She told her brother that "she had for a number of years felt a desire to go among the heathen" but had never shared this with anyone else because the subject was "delicate." Now she hoped that her brother might find out for her "whether it would be expedient for a female to go out unmarried as a missionary? would such a person be useful in any degree? and would they be accepted if they should offer."[6] Miss Potter, as it turned out, was rejected, but women in similar situations would continue to ask these same questions.

As the unevenness of Potter's descriptions of his wife and his sister suggest, single women had a more difficult task than married women in making an argument for themselves. But whether married or unmarried, missionary women responded to a sense of a call. Married women, like Mrs. Potter, might have their own agency and desires somewhat covered by that of their husbands. Why did Mrs. Potter want to go into the mission field? Her husband did not feel the need to explain as he did with his sister. The wives traveled to the mission field because of their husbands, and it was the men who were ordained as missionaries. Yet missionary wives, too, felt a sense of calling to mission work. This was evident in their decision to marry men who had decided to become missionaries, but apparently some may still have doubted.

For those "uncharitable" sorts who assumed women only went to the mission field "for the sake of a husband," Louise Battelle, an agent of the ABCFM, had a retort. Writing to the board in 1822, she asked if *The Missionary Herald* might be interested in publishing the story of Miss Ellsworth, a missionary to the Cherokee who had hoped to serve alongside her fiancé. She had planned to be a missionary wife, but ill health kept her intended husband home. Instead of remaining with him, she went out to her missionary work and gave up the promised marriage, an example that Battelle hoped many other women would follow. Ellsworth followed her calling to missions, not to the marriage that was the more obvious path of duty for American women at the time and that would have made entry into mission work easier.[7] The story itself is striking, but so too is the reason that Battelle wanted to relate it: her sense that some doubted the sincerity of women's commitment, attributing it to a desire for husbands rather than a fulfillment of one's own calling. Battelle herself was an interesting figure. As an agent of the ABCFM, she traveled to raise funds and interest in the mission movement, a role usually filled by men. So she may have had her own reasons for wanting women's virtuous motives to be respected, recognized, and celebrated. Like Miss Ellsworth, she too had found a somewhat unusual way to fulfill her sense of duty to the missionary cause. Ellsworth's story, she hoped, would prove that women had deeper motives than marriage.

Most of the women who applied in this way were unmarried, with no plans for marriage. This is despite the fact that marriage was the most straightforward entry for women into the mission field before the Civil War. Single women, too, could find a place in certain circumstances. Sometimes (usually in North America, but also in some overseas missions like Hawai'i and India) if they were relatives of or close friends with a missionary couple, in whose household they would reside, they might be able to go into the mission field accompanying them. Not infrequently, these women would note in their correspondence with the ABCFM their desire to remain unmarried for life. A single woman's application was far more likely to succeed if she was already known to a married missionary, though, as Miss Potter's application shows, success was still not guaranteed. In such a situation, she might be able to join the household of the married missionary couple, performing her work and, presumably, protected from any potential impropriety by virtue of her attachment to the family.

Hannah Thatcher's file from 1820 is exemplary of the sort of correspondence that would become more common from American women as the decades went on. After an opening inquiry from Ebenezer Kingsbury on her behalf, Thatcher wrote directly to Samuel Worcester. Her letter explained that she had been reluctant to write on her own behalf, for fear of "intrud[ing] upon a moment of your valuable time," and yet she "possess[ed] an ardent and increasing desire to devote [her]self to the service of the Lord among the heathen." For a year, Thatcher had felt this desire, especially after reading about women in the Brainerd and Eliot missions to the Cherokee who "were ready to sink under their burdens." Thatcher assured the ABCFM that she had "a strong and sometimes almost insupportable desire to devote the firm health and strength and all those faculties which God has graciously given me, to aid the friends of Zion in promoting the cause of my Redeemer among those poor wretches who are engrossed in moral darkness." She was prepared for frontier conditions, "privations and hardships and persevering industry," having come with her family from Massachusetts to "the wilderness of Penn[sylvania]" as a girl. She could spin, weave, knit, sew, manage a household, and teach in a mission school. She knew God would go with her, and she was ready to serve.[8] Like Thatcher, Ellen Stetson felt called after reading about the needs of the Choctaw missionaries at Eliot for more "female help" and accordingly "offer[ed] [her]self for this service." Stetson's letter noted that she possessed health, cheerfulness, and industry and had "long considered the extent of the sacrifice and the qualifications which are immediately necessary." She, too, was ready.[9]

Most women's letters of application spoke of their questions about whether they could be allowed to serve because of their gender. In light of this, it is remarkable that they decided to reach out anyway. Even though they had plenty of reason to doubt their welcome, they also found room for hope. After all, they could see some examples of women like themselves who served as teachers in mission schools, heard from visiting missionaries of opportunities to superintend missionary households, and read in missionary periodicals of the need for female labor. Missionaries were not simply ministers who worked overseas; missionary work, in fact, went well beyond preaching. Accordingly, it was very possible for Protestant women to imagine a role for themselves, if only they could be allowed. There were many opportunities for lay service, much of which resembled the sort of reform work that women were doing at home. If a woman could teach in a school or Sunday school at home, why might she not help to establish schools in the mission field?

Discussions of "missionary qualifications" provided a range of answers to this question. The 1828 address of the ABCFM's Prudential Committee on the topic seemed to open some possibilities. Though the five-page article in the ABCFM's periodical *The Missionary Herald* exclusively referred to missionaries as "he," it also twice acknowledged that women might be missionaries as well: "missionaries of all classes, and both sexes," it read, needed to be industrious, careful, and humble. Missionary teachers, "men and women," were both needed in the field.[10] But a few years later, Americans could read William Swan's *Letters on Missions*, which included no such flexibility. Swan was a missionary from the London Missionary Society, and his discussion on missionary qualifications included a defense of the need for well-educated missionaries familiar with Greek and Hebrew who would be well prepared for translation of scriptures from their original text. Such an education was out of reach for most American women at the time. Though he, too, emphasized the importance of qualities such as self-discipline and prudence, he was clearly envisioning men when he talked about who a missionary ought to be.[11]

This sort of double-talk revealed a movement that needed female labor but was not entirely comfortable with that need. Though leadership in the church was generally understood to be male, missionary work was theoretically gender neutral. To spread the kingdom of God would require many hands and a variety of talents. For those Protestant women who felt called to take part, the journey to becoming a missionary began with the ability to imagine an opening for a woman to serve and then the courage to ask.

The Paths to Application

Women's applications generally opened with a discussion of their years of thoughtful introspection. When the opportunity seemed open, a few of them took the step to reach out and ask if they might be called, after all. If so, they were ready. They had been thinking about it for a long time. Emily Root wrote "with a trembling hand" in 1826 about her desire to serve as a missionary. It had been more than five years since she had, while reading about "the sad state of the heathen world," felt a calling to serve. Yet the first time she had mentioned such an interest to a friend, she had been discouraged. For years afterward, she remained silent.[12] Miss Flora Post was ready in 1829 and offered her services after hearing that more female help was needed at the Haweis station.[13] Adeline Sadler had been preparing herself for mission work for two years by the time she reached out to the board in 1837.[14] Abigail Kimball was ready in 1834, after hearing that the ABCFM was in need of an assistant for Cynthia Farrar, in India. Other women's letters were remarkably similar in tone and content.[15]

Kimball's letters are striking on this point. More than many of the other women, she explained at length the sorts of issues that had kept her from reaching out initially. She had first come to be interested in mission work through "frequent reading and reflection" on the needs of the heathen. "I was delirious of doing something for the diffusion of the light of the gospel amongst them," she explained, "yet it seemed impracticable for *me* to think of engaging in so great a work. There were obstacles in the way. I was not possessed of the requisite qualifications, nor the means of obtaining them. However, I resolved to procure them if possible, that if I had a call to labor, I might be able to answer it." She left home to train to become a teacher to prepare herself for such work. Until she heard of the ABCFM's need she had hoped to teach in the "destitute West," but now the possibility of working in a "field . . . just such as I have long desired" compelled her to reach out. "If I can do any thing for the spiritual welfare of the degraded females of India, even though it be but little," she insisted, "I should rejoice."[16]

The men who helped Kimball reach out to the ABCFM revealed a wider network of other women deeply interested in the mission movement. These women, like the students at Mount Holyoke, might reveal their interest to a trusted adviser and wait for a path to be opened. They might let it be known to a minister that they would be open to marrying a missionary and thus join the "missionary conjugal network" that historian Dana Robert has described.[17] Or, if they planned to remain single, they might look for the few opportunities like this to inquire about options.

Kimball's pastor spoke of other women from her town, mentioning one other woman specifically (though he did not name her) who was "*very* desirous of spending her life among the heathen, and devoting her *all* to their spiritual good." There were others, too, who had "repeatedly" asked him about how to prepare themselves to serve as missionaries.[18] The unnamed women in this letter were joined by other similar women. James Robbins, for example, wrote to the ABCFM in 1821 about an "unmarried woman in this town who is desirous of devoting herself" to the Eliot mission station. Robbins wrote about the woman's age (forty), her health (not great, but able to endure fatigue), her educational qualifications (quite strong), her religious activities (church member, active in benevolent societies), and her marital and economic status ("I do not think she has now or ever has had any particular desire to be married"). But she was never named until the board expressed its interest in this anonymous candidate. Then, and only then, did she make herself known and share an extensive statement in which she discussed her faith and her property (which she was planning to turn over to the ABCFM).[19] Rev. Shubael Bartlett asked Jeremiah Evarts in 1822 if "a single woman of excellent and pious character, one who always expects to live single" and who "would be an excellent help in families for any kind of domestic business" would be of use at the Sandwich Islands mission. If the board could use such a woman, he promised to "describe her more particularly."[20]

Cynthia Thrall, who would serve as a missionary to the Cherokee, explained why these men and the women they wrote about were so reluctant to use names. Thrall wrote that it was "thought by very many to be a presumptuous folly for an unmarried female to expose herself unsolicited" to missionary work. Like the other women who wrote to the ABCFM, she had spent years thinking about "the duties of the Christian towards those who are perishing for lack of that knowledge which we have the means of possessing to overflowing," and she hoped to find a way to become active in God's service. She worried that it was inappropriate for her to offer herself and that the board may have considered whether it was "inadvisable to accept the *offered* services of a female," but she asked anyway.[21] To her delight, the ABCFM had no such objections and opened a path forward for her to answer the calling she had received.

Women's Voices in the Archive

These applications represent only a small portion of the voices of Protestant women that can be found in the papers of the ABCFM, the largest of the Protestant American missionary societies of the antebellum period. Women's stories are everywhere in these archives. Here we meet both the white women who would serve or donate as well as the filtered stories of the non-white women whom they would convert. American women's applications for mission service are scattered throughout the mammoth archives of the ABCFM. They can be found in the obvious places—the collection of missionary "candidates" or applicants—as well as mixed in among the extensive collection of "domestic correspondence files."[22] In these many archival presences and absences and the (mis)filing of women's letters, we are left with the question of what to make of all this.

Archives are not natural, of course. They are created by living and breathing human beings, and the idiosyncrasies of their organization reflect the ways in which those individuals organized their world.[23] These particular files were created in their own time, with letter books initially created for, and used by, ABCFM personnel in the nineteenth century. Here, they recorded their outgoing and incoming correspondence in one place or another based on where it fit in their own mental and institutional sorting. Letters from missionary candidates were bound together and indexed by applicant, as were letters from missionaries abroad and outgoing letters to the various mission fields, to the agents who traveled throughout the United States to raise money and awareness about the movement, and to local auxiliary societies. Miscellaneous domestic and foreign correspondence was similarly sorted, bound, and indexed for the reference needs of the ABCFM's officers and the future researcher. The Protestant mission movement generated a great deal of correspondence and paperwork, and the internal organization of those records remains in the current archive. The modern historian who wants to view these letters can examine the now-fragile bound volumes, carefully supported in book cradles, at Harvard University's Houghton Library. To find women's voices in these early nineteenth-century records, the historian has many points of entry. The confusion about where women's letters of application ought to be placed in these archives is accordingly a sign of the confusion that early nineteenth-century missionary organizations felt about what to make of the women who felt called to serve in world mission.

In light of this structure, it is worth thinking about the ways in which women put themselves forward for missionary service and claimed their place within it in these years in greater depth. Comparison can help here. British Protestant women, too, formed auxiliary societies, followed the news of missionary progress, and supported the broader project of Protestant missions. But the British mission movement was generally more uncomfortable about the place of women than the Americans: mission wives were the cause of a bit more concern and caution, and there were no fields open to single British women that paralleled the North American and Sandwich Islands missions offered to their American sisters. But most striking of all as we look at American women's application letters is the absence of similar exploratory letters in the London Missionary Society archives inquiring about whether, where, and when women could serve. Even in the archive of unsuccessful missionary applications, women are absent until the 1870s, when the women's board began sending out single women on their own. (A similar upsurge of women's applications is evident in the United States at the same time, for similar reasons.)

In the London Missionary Society (LMS) archives, documents relating to the applications of women missionaries from the early decades of the century are limited to brief discussions and testimonials on behalf of the wives of ordained male missionaries. Each wife required two testimonials: one (usually extremely brief) from a doctor attesting to the woman's health and ability to survive in a foreign climate, the other (sometimes a bit longer) from the woman's pastor attesting to her piety. The other thing that stands out in these files is the complete absence of the women's voices themselves; no testimonial from the woman herself was required or saved. In the testimonials, the same adjectives and many of the same biographical details are repeated over and over again to the point that almost no individual personality emerges from the files. These British mission wives are pious with a zeal for the gospel. They have been Sunday school teachers. And they are of good constitution. Why any of them want to go to the mission field, however, is unanswered, at least in the files sent to their mission boards.

A few examples here will demonstrate this dynamic. Two of the earliest LMS files stand out for mentioning wives who had their own desires for mission work: William Gregory and Walter Hawkins both became LMS missionaries in 1798, and both were already married. Gregory noted that his wife was "also united with a very great desire if the Lord wills [us] to go and should esteem it a peculiar favor if we were favored with a line which would rejoice our hearts to hear that yet there is room." Hawkins brought his wife and daughter to his examination with the directors of the LMS, who noted that the wife was "a gracious woman" who "more than acquiesced" and was "evidently engaged" in her husband's desire to serve.[24] These 1790s examples of already married men and their willing wives stand out as examples of couples who were united in a desire to serve, even if it was the husbands and their callings that were the main interest of the society. A few decades later, the records on LMS mission wives' applications were a bit different—these couples were not usually married yet. Their intended husbands were asking permission from the society to get married, and the testimonials sent to the society were an important part of that process.

The question of whether or not LMS missionaries could be married became a hot-button issue quickly, with some directors preferring single male missionaries, while many men (like their American brethren) preferred to go into the mission field with wives. Mission work was meant to be lifelong, and concerns about illicit interracial sexuality made the idea of traveling with a wife preferable to some. Accordingly, the 1820s saw a few examples of men asking the LMS about whether or not they could marry: one such letter never names his intended wife, only referring to her as "a female" throughout the correspondence.[25] Another file, from David Griffiths, featured a series of heated letters about whether or not he could be married: he wanted to be married and had told the LMS of this desire, yet they were sending him to a field (Madagascar) that would require him to go unmarried. For such a passionate series of letters about marriage, it is striking that Griffiths's arguments never discuss any particular woman.[26]

Indeed, a good number of the pre-1870s candidate files for the LMS feature no women at all; those that do contain brief testimonies and records entirely voiced by men. In 1837, for example, Rev. John Abbs wrote to the directors of the LMS to inform them of his wish "to enter into the Married state previously to leaving England." He was engaged to Miss Louisa S. Kipper and enclosed testimonials on her behalf. He awaited the directors' response as to whether or not he could, in fact, be married to her. The two letters testified to her character and health ever so briefly: Richard Griffin had known her for five years and believed her constitution to be well suited to the Indian climate. John Dryden, her pastor, had a bit more to say, including that she had an "irreproachable" moral character, served as a teacher in his Sunday school, and was attentive to "the means of grace." "Her zeal and heartiness in the cause of the Redeemer, I have frequently had occasions to observe and admire," he wrote, insisting that the deficiencies that existed in her education were well balanced by these positive qualities.[27] This type of file was typical of those that mentioned women at all.

In comparison to this earlier silence from LMS women, the post-1870 period is remarkable. In that year, the LMS Women's Committee began sending single women out into mission fields on their own, and the candidates' files of the LMS were suddenly flooded with the voices of women who felt called to the mission field. These women, like their American peers, could speak quite eloquently about their desires to serve. Emmeline Geller's file from the 1870s, for example, speaks not only to her own calling but that of other women as well. In 1875, she explained to the society that she had long been interested in the mission to China from reading reports in LMS periodicals about the need for female laborers. Now that she had heard that the LMS had decided to send out single women, she felt that her time had come. When she later had to end her relationship with the society due to her marriage, she could do so with the confidence that there were other women who were "already waiting and anxious for employment, either one of whom would I have no doubt be only too glad to be appointed to this station."[28] Based on the robust files from women in this later period, there were indeed a great many women anxious to be sent out by the LMS.

Comparing the ABCFM and the LMS archives in this respect raises some intriguing questions. Why do women's missionary applications, tentative as they might have been, appear regularly in the American files but not at all in the British files? Between this quick increase in applications from women as soon as single women could be sent and the contrast with the more robust collection of early nineteenth-century American women's letters, it would be quite surprising if English women were not actually interested in missionary service in similar ways to American women in the first decades of the century. The major difference here seems to be more likely in archival practices. That the ABCFM does include some (but not all) women's applications in their archive of applications (the "candidate files") is revealing of the ways that women were simultaneously welcomed as potential missionaries and set aside.

These divergent archival practices between transatlantic missionary organizations that tended to cooperate with each other should draw our attention again to the range of ambiguous ways that women found their place in the movement and that the movement found a place for women. As American missionary officials received women's letters and decided where and how to file them in the ABCFM's extensive archives, they revealed the logic that undergirded where women themselves fit into the mission movement as a whole.

Throughout all the archival pockets where women's voices can be found in the ABCFM papers, similar themes emerge, and prime among them is a *question*. Over and over again, correspondents ask if women could be welcomed in as missionary laborers. We can see women asking on their own behalf, but far more often we see women using an intermediary: a pastor, a brother, or sometimes even a female missionary agent, who you might have thought would already know the answer to the question of whether single women were needed.[29] Over and over again, we hear of women wondering to themselves for years about whether such a path was possible. And finally they asked, Could a *woman* work in the mission field? And the answers they got explain why the women's letters, far more often than those of male candidates, open with a basic question of possibility. There was no consistent answer; sometimes *yes*, sometimes *no*, sometimes *wait*.

And so they asked. Over and over again. The sheer volume of women asking the board if they might serve, the lack of consensus about women's proper roles, and the reality of a broad and diverse mission field that had different needs at different times and in different places demanded a range of responses— even in these early years. The ABCFM organized its application files together, with individual volumes sorted alphabetically within a given date range. Within the files, women were not set apart; their letters can be found among those of the young men who, like them, felt a calling to serve the mission movement.

Thirteen thick volumes make up the applications received by the ABCFM between 1810 and 1837. Within those years alone, 160 women's inquiries can be found within these volumes and elsewhere in the archive. Women's names appear alongside men's in the index, sometimes identifiable by a "Miss" before the name but sometimes not. Some were accepted to mission service, while others were rejected (nine out of seventy-nine total missionaries whose rejections were compiled in a separate volume before 1821 were women). Many more American women show up in the collection of general domestic correspondence, sometimes writing about donations but often asking about opportunities to offer themselves to missionary service. In all these archival spaces, the letters speak to both individual callings and institutional grappling with gender and mission work.

Geography of Women's Missionary Opportunities

The increased opportunities for American women relative to their British peers are first and foremost attributable to the large missionary operations among various Native American groups—particularly, in this period, the Cherokee, Choctaw, and Seneca. Yet the existence of nearby North American missions cannot be the only explanation for the Anglo-American contrasts we have been exploring, for single women were also being sent overseas: to the Sandwich Islands and to India, where ABCFM missions began looking for single female assistance in the late 1820s. When women specified where they wanted to serve, many of them did mention the "Western" missions to American Indians—but many others pointed to overseas missions or were clear that they would go anywhere in the world that the ABCFM might send them.

Such was the case for Cynthia Farrar and Abigail Kimball, who would be the single women sent by the ABCFM as assistants to Bombay in response to a request from missionary wife Mary Graves, in 1827 and 1834 respectively. It was Graves who noted the need for more female teachers during a trip to the United States in the 1820s, pushing back against dissenting voices who doubted the propriety of sending single white women to India. Graves was insistent, however, and found some support among American women who were excited to raise money for the support of a female assistant missionary to India (at least some of whom wrote to the ABCFM about creating auxiliary societies for this purpose), while others at Bombay and in the ABCFM's Prudential Committee were not sure that this was a good idea at all.[30]

As ABCFM Secretary Rufus Anderson explained to one correspondent, it was a tricky question. It was clear to him "that females might doubtless do much good" in Indian mission schools, but the question remained, he insisted, "whether on the whole, taking a large view of the subject, it would be desirable to send unmarried females from this country to act as teachers and superintendents of schools." He just was not sure. "The time may come when this would be expedient—possibly it has become already," but the ABCFM was not quite ready to act. It was to this undecided organization that Farrar and Kimball offered their services. Women at home and in India wanted to make a way for their missionary work, but the leaders of the ABCFM were not sure what to do with them.[31]

In spite of the geographic differences in where they would serve, Farrar's and Kimball's applications conform to what we have seen elsewhere. In tone and content, they read much like those of the women who served in North America.[32] They were ultimately able to go to India for the same reasons that other single women were able to go to work with Native Americans: married missionaries saw a need, and they had offered to fill it. They could live within already-established missionary households and go about working with and for the women of the "heathen world." Their success in these roles, and the excitement they generated among American women at home, would lay the groundwork for later generations. After the Civil War, frustration at the long-standing slowness to respond to women's overwhelming interest in mission work would lead to the formation of women's boards and the embrace of "woman's work for woman." Farrar, Kimball, and their sister missionaries in North America opened the door and demonstrated women's interest and dedication to the cause, even when they were not sure if the institutions of the missionary movement were built to support them.

Women's Voices

In various places within the ABCFM archives we can hear women's voices, placed in the official candidate files, mixed among the domestic correspondent files (a fate that, it should be noted, men's applications did not face), and responded to over and over again in the ABCFM's outgoing correspondence. In letters from male supporters, too, we can glimpse their whispered wonderings. Could unmarried women be employed as missionaries? The ABCFM wrote to women and men alike to explain their shifting answers.[33] Women wrote for themselves; they asked through male acquaintances, who sometimes did not even provide the women's names. Could women serve? Well, sometimes.

The archival placement of these applications is a helpful reminder of the overall ambivalence of women's role in Protestant missions: of the limited recognized role for women within the transatlantic foreign missionary movement even as the women who did serve as missionaries could be celebrated on both sides of the Atlantic. The mission movement was never shy about holding up women as important actors in and beneficiaries of the movement, but, for all of its celebration of women's participation, and for all of its financial dependence on women's contributions, it was never quite sure what to do with the flesh and blood women who offered themselves for service. The women, too, were not sure what to do with the callings that they felt. This ambivalence is evident in many moments and spaces, down to the very archives in which the history of the movement was recorded and preserved.

Although the comparisons within this chapter have focused on British Protestants, another comparison suggested by this book as a whole would be particularly interesting. Mormon women entered into mission work under very different circumstances later in the century. Though there were some limited options for Mormon missionary wives in locations like the Pacific earlier in the century, the story of Mormon women in missions is generally understood as a response to outside pressures. Anti-polygamy criticism had become a real problem for Mormon missionaries, as outsiders spoke of Mormon women as enslaved and oppressed by plural marriages. When male missionaries found that audiences were responsive to presentations by Mormon women whose very presence spoke to these critiques, women were welcomed into missionary work at the turn of the twentieth century. Like their Protestant counterparts, they quickly became active once a path was opened for them.[34]

The different understandings of missionary work within Protestant and Mormon frameworks can account for some, perhaps much, of this difference. But Protestant women's anxieties when they asked about missionary service as well as the evident silences in the archives that were caused by those concerns might suggest that there is much more to say about Mormon women's understanding about their place in missionary work. Protestant women could keep silent for years, sensing that there was work that God wanted them to do, even before structures were built to enable them to act. Might Mormon women, too, have wondered in silence if the way might open for them to serve, long before the church opened the door?

CHAPTER 3

Humanitarian Encounter in Late Ottoman Turkey
State, American Protestant Missions, and the *Christian Herald* Armenian Relief Fund

Devrim Ümit

On November 3, 1819, Levi Parsons and Pliny Fisk, the first missionaries under the American Board of Commissioners for Foreign Missions (ABCFM) to the Near East, set sail from Boston to Izmir (Smyrna).[1] Izmir had long been a well-known Ottoman port city in the Aegean coastal region of western Anatolia where American merchants did prosperous business and American citizens with good connections resided. However, the American touch in the Ottoman territories did not create instant magic the way the missionaries expected, especially in terms of conversion of the "heathen" to Protestant Christianity, though they at least did their best to get acquainted with Ottoman lands.[2] The period from the day that the first American missionaries landed in Izmir until the mid-nineteenth century was therefore mostly a preparatory episode, not resulting in any immense accomplishment. Missionaries were largely concerned with getting sufficient training in the field to be familiar with the land, its inhabitants, and their cultures, customs, and habits. As a result, they focused on language learning, traveling as much as they could, preaching in private, distributing Bibles and religious tracts, opening presses, and experimenting with schools.

Resting on "three legs" from the outset, American mission work was the evangelistic, educational, and medical work carried out in churches and chapels, schools and colleges, and hospitals respectively. For this early period, missionaries in Anatolia were largely situated in the big cities of Izmir and Istanbul.

In 1830, as they began to "wander" the interior of Ottoman Turkey, they established a station at Erzurum the same year, the first station in the eastern region of Ottoman Turkey, to be followed by another at Antep (now Gaziantep) in 1848.[3] These two cities, particularly Erzurum, soon became stopovers for missionaries who wanted to travel into Anatolia.

The period from 1850 to 1876 was defined by the rapid growth of American missionary work in the interior regions of Ottoman Turkey. Evangelical interest was no longer confined to metropolises like Izmir and Istanbul but covered distant provinces and their environs as well. The expansion of missionary work required dividing the field in 1857, and three years later the ABCFM subdivided their operations in the Ottoman Empire into "European Turkey" and "Asiatic Turkey."[4] While the former included the European lands of Ottoman Turkey, the Balkans, and Thrace, the latter was divided into three fields, namely western, central, and eastern Turkey.

The focus of this chapter is the eastern Turkey mission, which was put together from the earlier northern Armenian mission and the remnants of the Assyrian and Nestorian missions, including the main locations of Erzurum in the north, Harput in the west, Van and Bitlis in the east, and Diyarbekir and Mardin in the south. However, in 1870, when the activities of the ABCFM were largely and massively concentrated in Ottoman Turkey, the missionary work in Turkey and Syria was overseen under the separate management of the ABCFM and the American Presbyterian Board respectively.

The time period covered in this chapter, 1876 to 1909, was an era in which American Protestant missionaries established themselves as significant actors in Ottoman Turkey as the ABCFM solidified its position through mission work. This was to such an extent that Rev. James B. Angell, a member of the Congregationalist Church as well as an educator and diplomat, was appointed envoy extraordinary and minister plenipotentiary in Istanbul between 1897 and 1898, with the support of the board. In return, Ottoman authorities, both central and local, consciously acted to defend the empire by systematically frustrating and dispiriting the American missionaries. The case of the *Christian Herald* Armenian Relief Fund, a relief body sponsored by the New York–based *Christian Herald* newspaper in 1896 to help the Armenians of the eastern provinces in Ottoman Turkey, demonstrates that the Ottoman ruling class, by the last quarter of the nineteenth century, was no longer interested in maintaining their earlier forbearing and amicable attitude toward the American Protestant missionaries and their activities, including relief work, which became a bone of contention between the Ottoman establishment and the missionaries.[5]

The period 1876 to 1909 was defined by the thirty-three-year rule of Sultan Abdülhamid II, which was associated with authoritarianism and meticulous surveillance of state and social affairs. The Hamidian regime understood the Islamic religion and the social order of the empire to be the empire's foundation, and missionaries presented a direct threat to both. Attaching the utmost importance to protecting Ottoman traditions and dominating the public sphere, the Hamidian regime considered the universal evangelism of American Protestant missionaries a threat to its foundations and fiercely scrutinized the missionaries.[6] Moreover, in the last quarter of the nineteenth century, European intervention, failure to reconcile ethnic and religious differences, territorial disintegration, and a wrenching series of social and economic crises tore at the bonds holding the Ottoman Empire together. In the face of a crumbling empire and the American mission work reaching the level of inculcating and indoctrinating the infrastructure of the Ottoman state, Abdülhamid II fiercely countered the American missionaries and their various activities with new policies and regulations.

The ABCFM ventured into Ottoman Turkey and humanitarian relief as an extension of a broader and vibrant "benevolent empire" movement that gained popularity in the decades after the American Civil War. In the last quarter of the nineteenth century, American missionaries and establishments associated with the board covered the map of Ottoman Turkey, and the relief work in particular provided the missionaries with an excellent venue for outreach to non-Muslims, primarily the Armenians in Ottoman Turkey. The humanitarian encounter between the Hamidian regime and the American Protestant missionaries around the turn of the twentieth century also served as a microcosm of the encounter between the Ottoman Empire as the "last Muslim empire," struggling to maintain its fast declining place in world politics, and the missionaries of "Christian America," of which the internationalist pattern was largely articulated by the term "New Manifest Destiny." Therefore, this chapter, largely through the examination of Ottoman archival materials, will look into the case of the *Christian Herald* Armenian Relief Fund, a relief group organized in the United States in the late nineteenth century to help the Armenians of the eastern provinces of Ottoman Turkey, shattered by the Armenian uprisings and state-military reprisals, while demonstrating the dispersal of aid materials as a point of contention, particularly between the American Protestant missionaries and the Ottoman ruling establishment, only to be solved through an imperial decree of Abdülhamid II sanctioning the distribution of relief by means of Ottoman officials.

In early January 1896, the New York–based Armenian Relief Fund's Work of Succor, which had been organized earlier by a weekly newspaper, the *Christian Herald and Signs of Our Times*, was extended to six new "Relief Stations" in eastern provinces of Ottoman Turkey to give "aid to large of numbers of destitute Armenian families," and the relief was to be distributed by "faithful American missionaries" on behalf of the fund.[7] These stations included Erzurum, Erzincan, Harput, Diyarbekir, Mardin, and Gemerek.[8] The earlier Van station had an appropriation of $10,500 from the relief fund through several missionary agents and attracted the single largest extensive relief project for an estimated fifty to seventy thousand refugees in need. With the exception of Gemerek, these locations were where the relief work was mostly concentrated in accordance with the needs of the areas. Trabzon was not included in the list as the American missionaries expected to reach the province more easily via sea from Russia. Readers of the *Christian Herald* contributed the bulk of the relief fund in response to a series the journal ran of letters received by Armenians of diverse backgrounds. One letter from the patriarch of Istanbul relayed a "report" by the Armenian prelacy of Harput that depicted the devastating outcomes of clashing religious communities: "Churches have been destroyed and holy vessels crushed, and many Christians killed," it read, raising the alarm for Protestants in the homeland to send urgent aid. Distress, displacement, and hunger afflicted the survivors, who entreated missionaries for "bread to keep them from dying" and for refuge against further hostility. Monasteries now turned to rubble could not house these refugees through the coming winter. The attack on the monastery of Tadman left residents and guards "torn to pieces."[9]

Letters of American "sisters and friends" of Ottoman Armenians to the *Christian Herald* were also influential in drawing the attention of readers in the United States. Margaret E. Sangster wrote to the journal appealing to the women of Christian America "to come to the relief of the starving mothers and children of Armenia" as a duty of faith and urged that Armenia and Armenians, as Christians of "pure faith" encircled by "idolaters," be protected against the destroying "Islamic despotism" of "unspeakable Turk" and be relieved through the contributions of Christians, not as charity but as a "just debt." American missionaries, as the "true-standard holders and torch-bearers," were ready to guard the Armenians.[10]

The *Christian Herald* further reported through US minister Alexander W. Terrell in Istanbul that the Ottoman imperial government was finally permitting the American missionaries to distribute relief. This "last obstacle" confronting the American missionaries, who felt thwarted by official opposition and had been conducting the relief work at "the greatest personal risk," had been "removed" by the Ottoman permission, the paper assumed. Its report was a blow to the Ottoman embassy in Washington, DC, which, on the same day, wrote to the Ottoman Ministry of Foreign Affairs about the *Christian Herald*'s misperception of the Ottoman permission.[11] In contrast to the paper's claim, the embassy letter indicated the vehement opposition of the Ottoman government to the distribution of relief work among the Armenian residents of the imperial provinces under the exclusive auspices of the American missionaries without governmental inspection and surveillance. The letter further indicated the Ottoman officials' astonishment and confusion at how the *Christian Herald* could possibly have gotten the idea that the Ottoman government had granted permission. Pointing to the large amounts of money in the relief fund, the embassy expressed its concern that the more money the fund accrued, the more money would be under the control of the American missionaries.

"Encouraged" by the "grant" of the official permission, the *Christian Herald* now proposed the establishment of new stations, "all manned by American Board missionaries," in Bitlis, Antep, Sivas, and Urfa. Giving particular attention to Urfa, where the Kurds and Hamidieh cavalry had committed "frightful atrocities on the Christians," the *Christian Herald* generally hoped that, with readers' cooperation, they could open new stations weekly until the crisis abated.[12] When appropriations of the relief fund for these new stations were transmitted by cable to the general treasurer of the ABCFM in Istanbul, Judson Smith, corresponding secretary of the board, wrote to the paper with joy: "Our missionaries everywhere are in warmest sympathy with these distressed people [Armenians], and I am sure they will prove most welcome almoners of the gifts of the Christendom."[13] In the abovementioned dispatch to the Ministry of Foreign Affairs, the Ottoman embassy was also concerned about the *Christian Herald*'s plan for additional stations, as this would increase the influence of American missionaries on the Armenian population. The Ottoman embassy closely followed the issues of the paper. When the *Christian Herald* emphasized in its January 22 issue that Armenians in the Ottoman Empire were being persecuted for being Christian, not Armenian, the embassy updated the ministry the very same day.[14] Alexander Mavroyeni, an Ottoman ambassador of Greek descent, was also influential earlier in changing the mind of a "Mr. Howard" about his plan to set off for Ottoman Turkey to be involved in the work of the relief fund.[15]

The Ministry of Foreign Affairs transmitted the dispatches of the Ottoman embassy, given the dispatches' significant contents and concerns, to the Grand Vizierate. In his February 17 communiqué to the Grand Vizierate, Minister of Foreign Affairs Tevfik Pasha stated that although the Ottoman government did not permit relief organizations' agents to distribute aid, it allowed relief by local commissions established by Muslim and Christian dignitaries.[16] These commissions had actually been established to allocate the donations made by Abdülhamid II for the needy. The US Department of State was informed accordingly by the Ottoman embassy. The question of distribution of foreign relief at the hands of American missionaries was of such great importance to the Ottoman government that the Grand Vizierate, in its letter of March 2 responding to the Ministry of Foreign Affairs, asked the latter one more time to inform the US Department of State that the distribution of American relief would be allowed only through the local commissions.[17]

The Ottoman government was not the only party to resent the distribution of American relief by means of American Protestant missionaries. When relief work for Armenians of Eastern Anatolia was organized by Clara Barton of the American Red Cross earlier in the year, Catholic Ottoman Armenian citizens also protested denominational "discriminations" against recipients by the American Protestant missionaries.[18] In a letter of May 13, 1896, published in the Chicago-based *Chronicle*, Stefano Pietro X. Azarian, patriarch of Catholic Armenians, criticized Barton for distributing the relief work of the Red Cross and other societies through Protestant missionaries.[19] Despite the fact that aid collected by these societies was from all the denominations in England and the United States, Azarian alleged that the American Protestant missionaries were using their position and the funds to exclude Catholic Armenians.

In the aftermath of talks with Patriarch Azarian, Barton, in person, appeared to be responsive to the concerns of the Catholic Armenians. Based on the continuing reports of bishops from various centers, such as from Monsignore Avedis Turkian, bishop of Maraş (now Kahramanmaraş), the patriarch maintained his position that the Catholics did not want aid to be distributed "at the hands of the Protestant missionaries." If it was, they would be deprived of any aid and it would be impossible to ask for any support from the Protestant missionaries "without running into danger."[20]

Azarian suggested the distribution of aid through a mixed-denomination committee, at least one member of which should be a Catholic. Meanwhile, he also defied the statements that the bulk of the aid was sent to the French and English ambassadors in Istanbul with a counterclaim that the French ambassador had received nothing while the English ambassador and the American Bible House had the "principal management of the dispensation of funds."[21]

For different reasons, both the Ottoman central authorities and the Catholic Armenian population in the eastern provinces were against the distribution of relief materials of various benevolent societies through American Protestant missionaries, and both sought the establishment of mixed commissions, though with different configurations, for secure and fair distribution. As with other missionary journals and any other newspapers and journals of importance, the Ottoman embassy closely followed the *Chronicle* as well and promptly updated the Ministry of Foreign Affairs on relief work in Ottoman Turkey.

As the *Christian Herald* Armenian Relief Fund began to extend its relief work through American Protestant missionaries to include new stations, such as the district of Antep and the subprovince of Urfa (now Şanlıurfa), both located in Aleppo province, the Ottoman government took extra measures to limit the activities of the American missionaries and their influence on the local communities, especially on the Armenians. Upon notification of the Ministry of Interior Affairs by the Grand Vizierate on March 26, 1896, that "the American missionaries were trying to convert the Christian populace [*ahali-i Hristiyaniye*] to Protestantism and Catholicism," the ministry asked the governor of Aleppo to investigate and communicate the circumstances within the province and the latter authorized the local authorities to this end.[22] Subsequently, the subgovernors of Urfa and Maraş and the *kaimmakams* of Antakya and Antep reported back to the governor about the American relief work, foreign missionaries, and consuls as much as about the American missionaries, through whom the aid was being distributed, and their influence on Muslim and Armenian populations. The reports of the local authorities were soon transmitted to the Grand Vizierate by the Ministry of Interior Affairs. Meanwhile, on April 27, 1896, an "imperial rescript" (*ferman*) was issued to warn against the distribution of the relief by the American Protestant missionaries: "Since the aid, accumulated by the *Christian Herald* journal for the Armenians residing in the imperial provinces, is being distributed through the medium of American missionaries, the *missionaries use this as an opportunity to disseminate Christianity and to cause the Christian populace to incline towards Protestant and Catholic religions.* . . . Henceforth, it is vital to make all possible investigations by every necessary means and to communicate the consequences with due evaluations."[23]

The mounting concern of the Ottoman central and local authorities was for several reasons. First, the appropriations in the *Christian Herald* Armenian Relief Fund was reaching a significant level. The subgovernor of Maraş began his communiqué of June 10 to Aleppo province by calling attention to the high amount of $30,000 from the relief fund that had so far been distributed by American missionaries to the Armenian population in Ottoman Turkey.[24] This was perceived as an increase in the missionaries' direct influence on the Christian population in general and on the Armenians in particular. Ottoman authorities were further uneasy about the fact that the American missionaries and the Armenians were growing closer, to the extent of becoming "allies" (*müttefik*), especially since the outbreak of the "Armenian question" (*Ermeni meselesi*) in the last quarter of the nineteenth century.

Second, Ottoman authorities were also worried about potential exploitation of the Christian populace through aid, thereby converting believers such as the Armenians of the native Gregorian Church to the denominations of the relief workers, whether Protestantism or Catholicism. As articulated in the letter of April 27 by the Ministry of Interior Affairs, this was considered to be "incompatible with the policy of the Ottoman state since this development was recognized to be against the fundamental principles of freedom of religion and to be a source of conflict among the classes and subjects of the state" (serbest-i edyan-ı kaide-i esasiyesine ve sınıf ve teba beyninde her neden olursa olsun ihtilafı zuhuru hükümet-i senniyenin ahval-ı siyasiyesine mubayın).[25]

It is worth stressing that Ottoman authorities' understanding of the "freedom of religion" (serbest-i edyan) was different from the modern meaning of this principle in that it was recognized as a right of the Ottoman state to guard the religion of Islam against other faiths and beliefs. Based on a specific imperial decree, one was required, in the event of a "change of religion" (tedbil-i mezheb), to inform both the "head of the church" (reis-i ruhaniye) of the denomination that was going to be abandoned and that of the denomination to which the person was converting. Otherwise, conversion would not be officially authorized. The subgovernor of Maraş, in the concluding lines, showed his conviction that the missionaries had ill intentions: "It is within our knowledge that the American missionaries are committed to intrigue while they visit the Armenian localities of the Imperial Domains" ([Amerikalı] misyonerlerin bir vesile ile Memalik-i Şahane'nin Ermeni olan mahallerini gezerek ikayı fesaddan hali olmadıkları mahsus[dur]).[26]

Third, government officials were concerned that British and French diplomatic officials could now potentially cooperate with American missionaries, expanding the Ottoman surveillance net. The subgovernor of Maraş complained about the French vice consulate, whose "activities against the Sultan [Sultan-ı seniyye] and Muslim subjects [millet-i İslamiye] went far beyond those of the American missionaries."[27] He also criticized the Latin priests and the Catholic plenipotentiaries, but their activities were less of a concern than those of the French diplomat. In his letter of June 13 to Aleppo province, the kaimmakam of Antakya reported that, although there were no American missionaries in his locality, there was one particular British missionary who had been operating there for more than fifteen years.

Unlike the claims of the patriarch of Catholic Armenians during the American relief work, the kaimmakam of Antep, in his letter of May 9 to Aleppo province, expressed his concern that Rev. Americus Fuller, president of Central Turkey College in Antep, also known as Antep College, who was distributing relief materials, made no distinction between the Armenians on the basis of Protestant or Catholic millets.[28] There were two reasons for the Ottoman officials to be displeased by this particular development. First, as the Armenians, including the clergy, were becoming more politically active, the line between the Assembly of Clerics (Ruhani Meclis) and the Political Assembly (Cismani Meclis) became blurred. The bicameral system within the Armenian millet was a by-product of the Regulation of Armenian Millet (Ermeni Milleti Nizamnamesi) of 1863, popularly known as the Armenian Constitution, in accordance with which the Assembly of Clerics saw to religious affairs while the Political Assembly attended to executive and legislative affairs. Distribution of the relief materials without giving attention to the separation between the Protestant and Catholic Churches was seen by the Ottoman officialdom as encouraging the union between the Assembly of Clerics and the Political Assembly. Second, even though the millet system was abolished with the Reform Edict (*Islahat Fermanı*) of 1856, the Ottoman authorities were still sensitive to protecting the boundaries between Christian denominations, particularly in the case of Armenians, by separating churches, and they resented Armenian priests attending Protestant churches and vice versa. By this means, the Ottoman ruling class aimed to play down the nationalist sentiments among the Armenians of diverse denominations. As a result, American missionary contact with the Armenians was recognized as a threat against the Ottoman societal structure and state authority.

The rapid expansion of American missionary establishments and activities by the early 1880s resulted in their close surveillance by the Ottoman officialdom in conformity with imperial rulings. This was centered on the question of "conversion" (*tanassur*), a term used in reference to conversion to Christianity irrespective of the religion abandoned. If the conversion took place from Islam to Christianity, this was recognized as "apostasy" (*irtidad*) and was punishable in accordance with the "religious law" (*şer'i hükümler*) but not strictly criminalized based on the imperial law and regulations. Since relief work granted the American missionaries a prime opportunity for intimate association with the Ottoman Armenians, the Hamidian regime adopted a more cautious stance toward the mission relief work due to its potential consequences in terms of changes of church affiliation. Abdülhamid often issued imperial decrees for the "investigation" (*tahkikat*) of missionary activities throughout the Ottoman domains by respective local authorities, who were asked to report the findings of their inquiries to the Yıldız Palace, the official residence of the sultan.

The Ottoman government maintained its cautious stance toward the American missionaries' dispersal of aid as the American relief work largely targeted areas with an Armenian population. Unless informed in advance, the government did not approve the distribution of relief materials via missionaries, and the latter sought the cooperation of central and local authorities for the safety of their relief work. Both central and local authorities watched foreign relief activities closely. In accordance with central orders, local authorities kept the Ottoman government informed on a regular basis about relief work and missionary involvement. Given the importance and urgency attached to missionaries and their activities, provincial authorities preferred to inform the Grand Vizierate directly instead of going through the Ministry of Interior Affairs, which had previously been the routine method of bureaucratic communication.

Ottoman authorities harbored similar concerns and exhibited the same approach toward the British missionaries when it came to their activities influencing the Armenian population. During the Armenian uprisings of the mid-1890s in Sason, a district of Bitlis province, plans were made for relief materials that had been collected in London to be distributed to the towns of Sehhal and Feval through the British missionaries.[29] The British embassy in Istanbul communicated to this end with the Ottoman Ministry of Foreign Affairs. Based on reports sent by the inquiry commission established in Sason to investigate the events, the Cabinet (*Meclis-i Mahsus-u Vükelâ*) denied the British embassy's request. Copies of these reports were also presented to the sultan.

The minutes (*mazbata*) of the Cabinet highlighted a particular event reported by the Sason inquiry commission concerning an Armenian resident who "rebuffed" a sum of 2,000 Turkish liras granted by Abdülhamid II as part of a donation to the Armenian residents of Sason whose houses had been burned down during the uprisings. The Cabinet saw this as "rebellious behavior" (*hareket-i serkeşâne*) resulting from the "incitement and encouragement of some intriguers within the Armenian National Assembly" and therefore deduced that allowing the relief materials to be distributed by British missionaries would cause the Armenians to become even more "spoiled."[30] It was not common for Abdülhamid II or any sultan to make public donations, and it was virtually unheard of for an ordinary citizen to decline the sultan's aid. Consequently, in conformity with a specific imperial decree ordering the distribution of foreign relief materials through Ottoman officials, the Cabinet ruled that foreign relief materials within the imperial domains should be distributed in parallel with the way the sultan's relief supplies were being distributed in foreign countries, that is, through the officials of these countries.[31] The Grand Vizierate promptly transmitted the Cabinet decision to the Ministry of Foreign Affairs to be presented to the British embassy on June 27, 1895. The insistence of Abdülhamid II on the dispersal of foreign assistance through Ottoman officials suited the Hamidian regime since it was an opportunity for the legitimization efforts of the monarch to be integrated into the public sphere.

During the reign of Abdülhamid II between 1876 and 1909 the Ottoman Empire was in a political and economic recession, and the American Protestant missionaries, as the evangelical arm of a great power, were thoroughly establishing themselves among the non-Muslim populations of the empire, particularly the Armenians. The Ottoman ruling establishment set itself to counter the ambitious, determined, and expansionist activities of the American missionary enterprise in a broad range of domains from schools to relief work. They did not pretend that the American missionary was a temporary threat but rather viewed them as a long-term, formative challenge to the long-established fabric of state and society. Therefore, any activity associated with the American missionaries served as a site of conflict between the Ottoman Empire, whose place in the international arena was fading fast, and the United States, a nation quickly becoming a leading power and threatening to sweep into the realm of the Ottomans.

Consequently, the humanitarian encounter between the Hamidian regime and American Protestant missionaries was not without serious friction. In the late 1890s, when the eastern provinces in Ottoman Turkey were devastated by the vicious cycle of Armenian uprisings and state-military reprisals, relief work in particular granted the American missionaries a perfect opportunity to reach out to and engage with the Armenians in the region. The particular case of the *Christian Herald* Armenian Relief Fund, a US-based relief body mainly backed by American Protestant missionaries, in 1896 demonstrates the conflicting views of the Ottoman officialdom, Catholic Armenians, and American Protestant missionaries not only over the dispersal of aid but also over how the question was eventually settled in the imperial decree of Abdülhamid II sanctioning the distribution of relief materials through Ottoman officials. The voluminous Ottoman state files on the Armenian Relief Fund and other foreign relief work highlight how the Hamidian regime had become much more alert by the late nineteenth century to American relief work serving as a fertile ground for American Protestant missionaries to target the Armenians of the eastern provinces of the Ottoman Empire. Seeing American mission work of any kind as a substantive and long-standing challenge to the core elements of the Ottoman state and society, the Ottoman ruling establishment managed to impose its own set of rules for relief work in the last decade of the nineteenth century.

CHAPTER 4

Dueling Orientalisms
The Scottish Imagination in the Mormon Missionary Mind

Taunalyn Ford

Hugh Findlay (1822–1905), a Scottish Latter-day Saint, was taught and baptized by Parley P. Pratt in 1844. He lost his first wife and two sons in a diphtheria epidemic; in the midst of his sorrow, Findlay poured himself into work as church leader and missionary in Great Britain.[1] He received a letter while serving as a district president in Hull, England, from Elder Lorenzo Snow, then "President of the Italian, Swiss and Indian Missions" of the Church of Jesus Christ of Latter-day Saints. The letter dated September 1, 1851, began, "Dear Elder Findlay, How would it suit your feelings and circumstances to perform a Mission to Bombay India?" Snow, who would eventually become the prophet-president of the Church of Jesus Christ, was somewhat timid in his call to Findlay, writing, "I should like you to go on this mission if circumstances are favorable, and you think you could live through it." He warned that it was "no easy mission. A strange country, a hot climate, pestilential diseases, &c. &c., are no pleasant things to encounter."[2] Perhaps it was Findlay's lack of family to leave behind that gave him the courage to travel without purse or scrip to India late in 1851. By April 8, 1852, Findlay had arrived in India, according to a report in the *Bombay Guardian*. The article warned, "A Mormon has made his appearance in Bombay, bent on propagating the faith of the Latter Day Saints."[3]

Findlay was one of many Scotsmen in 1850s Bombay. After the parliaments of Scotland and England united in 1707 to create the Parliament of Great Britain, underprivileged Scots were drawn to the opportunities of British citizenship, such as membership in the English East India Company (EIC). After 1750, EIC employees from Scotland made up half of its total numbers.[4] Findlay and his fellow "Mormon" missionaries spent most of their time and resources proselytizing EIC soldiers stationed in India.

Scottish missionaries were a significant presence in Bombay when Findlay reached his field of labor. The Church of Scotland sent two "rising stars" to India in 1830: Alexander Duff (1806–1878) to Calcutta and John Wilson (1804–1875) to Bombay.[5] John Wilson stayed in Bombay until the end of his life and became fluent in the Marathi vernacular as well as Sanskrit and Zend (the liturgical language of the Parsees).[6] The Church of Scotland also sent John Murray Mitchell (1815–1904), a graduate of Edinburgh University and a prodigy in languages, to Bombay to join John Wilson as a missionary in 1838. He too mastered Marathi, Sanskrit, and Zend (Avestan). Mitchell's work in India was representative of the Scottish orientalist missionaries of the nineteenth century. He was a prolific writer, translator, missionary, and administrator of higher education.

These missionaries are referred to as Scottish orientalist missionaries because of their contributions to knowledge of the religions of India, their translation of scriptural texts into English and vernacular languages, and the literature they produced that educated the "occident" on the "religion" of the "orient" in India. They founded universities in India as part of proselytizing efforts and focused on higher education of the middle-class and upper-caste Hindus according to Duff's downward filter theory. The theory was based in the Scottish Enlightenment ideals that education would naturally lead to Christian conversion and that the influence of the higher classes would eventually trickle down the social ladder and result in the conversion of all Indians. The Hindu students of these Scottish missionaries became a new elite encompassing figures like Ram Mohan Roy, who instigated the Hindu renaissance in Bengal that would lead to the birth of nationalism. In the end, the objective of Scottish orientalist missionary work was to convince the native population in India of the supremacy of Protestant Christianity.

Jane Rendall makes the case that "the extent to which the Scottish Enlightenment offered a conceptual framework for the understanding of complex and alien Asian societies has been underestimated."[7] I suggest that the extent to which the Scottish Enlightenment influenced Mormon missionary work has likewise been underestimated. Findlay, the Scotsman, acted in ways that echo the Scottish orientalist missionaries of his time. Some of his practices mark him as more American in his approach to missionary work, but he clearly departs from the other Latter-day Saint missionaries in the East India mission in at least three ways. First, Findlay prioritized learning the language of the people—Marathi—and worked diligently to write a tract directly to them. Second, Findlay was careful to record information about the religious practices of the diverse traditions he encountered in Bombay and thus took part in the orientalist practice of creating "world religions." Third and finally, Findlay seemed more cognizant of his Scottish missionary peers as he emulated their orientalist priorities, responded to them in newspapers, challenged them to debates, and critiqued them. In the end Findlay rejected and was likewise rejected by his Scottish peers in spite of the ecumenical spirit of the time. Ultimately, Findlay, who had become more American, became an object of their orientalist glare.

Marathi and the Tract

One of Mitchell's books written as a missionary in India is called *Letters to Indian Youth regarding the Evidences of the Christian Religion, with a Brief Examination of the Evidences of Hinduism, Parseeism and Mohammedanism*. Findlay was unique among his fellow Latter-day Saint missionaries in his desire to write directly to the "Indian Youth" to explicate the importance of the *restored* Christian message. He was constantly recording his efforts to learn Marathi, at the same time as he preached among British soldiers. Finally, with the help of a paid tutor, Findlay mastered enough Marathi to oversee the translation of a small missionary tract, "To the Marattas of Hindoostan: A Treatise on the True and Living God and His Religion." It was his magnum opus, akin to Mitchell's *Letters to Indian Youth*, though on a much smaller scale.

The question of who was to be the object of Latter-day Saint proselytizing in India was broached often. Were they to preach to British members of the East India Company stationed in India or were they to take the message to the indigenous people? The impetus for nineteenth-century Latter-day Saint missionary work in India came in 1849 when two Europeans living on the subcontinent read missionary tracts and inquired about the church. Around the same time, two newly baptized British sailors, Benjamin Richey and George Barber, landed in Calcutta and introduced the gospel to some British members of the Plymouth Brethren sect of Christianity. Hearing of these occurrences, Lorenzo Snow felt that he should call missionaries to serve in India. Snow sent the first official—in other words, ordained and set apart missionary—Elder Joseph Richards, to Calcutta, and he baptized the first Mormon converts in India. Snow also sent William Willes to Calcutta just prior to calling Hugh Findlay to Bombay.

Latter-day Saint missionaries were also sent from the Great Salt Lake Valley in 1852. The millenarian spirit present in Mormonism of this era, and the belief that the "gospel of the kingdom shall be preached in all the world for a witness unto all nations; and then shall the end come," was part of the theme of a general conference of the church held in Salt Lake City in August of 1852. At this conference, Brigham Young called 108 missionaries to fields of labor all over the world, and nine of them were called to India or "Hindustan." The missionaries sent by Brigham Young in 1852 and those British missionaries sent to Calcutta were more inclined to teach the British and the few Indians who spoke English than to spend the time and energy learning the different vernacular languages spoken in the various cities where they worked. Some felt that when they tried to learn the language "they could not get the holy Ghost to help them," concluding that "the time [had] not yet come for India to receive the gospel" and that it was therefore not expedient for them to study languages.[8]

Hugh Findlay never seems to have questioned that he was sent to all people in Bombay, not just those who spoke English. He spent his scarce resources and time in language study. One entry in his journal reads, "I have this morning commenced rising with gunfire at ½ past 4 in the morning for my Maratha Studies as I am so often interrupted during the day."[9] In the end, Findlay was no more successful at reaching indigenous Indians than his fellow Latter-day Saint missionaries, but he never gave up on the pursuit of language acquisition. Like the other Scottish missionaries, Findlay envisioned learning languages and translating key texts as central to the Great Commission. Ironically, all that seems to remain of Findlay's tract, "To the Marattas of Hindoostan," is a copy of it in Marathi, with no evidence of the English original.

Constructing World Religions

Mitchell, speaking of the religious diversity in nineteenth-century Bombay, confessed that it was "tempting to denounce" these religions but argued that doing so "did little good. The question was what gave these systems their terrible power over human hearts."[10] Answering that question for the missionary/orientalist was the key that would unlock these hearts to the Christian message. According to Mitchell, "All of these systems had to be studied, and, if possible (no easy task), *understood*."[11] We should note that he refers to the religions to be studied as "systems." This use marks his participation in the larger project of labeling "oriental" religions with their "isms": Hinduism, Zoroastrianism, Buddhism, and Jainism. Then Scottish orientalist missionaries translated associated religious texts, compared them, and situated them "on a world religions map that remains essentially unchanged to this day."[12]

Even if the orientalist work of these missionaries was in the service of the Great Commission, they offer important glimpses of the lived religions they encountered. These Scottish missionaries interacted "extensively with Hindus,

Muslims, Parsis, Jews, Jains, Catholics, and tribal and aboriginal peoples living throughout western India." The same cannot be said of "Orientalists such as Max Muller and Christian ministers such as Fredric Maurice," both of whom "have become popular names for their studies of India's religions," and yet "neither of them lived in nor traveled to India," nor did they or scholars like "H. H. Wilson, interact *significantly* with the populations whose religions they were ostensibly describing."[13] Mitch Numark argues that the observations of Scottish missionaries "reveal the elements that made non-Christian religions *religions* distinct from and structurally equivalent to Christianity."[14] Numark also links their efforts at making these observations "scientific" with their Scottish education. I argue that Hugh Findlay can be added to this list of Scottish missionaries. I also argue that more work needs to be done among scholars of Mormon mission to see the links between the Scottish Enlightenment and the growth of Mormonism through Scottish converts and missionaries.

The detailed ethnographic observations that Findlay and the career Scottish missionaries recorded were also for the consumption of supporters back in Scotland and Christianity at large. Although worlds apart in their differing Christian theologies and training, their writings reflect a common orientalist missionary discourse of the period that included surprisingly rich descriptive detail and interreligious engagement. Findlay would often copy quotations from the local newspaper describing religious practices and festivals. It is highly likely that these descriptions came from the work of orientalist scholars in the area. Hugh Findlay clearly studied and looked to the work of these missionaries both to criticize, as a competitor in the war for the souls of the British soldiers and the native population, as well as to learn from their scholarship. Findlay's dedication to recording the practices of the various religions set him apart from his Mormon contemporaries in the Hindustan mission.[15]

There are numerous examples of Findlay recording in his journal descriptions of religious practices, such as his "Reflections started by the occasion of a Hindoo funeral procession." In this detailed description Findlay depicts a tower of silence "used by the Parsees or descendants of Persia who are numerous in Western India." He explains how in "large enclosures built to a good height, open overhead [these Zoroastrians in exile in India] deposit their dead, purposefully exposed to the vultures and fowls of the air to feed upon, with a chasm under and iron grating into which the mauldering bones drop."[16] Another entry outlines "a history of the female Hindoo costume" in detail to show "the clear fulfilment of the prophecy [of] Isaiah, chap. 3 and 2 Nephi 13."[17]

Not all Scottish orientalists of the period were seeking constructive understanding of the religions they were systematizing. There is another side "of the perception of India through Scottish discourse" exemplified by James Mill

(1773–1836), who wrote a six-volume *History of British India* that was "a recommended seminal text for the British personnel who came to rule India." His work spoke of the "inherent 'evil' and 'corrupt' nature of the Hindu and 'depravity', fueled by his superstition and 'primitive' religion." The other side of Scottish orientalism "justified the coloniser's sense of superiority that led to a sense of disinterest among the East India Company servants and the employees of the Raj in Indian culture."[18] There were times when missionary discourse also drifted into this darker side. The lack of success that Latter-day Saint missionaries had with indigenous peoples was often attributed to the corruption and depravity of the surrounding religions.

One of These Scots Is Not Like the Others

During the Second Great Awakening while Mormonism was in its infancy, the American Board of Commissioners for Foreign Missions (ABCFM) was organized. Inspired by the writings of William Carey and other missionaries in India, the ABCFM's first mission was established in Bombay.[19] They also sent missionaries to West Bengal, where the British missionaries already there "seemed perplexed by the lack of planning that American missionaries seemed to have completed prior to their arrival in India. American missionaries relied on Providence rather than planning and deference to the regulations in put in place by the East Indian Company."[20] Findlay and the other Mormon missionaries reflected this same "American" tendency. As David Golding has suggested, nineteenth-century Mormon missionaries were more pragmatic and "sensed a more existential preoccupation than their more established Protestant neighbors—their small numbers called for all hands on deck and gathering converts to a central community before an imminent apocalypse." The relatively short-term nature of their missions, coupled with a lack of formal training, made them stand out against Protestant missionaries.[21]

In 1825 the Bombay Missionary Union was formed and provided these ABCFM missionaries with important ecumenical links to their fellow Protestant missionaries. The Bombay Missionary Union consisted of four different mission agencies: the ABCFM, the Church Missionary Society, the London Missionary Society, and the Scottish Missionary Society, all working in diverse areas in Bombay.[22] According to Emily Conroy-Krutz, their "goal was to 'promote Christian fellowship, and to consult on the best means of advancing the Kingdom of Christ in this country,' and membership and participation in annual meetings was 'open to any Protestant missionary in the region.'"[23] Even Scottish missionaries, who endured a schism in the Church of Scotland in 1843 along with an accompanying rupture of mission in India, remained committed to an ecumenical Protestant approach. However, their perception of ecumenism did not encompass Mormon mission.

From the moment of Findlay's arrival in Bombay he was met with an antagonistic reception from the *Bombay Guardian*, a weekly Christian newspaper associated with the Bombay Missionary Union. In addition to the warning given of his arrival in early April 1852, the paper published a report on "The Mormons" in the Utah Territory on April 16, 1852. Findlay, who seems to have had no awareness of the practice of plural marriage, was greeted by an exaggerated account of Brigham Young's ninety wives, including a description of him driving down the street with "16 of them in a long carriage, 14 of them having each an infant at her bosom."[24] Findlay responded with a polemical letter to the editor on April 27, calling the *Bombay Guardian* to repent for publishing these lies. In it, he opines in a not-so-ecumenical manner that he and his fellow Latter-day Saint missionaries have come "with the fulness and power of the everlasting Gospel," expressing that he is surprised to find his "first opponents should be, not the votaries of idolatry or heathenism" but his fellow Christian missionaries, in a newspaper "published, professedly, for the extending of Messiahs Kingdom!"[25] This debate continued back and forth in the *Bombay Guardian* through June 1852. Findlay continued to write lengthy and verbose letters denying the practice of polygamy and declaring the doctrines of the great apostasy and the restoration of the gospel. The *Bombay Guardian* responded by warning, "The enemy is now *within* the Camp," inviting the Scottish missionaries who had put to rest the "controversy on the Zend and Sanskrit mythology" to take on Findlay.[26]

The editors of the *Bombay Guardian* mocked Findlay and painted him as clearly oblivious to what was going on in the Utah Territory because he had never even been to the headquarters of the American religion he was representing in India. They were appalled by Findlay speaking of the priesthood in a way reminiscent of Roman Catholicism and declared that "Mahommedanism is not near so transparent a lie as Mormonism."[27] The stakes rose as the first Mormon baptism was performed in June 1852. Findlay failed to gain permission to preach and hold meetings in the military boundaries of Bombay and left for Poona (now Pune) approximately one hundred miles southeast to continue his work. In the end, Findlay and the Mormon missionaries were working against what Conroy-Krutz has described as the "Anglo-American culture" built on "Enlightenment concepts of progression of mankind from savagery to barbarism and finally to civilization the highest form of social organization."

Mormon missionaries were viewed by their Protestant contemporaries as having yoked themselves to Catholic priesthood and as worse than "Mahommedan" polygamists.[28]

On July 19, 1855, the East India mission president received a letter from Church President Brigham Young. It read, "Come home, and bring as many of the Saints with you as are ready to come and leave the rest in the best possible state you can." On October 31, 1855, a notice in the *Deseret News* from the First Presidency read, "The East Indian missionaries have returned or are on their way hither, having faithfully preached the gospel to that benighted country but with little apparent success." In 1856, the mission was officially closed, leaving approximately sixty-one members in all of India, with eleven church members eventually immigrating to the Salt Lake Valley. Those who were "gathered" to Utah were mostly British, with the exception of Elizabeth Xavier Tait, who was married to a British solider.

The next chapter in Indian history pivots on the Sepoy Mutiny of 1857 and the beginning of the British Raj on the subcontinent. Historians mark the Sepoy Mutiny of 1857 as an important moment in the Indian quest for independence. The future of Indian Christianity would be characterized by postcolonial ecumenism. In retelling the story, Latter-day Saints see the closing of the Hindustan mission as providential because conditions in their fields of labor were increasingly dangerous for people of European descent.[29]

Subhashis Pan has recently argued that there was something unique about Scottish orientalists like Duff, Wilson, Mitchell, and others, "who studied and observed the richness of India in the field of economy, education, culture and religion." Pan's main contention is that "in the context of India when we talk about 'Scottish Orientalism', we need to focus on the already blurred identity of being 'Scottish' in the dominant English field." According to Pan, Scottish missionaries and scholar-administrators "shunned European superiority" and endeavored to define "India in its own terms."[30] The same blurring of Scottish identity in Mormon history is something historians might consider. Findlay's writings and priorities in his missionary work reveal an echo of the work of Scottish Christian missionaries in spite of the ways he fought against them in periodicals and public meetings. Acknowledging the Scottish orientalist influence on Findlay's performance of missionary work as well as the ways he and his fellow Mormon missionaries differed is an intervention into uncovering the Scottish influence on Latter-day Saint thought in general and specifically in understanding Mormon missiology in the last half of the nineteenth century.

CHAPTER 5

Shoshone Worlds, Bannock Zions
Protestant and Latter-day Saint Missionary Work among the Shoshone and Bannock

Amanda Hendrix-Komoto

In 1884, the Church of Jesus Christ of Latter-day Saints opened a temple in Logan, Utah. For white Saints, the temple consecrated the valley. *The Deseret News* proclaimed that it offered the Saints a view that extended "from the mountains of Paradise on the South, to Marsh Valley, in Idaho, on the north." Ascending its steps allowed individuals to see "Providence, Millville, Hyrum, Paradise, Wellsville, Mendon, Newton, Oxford, Lewiston, Smithfield, Hyde Park and Benson." The authors considered "the view from [its] towers" to be "one of unsurpassed loveliness and beauty, embracing not only the quiet charm of villages and fields lying so peacefully beneath the eye of the observer, but the grandeur and sublimity of our glorious old mountains."[1] From the temple, Latter-day Saints could look at the mountains and valleys of Utah and Eastern Idaho that formed Zion.

Over twenty-five thousand local Latter-day Saints assisted in the temple's construction, quarrying stone and felling lumber from nearby canyons.[2] One of the community groups who volunteered was the Shoshone Latter-day Saint community of Washakie, Utah. Members of the Northwestern Shoshone founded the community after their conversion to the restored gospel. In 1863, the United States Army murdered three hundred Northwestern Shoshone as they camped near the Bear River. The attack was originally framed as the Battle of Bear River but eventually became known as the Bear River Massacre.

Close readings of nineteenth-century church records reveal the importance of the Logan Temple to the Northwestern Shoshone. Its construction allowed Shoshone Saints to participate in temple rituals that promised salvation to family members lost to colonial violence. The church's archives hold a register documenting the names of Shoshone Saints who came to be baptized for the dead, many of whom had died in the 1863 massacre. The baptisms connected the living Saints to their dead, allowing them to solidify family ties that had become increasingly tenuous during the process of colonization. According to a 1945 oral history, a Shoshone woman had received a vision that connected the work that the Northwestern Shoshone were doing in the temple with the trauma they had experienced during the massacre. She saw "how their bodies had been disposed of" and "where they were killed."[3] The Latter-day Saint temple became a site of healing and restoration. In 2013, the Northwestern Shoshone read the names from the temple records at the Bear River Massacre site as a way of commemorating those who had died.[4]

The Northwestern Shoshone saw these rituals as deeply meaningful. Not everyone shared their vision or that of white Latter-day Saints. Southeastern Idaho was a contested space in the late nineteenth century. The Fort Hall Indian Reservation lay just outside of the Zion that the Saints imagined from the top of the Logan Temple. Although the Bureau of Indian Affairs had placed the reservation under the care of the Methodist Episcopal Church in 1867, the Methodists never began a serious missionary effort and left the task of evangelizing the Shoshone and the Bannock to others.[5] In 1887, the Connecticut Indian Association finally sent Protestants Amelia J. Frost and Ella Stiles to the Fort Hall Indian Reservation. They worried about the influence of Latter-day Saints on the reservation. In 1906, Frost published an essay in the Presbyterian *Home Mission Monthly* warning that both "the Mormons" and "liquor" were present among the Shoshone and Bannock.[6] Her fears were part of a larger concern among the communities of Pocatello, Blackfoot, and Firth that Latter-day Saints were becoming increasingly common in communities that had once explicitly been Protestant.

This chapter sketches the contest Latter-day Saints and Protestants waged over the souls of the Shoshone and Bannock in the late nineteenth and early twentieth centuries. Much of the contest focused on rituals such as baptism, Christian marriage, and temple work. Latter-day Saints believed that these rituals would produce tangible effects on the behavior of Indigenous converts. For Protestants, these rituals served a different role. Sacraments like baptism allowed converts to reaffirm their faith and make public their acceptance of Christianity. The registration of marriages allowed Protestant missionaries and federal officials to make certain that Native Americans had adopted white standards of domesticity by ensuring that they were not practicing polygamy and that they considered the relationships permanent, lifelong matches. Contemporary descriptions of marriage also suggested that European-style weddings had the ability to enforce white expectations of domesticity. The reality was never so easy. The Shoshone and Bannock made their own meanings out of the Christian gospels they encountered. They would create alternative Christianities that foregrounded their own needs and allowed them to survive in the new world that the Latter-day Saints and Protestants had created.

In some ways, this chapter blends academic and family history. In the early twentieth century, my great-grandmother, Annie Jane Graham, married a Shoshone man named Edward McCarey Edmo. They chose to baptize their children at the Episcopalian mission, and those children later attended boarding schools for Native Americans. As a result of my great-grandmother's death in 1969, I knew little about her first marriage and had a distant relationship with her children. She divorced Edmo sometime in the 1920s and married my great-grandfather, a Mexican American man named Antonio Alejo Aguilar. The racism that my great-grandfather faced as a refugee after the Mexican Revolution convinced him that it was safer for his children and grandchildren to hide their ties to Idaho's Latino community and to pass as white if they could. My red hair and light skin meant my great-grandfather was hesitant to tell me anything about the experiences of his Native stepchildren or even his own experiences in Mexico. This chapter combines an academic story about the effects of missionary work on Native communities with an attempt to understand my own family history. It is also an attempt to tell a history about religion in Southeastern Idaho that foregrounds Native rather than settler history. It begins, then, not with the arrival of the Saints in the Great Basin and the Cache but with a story about Otter and Muskrat.

The Shoshone storyteller Ed Edmo told a story about the creation of the world.[7] According to his telling, the world was initially filled with water. The Great Spirit lived in the water and had three children, whom he called Otter, Muskrat, and Beaver. One day, Otter leapt into the water and encountered beings called fish. Muskrat then went into the water and fell in love with a "water girl who winked at him," but he "ran out of breath" and had to return to the surface. Finally, Beaver dove into the water and swam past the fish until he came to the bottom and collected "a ball of mud." The Great Spirit grabbed the ball of mud from his son Beaver and began to sing and turn it until "it got big [and] as round as the world today." Then he created "mountains and trees, plants, insects, animals" and "rivers and lakes." In a final act, he fashioned people.[8]

The story that Edmo weaves about the creation of the world is at odds with how white settlers describe Southeast Idaho. The Idaho author Annie Pike

Greenwood described the area as a barren landscape, occasionally broken by a well-maintained Latter-day Saint farm or a few "jutting hills of lava."[9] The irrigation pipes that high school students and migrant workers lay each summer have allowed local farmers to successfully grow sugar beets, wheat, and other crops, but few people would name water as one of the region's defining features. My own memories of Southeastern Idaho mirror Greenwood's. I see myself as kin to sagebrush and lava rather than rivers and otter. Water, however, is important to local folklore. My stepfather once told a story about drowned Shoshone infants who haunted local waters and threatened to drown those who came too close. It wasn't until I was older that I realized this folklore likely drew from Shoshone oral traditions, which warned listeners about water spirits that could imitate the cries of human children.[10] Together, these stories emphasize the importance of water in an arid landscape and its danger.

In Southeastern Idaho, local Native Americans adapted their seasonal rounds to this landscape to take advantage of the harvests that were available. The bodies of water that did exist—the Snake and Portneuf Rivers, the Bear Lake, and Shoshone Falls, to name a few—may have seemed powerful. By the eighteenth century, the Shoshone and the Bannock had developed complex societies well suited to the area's climate. According to the historian Stephen J. Crum, the region's environment made it difficult for the Shoshone to "overpopulate their country" or "concentrate in large numbers in one particular place over a long period of time."[11] He described a world without "competition" over resources, in which the Shoshone ate a wide variety of foods. "Jack rabbit, cottontail rabbit, ground hogs or woodchucks, sage hen, antelope, and deer," as well as "chokecherries, yampa roots, and pine nuts," fed the Shoshone people and allowed them to maintain their families.[12]

The arrival of Europeans in the Americas transformed Shoshone society. In 1781, the Blackfeet attacked a Shoshone encampment, only to discover that smallpox had decimated the group. A Cree man named Saukamappee resided with the Blackfeet at the time and described their horror: "Our eyes were appalled with the terror; there was no one to fight with but the dead and the dying, each a mass of corruption."[13] The Blackfeet, of course, soon experienced their own outbreak. The virus had first entered the American continent through voyages from European nations. Trade between Native communities spread the virus throughout the Americas. Smallpox devastated the Blackfeet. "It was no longer with the song and the dance," Saukamappee wrote, "but tears, shrikes, and howlings of despair for those who would never return to us."[14]

When the Latter-day Saints entered the Great Basin in 1847, white settlement had already transformed the region. The Comanche had developed an equestrian lifestyle that allowed them to enslave members of other Native communities.[15] The fur trade had also brought white traders to the area who sexually exploited Native women to gain access to trading and kin networks.[16] The presence of Latter-day Saints accelerated rather than initiated these changes. White settlers often established communities near major bodies of water, disrupting foodways that had sustained Native peoples for generations. Native people in Utah and Idaho sometimes responded by raiding white communities. Stealing cattle allowed them to feed their families. It was also a symbolic attack on colonialism itself. Scholars like Pete Silver have demonstrated that violence against white settlers in the United States often focused on European homes.[17] These attacks often became symbolic assaults on white families and the idea of domesticity. Cattle embodied the destruction of Native foodways. As a result, these attacks came to stand in for larger Native American grievances against the encroachment of their lands.

When the Saints arrived in Utah, they had an elaborate theology concerning the history of Native Americans. Nineteenth-century interpretations of the Book of Mormon suggested that the Shoshone, Ute, and other Indigenous peoples in the United States were descendants of American Israelites. The Saints believed that Native Americans had descended into savagery but would eventually be redeemed. This redemption was racialized. According to nineteenth-century Mormon folklore, God had marked Native Americans with dark skin to separate them from the light-skinned faithful. Upon their redemption, their skin would again become "white and delightsome."[18]

On its face, the meaning of this statement was ambiguous. For nineteenth-century Saints, however, becoming white and delightsome meant adopting white understandings of domesticity. This understanding of missionary work meant Latter-day Saint missionary work mirrored that of other Christians despite differences in theology. In 1880, the Latter-day Saint *Woman's Exponent* published the minutes of a relief society in Indianola, Utah, in which both white and Native American women participated in the meetings. The testimonies that Native women offered of their faith highlight the degree to which Latter-day Saints were concerned with the hygiene and housekeeping abilities of Indigenous converts. According to the article, a Ute woman named Mary Tackipo testified that "she was learning to keep house." She felt it was "better than her former way of doing." Hannah Moritze expressed that she "was anxious to learn how to keep house and keep herself clean," while Phoebe Onump "encouraged the sisters to diligence."[19] Although these testimonies are summarized in the document and cannot provide us with the nuances of the Ute women's speeches, they do suggest the degree to which Latter-day Saint missionaries focused on how Native converts cared for their bodies and homes.

They also suggest that Latter-day Saints believed that baptism and other rituals had tangible effects on the behavior of Native converts. One Native woman said that she "felt different altogether since she had been baptized." Before her baptism, she had wanted "to learn how to be a good Latter-day Saint, but was rather slow."[20] Although her testimony did not describe the changes she experienced in detail, its phrasing suggests that she experienced renewed vigor in her faith as a result of her decision to be baptized. To symbolize this transformation, Latter-day Saint missionaries sometimes gave Native converts new names upon baptism. In 1854, several men traveled to Southern Utah to proselytize among the region's Native peoples. In his diary, Thomas D. Brown wrote down each convert's "Indian name" and then the new name they had been given at baptism. Tockwits Macoveooks became James, and Sawowats became Thomas.[21] This practice mirrored Latter-day Saint temple rituals in which individuals received new names to be used upon their entrance to heaven. It is possible that the Saints saw themselves as revealing the true names of their converts through divine revelation. The missionaries also provided new converts with a "clean garment" after baptism. The practice was meant to make the internal changes that accompanied baptism visible. According to Brown, Parley P. Pratt exhorted them to adopt the practice: "Would you leave the outside dirty but get the inside sweetened up?"[22] The implicit answer was no.

Although they were considered "friendly" Indians, the Shoshone initially rejected Latter-day Saint missionary work.[23] It was not until the 1863 Bear River Massacre that they converted in large numbers. After the massacre, the Northwestern Shoshone fought to support their families and often faced starvation. The historian Scott Christensen has suggested that one Shoshone leader received a vision telling him that his people must embrace the restored gospel if they wanted to survive.[24] As a result of this vision, members of the Northwestern Shoshone requested that the Saints send a missionary to them. Within a few years, many Northwestern Shoshone had converted to the church.

The elder's vision transformed what had been a faith that emphasized the power of white Latter-day Saints to redeem Native people into one that recognized Indigenous spiritual power. Throughout the nineteenth century, the journals of Latter-day Saint missionaries emphasized their ability to heal the sick and to demonstrate the power of God through the laying on of hands. In his diary, Brown describes healing and blessing the bodies of Native Americans. The missionaries' ability to do so was mentioned not as evidence of the faithfulness of Native people but as a demonstration of the work of Latter-day Saint missionaries and their own spiritual power. The elder's vision suggested that God had revealed himself to Native Americans just as he had spoken with their Israelite ancestors. Shoshone Saints eventually built a community called

Washakie in Northern Utah. For the Northwestern Shoshone, it was a Native American Israel.

Photographs from the decades around the turn of the twentieth century show members of the community standing in front of tepees holding their children still for photographs. In one photo, a man rests his hands on a child's shoulders. They are both wearing hats and Western-style clothing, while a woman wearing traditional clothing stands to their left distanced from the men.[25] In another, a girl emerges from the mouth of a tepee. She is wearing a calico skirt and is holding something to her mouth. The trees in the background of the photo reveal that her family is camping in Logan, Utah, likely to attend Logan's semicentennial parade in 1909.[26] The photographs read like an anthropological text, showcasing a white gaze. They also, however, represent the connection that the Northwestern Shoshone felt to the Logan Temple. The ability of the Northwestern Shoshone to participate in temple rituals reaffirmed the faith of many residents of Washakie, Utah. The rituals they performed sealed them to the relatives they had lost in the Bear River Massacre, allowing them to recreate important family ties that colonialism had severed.

Membership in the Latter-day Saint community became an important part of the identity of many of the Northwestern Shoshone. Men like Moroni Timbimboo became Native American bishops and encouraged their children to participate in activities with other Saints. Not all Shoshone, however, found peace in the restored gospel. The Shoshone Chief Pocatello originally converted to the Church of Jesus Christ of Latter-day Saints in 1875. He soon became disillusioned, however, after the church failed to protect the Shoshone community during disputes with local white communities. He ultimately agreed to move to the Fort Hall Indian Reservation. He was likely not the only Shoshone disappointed with the promises of the church. Although Latter-day Saints believed that the Shoshone were American Israelites, they often treated Native Americans no better than other white Americans. A local Latter-day Saint leader named Peter Maughan responded to the Bear River Massacre by telling Brigham Young that he felt he was "clear of their blood."[27]

For much of the nineteenth century, Latter-day Saints were the only Christian denomination engaging in serious missionary work among the Shoshone. In the late 1880s, Amelia J. Frost traveled to Idaho to begin missionary work on the Fort Hall Indian Reservation. Like most Protestant missionaries, she saw her mission as giving Native Americans access to the gospel by providing them with the opportunity to learn how to read, and she began the process of translating the Bible into their language.[28] Writing in the Presbyterian *Home Mission Monthly*, *Frost* described the Shoshone and Bannock as being drawn to her charisma. "Several Indians became so anxious to learn what the man knows about the creation of this world," she reported, "that they would sit hour after hour to hear from the Book." Frost emphasized that the people who came to hear missionaries speak "thought it no hardship to stay till the small hours of the morning to hear, and then ride several miles to their homes in cold and storm."[29]

The descriptions that the Presbyterian magazine offered of the Christian faith of the Shoshone and the Bannock do not emphasize baptism to the extent that Latter-day Saint records did. Instead, it focused on the charisma of individual missionaries and the adversity that individuals were willing to experience to gain access to the gospel. In 1900, several Nez Perce men traveled to Fort Hall as Presbyterian missionaries. The magazine emphasized the animosity that the two communities had felt toward each other. "In the olden days," the magazine informed readers, "the Nez Perces and these Indians were enemies. Raids were made into each other's countries, horses stolen, etc." Yet, Christian love inspired a Nez Perce minister to come to Fort Hall and tell the assembled, "You are as my own."[30]

Baptism and other sacraments, however, were not unimportant to Protestants living on the reservation. After my great-grandmother divorced Edward McCarey Edmo, he married a Nez Perce woman named Rachel Cook. On October 4, 1939, *The Salt Lake Tribune* reported that she had given birth to a boy with "royal blood" at Fort Hall.[31] She called him Edward McCarey Edmo Jr., after his father. The child's grandfather was the Nez Perce minister Joseph Cook, who had left his own community several years earlier to serve the Shoshone and Bannock.[32] According to the *Tribune*, this lineage connected the baby both to Hin-mah-too-yah-lat-kekt, more famously known as Chief Joseph, and to the first Native evangelists.[33] The baby's hospital birth seemed to link him to the future of both the Nez Perce and the Shoshone. In the early twentieth century, Christian missionaries worked with federal officials to encourage Native Americans to submit to the care of Western physicians. Women were also encouraged to forgo Indigenous birthing practices for hospital care. In choosing to give birth at a hospital, Rachel had given her imprimatur to the practice. Her relationship to Chief Joseph further suggested that Native Americans had a place in the future as well as the past. Perhaps equally importantly, the baby had been christened. The christening reaffirmed the Edmos' commitment to Christianity and to the civilizing project.

Marriage also played an important role in regulating Shoshone life. Christian missionaries frequently accused Native Americans of having little regard for marital bonds. In one of the issues that praised Amelia Frost's missionary work, the *Home Mission Monthly* told readers that when a Native man "grew tired" of his wife he had the option to just "throw her away."[34] It then contrasted the "old squaw slip" that Native woman wore with the bride's wedding dress—"a pale blue dress, beautifully made, over the whitest of embroidered skirts." It assured readers that the minister "tied the knot good and tight" as he was "strongly opposed to divorce."[35] The descriptions the magazine offered of the differences between traditional Shoshone weddings and those influenced by European traditions implied that the ceremony itself would transform the way that spouses treated each other. The Ojibwa historian Brenda Child has argued that the requirement that Native Americans submit to Christian marriage was a way of disciplining their families. It brought the families before the state and ensured that they were willing to accept its authority.[36]

The missionaries who worked at Fort Hall sometimes published in local newspapers. In 1907, for example, *The Idaho Republican* republished Frost's article from the *Home Mission Monthly*.[37] The result was that local newspapers served at times as advertisements for the mission. Even when they didn't publish the words of the missionaries themselves, newspapers frequently adopted their perspectives. *The Idaho Republican* attributed the progress of Native Americans to missionary work. In one article it described the school that the Episcopal mission ran as a place where "girls are taught everything in the line of cooking and housekeeping."[38] When Edna Biller visited the mission in 1921, the newspaper reported that she had been "impressed" with its "fine work."[39] Other newspapers echoed the sense of progress on the reservation. The *Twice-A-Week Twin Falls Times* described the longtime missionary S. W. Creasey as a man with "two striking and unusually salient characteristics . . . spirituality and simplicity." It welcomed his stay in Twin Falls but recognized that his "life work [was] among our Indian wards."[40] In 1922, the *Bingham County News* described the singing of one of the mission's choirs as "sweet and pleasing."[41]

Newspapers could be optimistic about the ability of Native people to integrate into American society. *The Idaho Republican* carried stories about the progress that the Shoshone and Bannock had made in agriculture, handicrafts, and literacy. When Tommie Cosgrove enrolled his daughters at St. Mary's Academy in Salt Lake City, the newspaper reported on the courses they selected and called them "good, faithful students."[42] In one article, it described the creation of "Chief ManySeeds," a portrait of an imagined Native American leader that had been made from "garden seeds and grain." According to one newspaper, "his dignified profile stood out in shaded kernels of wheat and was lined with barley seed. His beedy eye was created out of asparagus seed, and his feather headdress was made of oats and lettuce." The newspaper believed that "he stood out in seedy perfection, a tribal chief, having a certain vegetable repose that spoke for the domestic evolution of the red man."[43]

Of course, the realities of life on the Fort Hall Indian Reservation and in the towns that surrounded it were more complicated than these descriptions admitted. Blackfoot's newspapers at times celebrated the racial mixing that occurred in the region. According to *The Idaho Republican*, Blackfoot's white settlers and Fort Hall had exchanged food and attended each other's festivals. The Shoshone-Bannock had developed a taste for "watermelon and sweet potato," while local settlers had learned to enjoy "venison and Camas root."[44] Likewise, white settlers frequently traveled to the reservation to watch Native horse races, and the Shoshone-Bannock returned the favor by visiting the state fair and participating in its contests.[45] Although most of the images the newspaper presented of racial mixing were platonic, one article ended with an overt acknowledgment of sexuality. In the last paragraph, it admitted that "the sons of white men love to be entertained by an Indian princess." It assured readers that "the romance of Smith and Pocahontas" had "not lost its beauty nor its sweetness by being re-enacted today in the cabins and the tepees in Burns' woodlands on our local reservation."[46] *The Idaho Republican* assumed that Native Americans who married white settlers would assimilate into white society. The stories of children living on the reservation, however, tell a different story. In a history of Blackfoot, Idaho, my uncle Buster remembered his childhood. He had a pet porcupine and fished for crawdads. He ate "June bugs and grasshoppers" because he had heard that the Shoshone once considered them essential to survival. Like many Shoshone boys, he found himself attracted to the rodeo and rode broncos like his father.[47] His aunt Lillian had also married a Native man, and, according to family histories, dressed as a Native woman to participate in rodeos.[48] An undated family photograph shows a Shoshone man riding a bull in front of a wall. His braids are flying up and his hands are outstretched. It may very well be Buster.[49]

The marriages were also sometimes less binding than the missionaries presumed. Although my great-grandmother was a member of the Episcopalian Church of the Good Shepherd, she chose to leave her first husband after bearing several of his children. It is unclear from remaining records whether or not she ever formalized their divorce. At some point, she began a long-term relationship with a Mexican immigrant. Although the newspapers called her Mrs. Aguilar, she did not formalize her new relationship until the 1960s, when they already had grandchildren together. She was not the only one whose life departed from Christian norms. Her first husband remarried soon after their separation—first to a Nez Perce woman named Rachel Cook, as described earlier, and then to a Native Hawaiian woman. He also critiqued Christianity later in his life, telling an Idaho newspaper that he didn't understand why Christians "gossiped."[50]

Although my great-grandmother and her first husband had baptized their children, they could not protect them from the racism of the United States government or its agents. In the early twentieth century, Native children were often forced to attend boarding schools. My great-grandmother's children were no exception. Her daughter June attended the Chemawa Indian School in Salem, Oregon, where the young woman would have received vocational training. Although Buster maintained his love of flute-making and rodeo, he attended Sherman Institute, the same boarding school as his sister June.[51] According to family stories, Annie Jane was reluctant to let her children attend boarding school. She likely felt that as a former journalist and schoolteacher she was well equipped to ensure that her children were well educated. Ultimately, however, none of that mattered. In the words of my mother, "She didn't have a choice."[52]

The forced removal of Native children broke up the families that missionaries had argued Christian marriage and baptism had made sure. Annie Jane's daughter Laura sent a letter to her half sister letting her know that it would be a while before they saw each other again. "Dearest Tonia," she wrote, "I just decided to write you. Why didn't you answer my letter? . . . Honey I won't be home for a long time. Dave won't come after me because he didn't bring me down. He just took me to Fort Hall and I went down here." She ended the short note by asking about her sister's dolls. "Tell Ella, Stella, Rosita and Mamie Marylou I said hello and to write. Love and kisses, your Sis, Laura Edmo."[53] The two sisters would have maintained their close bond if they had been allowed to grow up together. Although the sisters still spoke, it would be years before Laura returned to Idaho. She sent her mother pictures of her husband and children with pictures of palm trees in the background.

Although the Northwestern Shoshone did not move to the Fort Hall Indian Reservation, they also traveled to boarding school. Mae Timbimboo attended the same boarding school as Laura. Although she remembered the Sherman Institute as a place surrounded by "magnolia trees" and "orange blossoms," she also referenced the pain that some of the other children felt. She remembered one girl who had been forced into a truck while she was herding sheep and driven to the institute. When she cried, one of the staff came in and asked, "What are you crying for? Are you lonesome for your sheep?"[54] Mae's grandmother was also worried that Mae would forget how to speak Shoshone. Mae reveled in the experience of being in Southern California, but when her grandmother died she longed to be connected with her and with the traditions that had given her birth. Her desire reveals the tensions at the heart of missionary work among the Shoshone and other Native people. The Book of Mormon and Logan Temple rituals had promised to bind Native people to their ancestors and families. The Northwestern Shoshone found deep meaning in these rituals after the Bear River Massacre. Likewise, Protestant missionaries had believed that Christian marriage and baptism would transform Native families. Ultimately, however, this missionary work also tore families apart. The boarding schools that my great-grandmother's children and Mae Timbimboo attended were part of the same civilizing mission that the missionaries had promoted. Although Mae Timbimboo remained a Latter-day Saint, she turned not to temple rituals to connect with her grandmother but rather a Ouija board.[55]

Mae's use of the Ouija is in some ways a metaphor for the ways the Shoshone and their kin the Bannock responded to missionary work. Christian missionaries, no matter their denomination, had believed that rituals would Christianize converts, transforming their family structures, understanding of God, and relationship to the world. Some of the Shoshone embraced the Church of Jesus Christ of Latter-day Saints and welcomed Amelia Frost. As they did so, however, they infused their new religious faith with their own meanings. The Northwestern Shoshone did not understand sealings and baptisms for the dead in the same way as white Latter-day Saints, and Rachel Cook likely rejected the *Salt Lake Tribune*'s description of her baby's baptism. When the Ouija board refused to perform for Mae and her friends, they "beat the heck out of it."[56] The Shoshone created alternative Mormonisms and Christianities that fit their own needs, and in so doing, they adapted to the new world that the Christian missionaries had created just as they had adapted their seasonal rounds to the arid environment of Southeastern Idaho generations before.

CHAPTER 6

Traveling Elders
The Latter-day Saint Gaze on Africa in the Early Twentieth Century

Jeffrey G. Cannon

Across the world, the iconic image of Christian missionaries in Africa is David Livingstone pinned to the ground by an enormous lion (figure 1). The fierce lion, the foreign landscape, and the dark-skinned Africans evoked an Africa that was exotic and fundamentally Other to Livingstone's British readers. It was first published in London as an illustration in Livingstone's phenomenally successful *Missionary Travels and Researches in South Africa* in 1857, and it entered the American consciousness the next year when the book was republished in New York.[1] This chapter places the Latter-day Saint gaze on Africa within the broader Anglo-American Christian imagination of the continent. As Christraud Geary has observed, missionary images of Africa are part of the colonial discourse of the Other.[2] This is true of American Latter-day Saint missionary images of Africa as well, despite the fact that the United States did not have a formal colonial stake there. The image of Africa and its peoples presented by and to Latter-day Saints in the early twentieth century was one of an exotic Otherness made accessible through the modernizing influences of the British Empire.

The first Latter-day Saint missionaries assigned to Africa landed at Cape Town on April 6, 1853, to initiate a missiological tradition on the continent that differed from that of the broader Anglo-American missionary project in both theology and practice. Beginning in the mid-nineteenth century, leaders of the Church of Jesus Christ of Latter-day Saints began instituting a policy that

FIGURE 1. *The Missionary's Escape from the Lion*, from David Livingstone, *Missionary Travels and Researches in South Africa* (1857), 12–13.

barred men with Black African ancestry from ordination into the otherwise nearly universal male priesthood. Brigham Young's earliest recorded comments on the policy were made in the same year missionaries were first sent to the Cape Colony.[3] The missionaries were withdrawn in 1865 without explanation. When the mission reopened in 1903, the policy was reiterated to the first of the returning missionaries by European Mission president Francis M. Lyman.[4] How the missionaries in South Africa would deal with the particular challenges arising from the church's policy regarding Africans may have been on Lyman's mind as he elaborated on the place of Africans in the economy of salvation in an editorial published in December 1903 in the *Latter-day Saints' Millennial Star*, which he edited as president of the European Mission. He rejected arguments that Africans were not descended from Adam or entitled to salvation through Christ: "We look on the negro as a human being, a child of Adam, who with all other members of the human race will be resurrected from the dead. Like his white brother the negro is capable of having belief in the Lord and has a consciousness of sin. Where sincere faith and repentance are manifested and all conditions are proper, negroes may be baptized and receive the laying on of hands for the gift of the Holy Ghost."[5]

Notwithstanding, Latter-day Saint efforts in Africa focused on the white populations. These efforts were carried out by a small, untrained, and frequently changing cadre of missionaries, mostly from Utah and the surrounding states. As David Hollinger notes, "The long-term, family-intensive immersion in foreign societies that so marks the Protestant missionary project was entirely lacking in the Mormon missionary project."[6] These significant differences made the Latter-day Saint experience distinctive among the missionaries laboring in Africa; still, important similarities remain.

It has been noted that missionary reports of Africa constituted one of the primary sources for Protestant ideas about the continent.[7] Nevertheless, comparatively little work has been done on the effects of the Latter-day Saints missionary enterprise on perceptions of foreign societies within the Latter-day Saint community.[8] This chapter attempts to address that lacuna by examining how Latter-day Saint missionaries in early twentieth-century South Africa portrayed the continent to those at home. Three years before the missionaries returned to the continent, the Kodak company introduced its Brownie camera in 1900, democratizing the art of photography and image-making of Africa. Missionary photographs and descriptions of South Africa and the missionaries' activities were frequently published in the church's *Improvement Era* magazine. Missionaries also sent photographs they had taken and commercially produced photographic postcards directly to friends and family at home. These photographs and descriptions reveal how, given few opportunities for meaningful contact with Black South Africans, the missionaries' views of them changed very little. However, their more frequent and intimate contact with white South Africans engendered a greater sympathy for them and their place in South Africa and its history.

The *Improvement Era* began publication in 1897 as an attempt to reach the church's young men and during the first years of the twentieth century carried on a ministry to a primarily male readership. In 1908 it became the official organ of the church's seventies quorums, responsible for proselytizing, and in 1909 it added the constituency of the church's other bodies of the all-male lay priesthood.[9] Consequently, the magazine had a highly masculine tone, reflecting the gendered nature of Latter-day Saints missions in the early twentieth century. Noticeably absent from the descriptions of Africa in the *Improvement Era* are the voices of women. Although Latter-day Saint women were first officially called on missions in 1898, their numbers remained relatively small. With the exception of mission presidents' wives and daughters, the Latter-day Saints missionary enterprise in Africa was still an all-male affair, and missionary reports reflect that reality. The church's women's organizations published their own *Relief Society Magazine* and *Young Women's Journal*. The latter was merged with the *Era* in 1929.[10]

Latter-day Saint missionaries' reports, like those of other Christian denominations' missionaries, bare similarities with travel narratives popular at the time. When Franklin J. Hewlett was called as president of the Latter-day Saint mission at the Cape in 1911, the *Improvement Era* noted his previous contributions to the magazine reporting his travels, no doubt hoping he would make similar reports of his travels in Africa.[11] When the magazine published Hewlett's first submission as mission president, his byline noted his previous contribution as a travel writer before assuming his position as mission president.[12] The missionary and travel genres had well-established links. John Murray, who published David Livingstone's books in England, was primarily a publisher of travelogues. Across the Atlantic, travel narratives were popular reading for middle-class Americans in the early twentieth century.[13] Viewing it as more than movement from one geographical location to another, this chapter employs Syed Manzurul Islam's definition of travel as an "encounter with otherness and difference."[14] He classifies travel into two types: "sedentary" and "nomadic." While physically moving through geographical space, the sedentary traveler is unchanged by the experience and, thus, has not traveled at all. The nomadic traveler, on the other hand, moves not only physically but psychologically toward the Other, causing a "fracture" in the boundaries between the self and the Other.[15] Casey Blanton writes that the primary theme of travel writing is, in fact, the self, whose "well-being and eventual safe homecoming become the primary tensions of the tale"; "the traveler's encounter with the other is the chief attraction."[16] For Islam, to return unchanged would be unethical and hardly worthy of the name "travel." That is, however, what much of travel writing reveals. As Steve Clark writes, "The Europeans mapped the world rather than the world mapping them."[17] The travel writer's focus on the exotic and the strange reinforces the norms of the traveler's home society, rather than breaking down barriers and expanding the traveler's or reader's conceptions.[18] With missionaries spread across the globe and the frequent inclusion of their reports in the *Improvement Era*, Latter-day Saints had ample exposure to this genre and the world outside the Intermountain West.

In their descriptions of Africa as exotic Other, Latter-day Saint missionaries in Africa at the beginning of the twentieth century exhibited aspects of both nomadic and sedentary travel. Their descriptions of Black Africans follow the familiar tropes of Africans as savages and the country as wild and untamed seen in images like that of Livingstone with the lion. There is little evidence that Latter-day Saint missionaries made any attempt at breaking down the boundaries between themselves and Africans. As their time was hardly spent with Black Africans but rather devoted to white settlers, the missionaries' reports reveal the much greater influence of the settler community on their perceptions of the country. At a time when the United States was stretching its imperial legs after the Spanish-American War, the missionaries presented settler colonialism as a positive force. In addition, many of the young missionaries were themselves the sons and grandsons of the pioneer settlers of the Intermountain West, who possessed the land by virtue of the doctrine of discovery discussed by Kathryn Gin Lum in chapter 1. The space between themselves and the white South African settlers was far smaller and easier to cross than that between the missionaries and Black South Africans.

"Black" South Africa and the "Dark Continent"

The South African Mission was not a coveted assignment for Latter-day Saint missionaries in the early twentieth century. Perceptions of Africa as "the Dark Continent" pervaded the American imagination. One young missionary, Orson M. Rogers, wrote to the *Improvement Era* in 1908, saying, "There are many young men at home who look upon South Africa as one of the worst places in the world for a mission, and many times at the mere mention of the name they shudder, and think of cannibals, Hottentots, and Zulus. When some of my friends learned that I had been called to this 'dark continent,' they began to pity me, and to offer condolence."[19] Opinion at home had not changed much eight years later, when another missionary wrote, "South Africa! Almost the first thought we have when those words are uttered is: 'Oh that's the home of the n——!' I know, for I had much the same idea."[20]

The Western image of Africa has evolved over time as the West has interacted with the continent. Both Africans and the West developed ideas of what Africa is through their interactions with each other.[21] Victorian-era Europeans and white Americans created and reinforced ideas of Africa through their use of photography and colonial exhibitions by constructing a counterpoint against which European identities were created.[22] V. Y. Mudimbe argues that "Africa" exists only as an invention of the West.[23] In doing so, he follows Edward Said's argument that the "Orient" was also an invention of the Western imagination.[24] "Africa grew 'dark'" in the Western imagination, according to Patrick Brantlinger, as the light shed on it by Victorian explorations "was refracted through an imperialist ideology."[25] According to Paul Landau, the popular images of Africa seen in the Global North constitute what he calls "image-Africa," which is not the continent as it is but as it has been portrayed.[26] Owing to their unique theology and practice, Latter-day Saints developed a distinctive "image-Africa."

Ironically, David Livingstone may have done more than anyone else for the image of Africa as a wild and dangerous place. His discoveries and adventures were headline news around the world and were even reported in the Latter-day Saint church–owned newspaper in Salt Lake City, the *Deseret News*.[27] The illustration of Livingstone with the lion became a staple in the iconography of

Christian missions in Africa, but Livingstone disliked it and the message it communicated.[28] While never fully breaking down the boundaries between himself and Africans, Livingstone approached Islam's definition of nomadic travel in the sense that he did attempt to understand the Africans he encountered and was changed by the experience. He was conscientious about the image of Africa he portrayed, objecting to sketches intended to illustrate his own books when they made Africans look "hideous" or "apish." He complained to his publisher that some artists did not seem able to draw Africans without caricaturing them.[29] Nevertheless, it was Livingstone who prepared the way for the term "Dark Continent" to be affixed to Africa, despite describing scenes "so lovely [they] must have been gazed upon by angels in their flight."[30] He created a nineteenth-century media frenzy when he lost contact with the outside world and Henry Morton Stanley, commissioned by the *New York Herald*, "found" him in present-day Tanzania on November 10, 1871. Stanley's account, published the following year, became a bestseller. He later capitalized on his fame by exploiting the mystique of Africa with book titles like *Through the Dark Continent* (1878) and *In Darkest Africa* (1890), which were published in Britain and the United States. Livingstone cemented the wild-and-dangerous-Africa image in 1873 by dying in what is now Zambia. Members of his African entourage transported his body to London, where he was buried in a quasi-state funeral at Westminster Abbey. Thirty years later, an illustration of the monument built at the site where he died was published in newspapers across the United States, including the *Deseret Evening News*, demonstrating Livingstone's enduring and far-reaching legacy. It was the same year that Latter-day Saints missionaries returned to Africa. While some papers chose to remember Livingstone primarily or exclusively as an explorer, the Latter-day Saints church-owned paper heavily emphasized his role as a missionary.[31]

The perception of an exotic Africa was a prominent feature in Latter-day Saints missionary reports. After more than two years in the mission field, by June 1909 missionary Orson Rogers fancied himself something of an expert on the Black populations of South Africa and wrote an article for the *Improvement Era* titled "Native Races of South Africa."[32] The ten-page article features seven images that demonstrate the missionary gaze that was communicated to Latter-day Saints in the United States, largely in the Intermountain West. The first photograph is of Rogers himself (figure 2).[33] It was not unusual for the *Era* to print pictures of authors. This was also a popular convention of book-length Protestant missionary narratives.[34] Beginning the article with an image of a young, white missionary from Utah further exoticized the Africans pictured by setting a normative baseline to which the other images were compared.

FIGURE 2. "Orson M. Rogers," *Improvement Era* (June 1909), 625.

The missionaries' portrayal of Africa was heavily influenced by local white attitudes. Juxtaposed against the image of Rogers in his suit and tie, the next image is of an intentionally stereotypical African, labeled simply "A K——"[35] (figure 3). This image and its caption are problematic for several reasons, not least of which is the word k——'s derogatory connotations in the twenty-first century. While arguably less derogatory in 1909, it was still heavily value-laden. Its use by Rogers derives from a long and troubled history. The word entered the English language through Portuguese slave traders, who, in turn, borrowed it from Arabic, in which language it means "unbeliever." The Portuguese, however, applied a racial component to it, which filtered into its usage in Dutch and English.³⁶ In the early days of white settlement at the Cape, Dutch settlers identified themselves as "Christians" and Africans were "k——"—unbelievers—even if they accepted Christian baptism. Africans were inescapably outside prevailing Dutch-settler conceptions of a racialized Christian identity. Even under English rule, the appellation remained, though it took on different meanings, including one granting higher status than the "Hottentots" (Khoisan) and "negroes" (other Africans, primarily those from West Africa).³⁷

During missionaries' relatively short tenure in the mission field, the knowledge they gained of African societies was superficial and often flawed. In an article that claims to be describing the "different races of people" in South Africa, Rogers unhelpfully and incorrectly lumps nearly all of South Africa's Indigenous peoples into one category. "The predominant native race of South Africa is that called the K——," he wrote. "As there are nearly as many nations of them as there are of Indians in America, I shall treat them as a whole, only mentioning that some of the well known names of tribes are, Zulus, Griques, Fingoes, Bantu and Basutos."³⁸ He also misuses the Bantu classification, which is not a specific ethnic group but a grouping of peoples with related languages, to which the Zulu, Fengu, and Sotho all belong. The Griqua are of mixed ancestry, primarily Khoisan and European. Rogers seems to have lumped all of South Africa's ethnic groups of African origin together under the one name, which he used analogously to contemporaneous American usage of the terms *black*, *colored*, or *negro*. Regardless of their cultural and genetic diversity, all of them would have fallen under the shadow of a theological Blackness because of the one-drop rule forbidding priesthood ordination of anyone with African ancestry, no matter how distantly removed.³⁹ Active proselytizing of those with Black African ancestry was thus proscribed in South Africa.

In addition to the attitudes and vocabulary he acquired in South Africa, Rogers was also influenced by existing beliefs about Africans he brought from home. While conflating designations of African peoples, Rogers placed them into a single category his readers understood: descendants of the biblical Ham. Responding to what he called the "theories of scholars," Rogers declared that "some are worthy of consideration." However, perhaps in an attempt to establish his own orthodoxy, he stated, "I believe that all of the negro races are children of Ham."⁴⁰ The widely held belief that Noah's son Ham was the ancestor of African peoples had entered Latter-day Saint racial discourse as early as 1831.⁴¹ Rogers's fellow missionary, Alma T. Jones, who took many of the photographs in the article, had earlier that year called South Africa "Ethiopia, the land inhabited by the sons of Ham."⁴² References to Africans' supposed

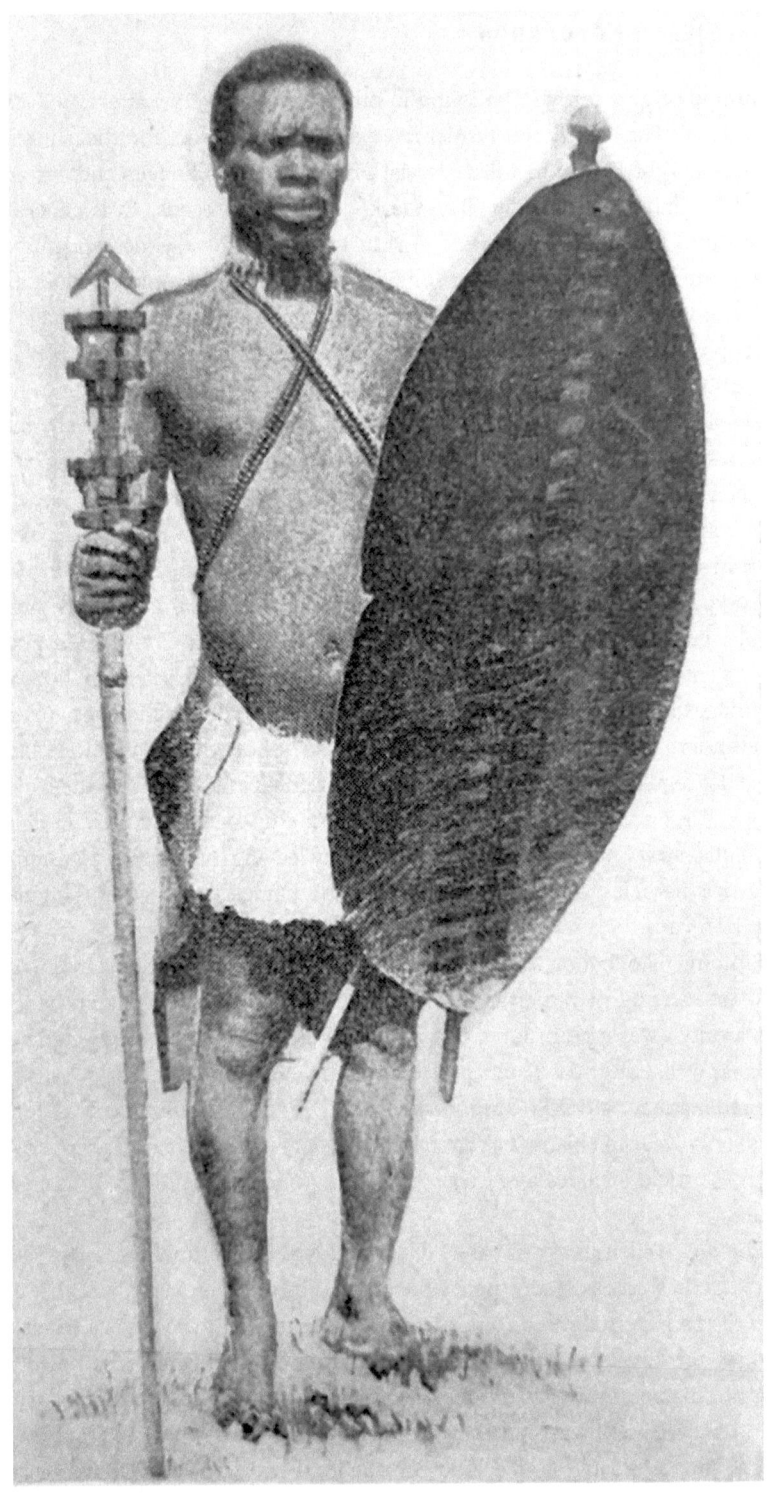

FIGURE 3. "A K——," *Improvement Era* (June 1909), 626.

Hammitic origins can also be found in other contemporary Latter-day Saints periodicals. The *Relief Society Magazine* included a lesson for the church's women in February 1918 titled "Racial History: Ham: His Descendants and Tribes."[43] Under the heading "The Dark Continent" it reads, "It is generally understood that the continent of Africa was settled by the descendants of Ham," after which a short description of some of Africa's people is included.[44]

Along with the caption and racial ideas surrounding figure 3, the image itself is problematic as a representation of missionary interactions with Black Africans. It is significant that out of all the depictions of South Africans in this article, this is the only image that is not a photograph apparently taken by missionaries.[45] That would seem to indicate that the missionaries had not personally seen anyone dressed in such a way (at least not with any frequency), or else they would have photographed him instead. Its inclusion in Rogers's article is illustrative of the missionaries' reliance on secondhand information and stereotypes for their knowledge about Black Africans. The image fits within a popular genre of ethnographic images intended to illustrate typical examples of Indigenous costume in which names were not considered important because the images represented types rather than individuals. Beyond images created for ethnographic purposes, scholars of mission photography in Africa have noted the regularity with which Africans were denied individuality by being left nameless in photographs.[46] Most likely unwittingly, Rogers and the editors of the *Improvement Era* followed this convention by leaving the subjects pictured in the article nameless as well, showing readers unnamed types rather than individual Africans.

Clothing, like that of the man pictured in figure 3, was an important indicator of modernity, or rather a lack thereof. A dichotomy of "savagery" versus "modernity" was a common trope of Protestant missionary photography in Africa as well. Latter-day Saints missionary June Sharp noted in his journal that "the red blanket natives [a common descriptor for those holding to traditional ways] only wear the blanket about their shoulders and often not that much."[47] Rogers's article includes a shirtless young boy photographed by Alma Jones (figure 4).

The boy is identified only as a "K—— lad who had drunk a quart of sour milk."[48] His shirtless state implies poverty, cultural difference, or both. The reader is perhaps supposed to think the boy's distended stomach is a result of drinking too much. Calling out the fact the milk was sour may also be an attempt to highlight poverty, but milk is often intentionally soured in Africa and noting that the milk was sour may simply be highlighting what missionaries or editors saw as strange and exotic African foodways. The boy is manifestly Other. Poverty is also highlighted in the article's other images, in which, al-

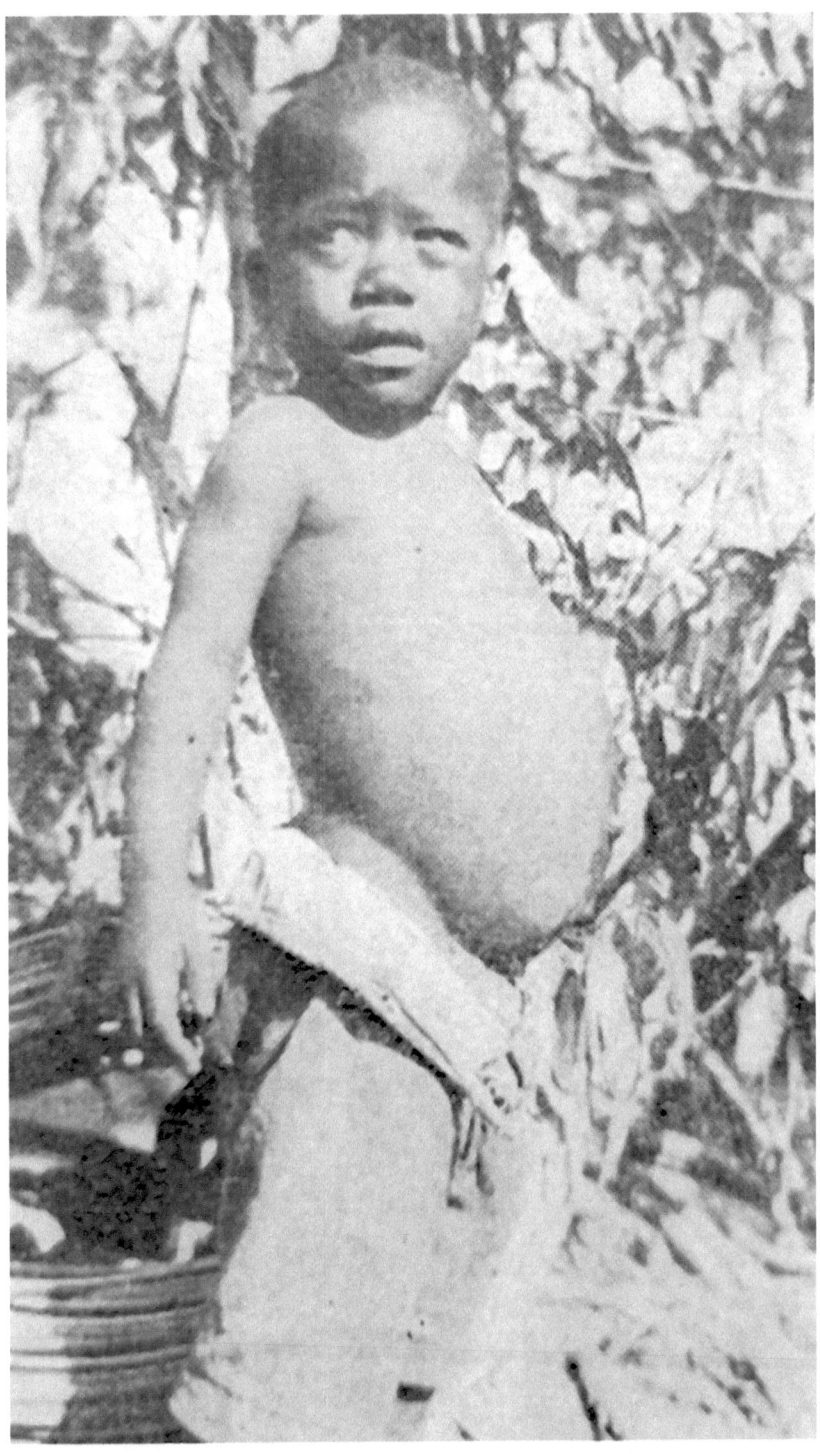

FIGURE 4. "K—— lad who had drunk a quart of sour milk," photograph by Alma T. Jones, *Improvement Era* (June 1909), 627.

though all the subjects are dressed in Western clothing, their clothes are clearly old and tattered (figures 5 and 6).[49] In contrast, the clothing of white South Africans is rarely mentioned.[50] Clothing was used by both British and American missionaries as well as settlers as a marker of conversion and civilization.[51] June Sharp's use of the phrase "red blanket natives" indicates that the missionaries had also adopted at least some of the notions of Western clothing as a marker of "civilization."

Another indicator of the lack of modernity was African architecture. There are two images in Rogers's article featuring rondavels, or traditional African buildings made from wattle and daub. Figure 7 shows one under construction and figure 8 shows a completed structure. Latter-day Saints missionaries found these buildings interesting, as is apparent in the two images featured in this article. Examples also appear in the missionaries' individual photograph collections.[52] Indigenous construction was an interest of Protestant missionaries as well; their reports and photographs also include accounts of African building styles and methods.[53] Featuring these buildings exoticized African technology and domesticity.

Images of Africans in traditional dress juxtaposed with them wearing Western clothing and of African construction compared to Western building styles

Figure 5. "K—— boys at Capetown," photograph by Alma T. Jones, *Improvement Era* (June 1909), 628.

Figure 6. "K—— boys," photograph by Alma T. Jones, *Improvement Era* (June 1909), 630.

Figure 7. "K—— hut in course of construction," photograph by Alma T. Jones, *Improvement Era* (June 1909), 629.

FIGURE 8. "K—— hut, King William's Town," photograph by F. A. Sheffield, *Improvement Era* (June 1909), 633.

were staples in Protestant missionary photography. The Protestant missionary experience centered on the mission station, which placed Africans in semiwesternized environments where they wore Western clothes, lived in Western buildings, and learned in Western schools. The brick and stone construction of the missions was another marker of "civilization" and modernity.[54] Africans were trained to make bricks, cut stones, and put them in place to build Western-style buildings as part of the "civilizing mission." Images of the stations and their residents became important tools of missionary propaganda, showing the "progress" that missionaries had made among their African converts.[55] These types of images were wholly missing from Latter-day Saint representations of Africa.

Unlike their Protestant counterparts, Latter-day Saint missionaries had no interest or stake in the civilizing mission and therefore no interest in portraying Black Africans as advancing toward any civilizational goals. Rather, a portrayal of stasis better supported their theological paradigm and the colonial narrative of progress in Africa through the agency of white settlers. This is well demonstrated in its contrast to Latter-day Saint thought concerning Native Americans. Latter-day Saint theology assigns Native Americans to the sacred Israelite bloodline, within God's covenant of salvation. Africans, on the other hand, were placed outside the salvation economy. At least until the "curse" was lifted, the missionaries saw little that they could do for them.[56] As such, the before-and-after images that are so ubiquitous in the images of missionaries from other denominations in Africa do not feature in Latter-day Saint missionary photography.

With little personal contact, Black Africans remained exotic and Other for American Latter-day Saint missionaries in the first decades of the twentieth century. Frequent contact normalized other peoples for Protestant American missionaries in Africa and elsewhere.[57] But visits to primarily Black African areas, or "native locations," were not the norm for Latter-day Saint missionaries in early twentieth-century South Africa. Alma Jones wrote to the *Improvement Era* that "although the majority of the people here are colored [Black], yet our labors are almost exclusively confined to the white people." This precluded the inclusion of images of Latter-day Saint missionaries preaching to Black Africans, which was a frequent trope of Protestant missionary photographs. More typically, Latter-day Saint missionaries' contact with South Africa's Black populations was limited to transactional relationships like hiring Black men to clean the mission hall or to transport goods.[58] Missionary June Sharp wrote in his journal about a rare visit by several of the missionaries to the "location" outside King Williamstown (now Qonce) on July 21, 1914: "We went thru the Location and got several typical scenes of native life.... After an interesting trip returned and had dinner."[59] Their visit, which produced images similar to those in Rogers's article, was more in the guise of tourists than working missionaries and reflects Syed Manzurul Islam's definition of "sedentary" travel.

There are several notable exceptions of Latter-day Saints with mixed-race ancestry for whom familiarity did breed affinity. Paul Harris (figure 9) was what South Africans call "Coloured," rather than Black. In the racial hierarchy of early twentieth-century South Africa, "Coloureds" inhabited a space between white and Black identity. During white rule, so-called Coloured South Africans attempted to claim some benefits of whiteness by emphasizing their European origins. They lived in European-style houses, ate European-style food, and wore European-style clothing.[60] Harris was baptized and confirmed by missionaries in Johannesburg in 1910.[61]

Because of the white church members' prejudices in the branch, missionaries provided separate meetings for Harris.[62] The missionaries reported that Harris had "the biggest heart" and that his wife, who was not a member of the church, was "very friendly towards us."[63] Another member, William Daniels, was also categorized as Coloured. He was baptized in 1915 after a face-to-face interview with Joseph F. Smith in Salt Lake City. The son of Mission President Nicholas G. Smith recalls his father openly showing affection to and even

FIGURE 9. Paul Harris. June B. Sharp photograph album, Church History Library, Salt Lake City, Utah.

hugging Daniels in public.[64] Indeed, June Sharp's photograph collection at the Latter-day Saint Church History Library includes images of Daniels with Smith's family and others (figure 10). Tensions relating to their attendance in the largely white congregation in Cape Town forced the Daniels family to create their own branch, frequently called the "Branch of Love."[65] The Daniels family welcomed the missionaries, who often described their meals with the family and William Daniels's insistence on the missionaries' use of proper table etiquette.

FIGURE 10. William Daniels (back row, third from left) and others. June B. Sharp photograph album, Church History Library, Salt Lake City, Utah.

The Harris and Daniels cases demonstrate what Gordon Allport called "the nub of the matter," that contact with another group was not enough to diminish prejudice unless the parties worked together toward a common goal.[66] In these limited instances, the missionaries, who were outside the usual South African racial hierarchy, met with the Harris and Daniels families on relatively equal footing due to their membership in the church. Nevertheless, although these families feature in missionary journals and photo albums, none of them was mentioned in church magazines where Latter-day Saints outside South Africa could learn their names during this period. The Coloured population, as it was defined in South Africa, was barely mentioned in the missionaries' published reports as a distinct group, effectively excluding them from the Latter-day Saint gaze on Africa and preserving the dichotomies of Black/white, savage/modern.

"White" South Africa, a Modern Country

Most Latter-day Saints in South Africa were white, and the missionaries saw the presence of the English and Afrikaners in South Africa as essential to the country's modernity. With some surprise, George W. Simons wrote in 1908 that "South Africa is a much better place than I imagined. There are many white people here, among whom we work."[67] White settlement was believed to create a more effective utilization of African resources by taming the land, animals, and even peoples. In this way the missionaries' thought bore similarities to that of American missionary theorist Josiah Strong, who argued that English settlers paved the way for Christian civilization in America.[68] Strong maintained that Anglo-Saxons—especially in America—were key to the world's future.[69] Rather than Strong's American exceptionalism, Latter-day Saint missionaries in South Africa adopted an eclectic version of development in Africa, viewing the history of British and Dutch colonialism as a narrative of untrammeled progress.[70] In some ways, they saw parallels with their own history and the transformation of the deserts of the Intermountain West. However, while Latter-day Saint missionaries celebrated the progress narrative in South Africa, they did not link it explicitly to the settlers' Christianity, which they saw as corrupt, or "apostate." Their reports reveal a somewhat secular civilizing mission at work. In some cases, they read more like travel brochures than missionary accounts.

Early twentieth-century Latter-day Saint missionaries in South Africa uncritically accepted the progress narrative cultivated by colonial and commercial interests. In August 1909, the *Improvement Era* printed an illustrated essay by Mission President Henry Lee Steed that described building after building in Cape Town.[71] The end effect, Steed hoped, was to "show that African cities are modern and up-to-date, rivalling those found in other new countries."[72] The photographs begin with a statue of Jan Van Riebeek, the first governor of the Dutch East India Company's outpost at the Cape of Good Hope in 1652 (figure 11).

Van Riebeek's "first work," according to Steed, was to take the modernizing steps "to build the fort of Good Hope for protection from attacks by sea, and from natives on land . . . [and] to exterminate the wild beasts from the surrounding country."[73] Buildings like Van Riebeek's fort had both symbolic and practical importance, asserting European dominance as well as keeping out both nature and Indigenous peoples.[74]

Many of the images in Steed's essay come from commercially produced postcards, featuring impressive buildings like the railway station, which was considered modern in not only its engineering and aesthetics but also its very purpose as a terminus for the railroad (figure 12).[75] Similar postcards can also be found in the photo album of June Sharp, like figure 13, showing the Cape Town city hall against the background of Devil's Peak.[76]

Contrasting Western construction and other technologies with Africa's natural features was a common iconographic and literary trope. One of the greatest symbols of Western technology, modernity, and empire was the railroad. Shortly before the missionaries' return to the country, the expansion of railways and their necessity for domestic industry and international trade

FIGURE 11. "Statue of Van Riebeek, Cape Town," *Improvement Era* (August 1909), 768.

Figure 12. "The Railway Station, Cape Town, Africa," *Improvement Era* (August 1909), 771.

Figure 13. "City Hall, Cape Town." June B. Sharp photograph album, Church History Library, Salt Lake City, Utah.

brought comment in the United States from the *Scientific American* magazine in 1902, noting a shortage of "native labor."[77] South Africa's modernity, which was enjoyed by the white settlers, was dependent upon the supposedly "savage" Black African majority. The Cape-to-Cairo railroad scheme championed by mining magnate and politician Cecil John Rhodes was the great attempt to control the continent's geography and exploit its resources with global implications. The *Scientific American* reported in 1903 on the importance of the route for the world supply of coal.[78] Orville W. Cutler, who began his mission with visions of a wild backwater, came to see South Africa as a land of great potential.[79] He wrote that the railway "might well be called the road of a thousand wonders, for according to its constructing engineers, it will lead past lions and giraffes; it will extend from civilization to barbarism." While other parts of Africa may have still been wild, Cutler saw South Africa as something different. He described the proposed route that would take passengers from what he called "the earliest civilization" in Egypt, where trains "may cross the very footprints of our Savior," "on to the great lakes of equatorial Africa," through the "dim forest lands where pygmies dwell," and "the haunts of lions, which sometimes try to tear the drivers from their engines," to South Africa's "land of gold and diamonds" and finally to Cape Town.[80] "South Africa!" he exclaimed, "the land of 'unlimited possibilities;' the land of a thousand undeveloped resources; the land where fortunes await to be made, is [importantly to Cutler's view of modernity] fast becoming the home of the white man." Noting the sacred bloodline in contrast to those excluded from the covenant, he continued, "There are good, bad and indifferent people here—its population is made up of all colors and nationalities; but, through it all, there still runs the pure blood of Israel, who must be 'hunted and fished' and brought up to the land of Zion."[81] Cutler connected modernity and religion in a distinctively Latter-day Saint way, which was significantly different from popular ideas about the civilizing mission.

The train featured prominently in articles from Mission President Franklin J. Hewlett. When he and his wife, Emily, arrived in the country, an assignment to the South African Mission was still regarded with derision.[82] A man of business who spent several years on the Salt Lake City council, Hewlett was quick to note modern public works in South Africa's cities, such as Pretoria's paved roads, public baths, sewage system, and electric car line. He also noted "massive structures," such as the "stone and brick post office ... which cost $512,000, and a museum and library, $590,000."[83] The value of investment was significant to Hewlett, who often included costs in his reports. Travelers crossing the country's vast open spaces by train passed industrial areas like "Germiston, the great smelting city, with its tall chimneys belching out the blackest smoke."[84]

The image is not environmentally friendly, but it is modern, which is the central theme of Hewlett's writing.

In Hewlett's descriptions, South Africa was not totally unlike Utah or the United States. "The wide streets, running water, and nice rows of shade trees" of Pretoria, he wrote, "remind us in many ways of our Salt Lake City, nestled under the shade of the Wasatch."[85] Another of his articles discussed the creation of the Union of South Africa in 1910 from the former Cape and Natal colonies and the Boer Republics. He referred to the Union as a "new U. S. A." and "United States, Jr."[86] He further likened South Africa's racial questions to those in the United States, calling it the "worst problem of the future" and stating "the more it is stirred, the darker it frowns." He asked, "In all sincerity, will this new U. S. A. make history repeat itself like its older namesake, by the baptism of blood?"[87] In another parallel, he compared the Boer leader Paul Kruger and the Afrikaners' inland trek to Brigham Young and the experience of the Mormon pioneers.[88]

Yet it was Kruger's nemesis Cecil Rhodes who was the personification of the modernizing-Africa idea for many early twentieth-century imperialists and, notably, many Latter-day Saints as well. Rhodes's home embodied the most persistent elements in the propaganda presenting South Africa as an oasis of modernity in Africa. When the editor of the *Improvement Era* asked Mission President Ralph Badger for photographs and descriptions of local scenes, Badger chose Rhodes's home, Groote Schuur, located on the slopes of Devil's Peak (figure 14). He focused on the architecture of the home and the grooming of the extensive gardens.[89] Badger described the veranda surrounding the house as "a characteristic of the best houses in semi-tropical climates, where one of the luxuries of life is to live in the open."[90] Sitting on his veranda, Rhodes would have looked out at his gardens, a potent symbol of Western domination of the African landscape. Protestant missionaries in the nineteenth century had also seen gardening as a metaphor for cultivating African souls.[91] One particularly interesting feature of Rhodes's gardens, though it was not photographed, was what Badger called "the nucleus of a zoo," including three lions, "ugly gnus, graceful elands, koodoos, hartbeests, zebras, gemsboks, llamas, and ostriches."[92] Africa's wilds were thus enclosed and brought under Western control.

Rhodes came to occupy an almost mythical status for Latter-day Saints. More than once, he was compared to Brigham Young and the colonizing effort was compared to the gospel itself. As a boy in Utah, future Mission President Nicholas G. Smith was told by one of his teachers that "Cecil John Rhodes is one of the greatest men that ever lived."[93] After arriving in South Africa himself, Smith wrote to the *Era* that "Rhodes was about such a man as our beloved

FIGURE 14. "Rear of Groote Schuur," *Improvement Era* (February 1908), 261.

Brigham Young, and through the kind treatment of the natives, he secured the land, and then set about to build railways and telegraph lines."⁹⁴ When Utah's first recipient of the Rhodes Scholarship at the University of Oxford wrote of it for the *Improvement Era*, he saw in Rhodes a sort of quasi–Latter-day Saint: "After all, the ideals and aims of the worldly-minded colonizer of South Africa were not so very far removed from some of the highest ideals and principles taught in our own faith."⁹⁵ In an address to the parents of young men in the Salt Lake Tabernacle, B. H. Roberts used Rhodes as an example of a useful manliness in the service of the British Empire and Anglo-Saxon culture that Rhodes believed were the pinnacle of civilization.⁹⁶

The controversy over Rhodes's legacy is completely lacking from Latter-day Saint missionary reports. The missionaries in South Africa were not required to speak Dutch, or the vernacular Afrikaans, until 1958, and their lack of knowledge limited their interaction with Afrikaners and Afrikaans literature, which were much more critical of Rhodes and British colonialism.⁹⁷ F. W. Reitz's Dutch-language polemic *Een Eeuw van Onrecht* (*A Century of Wrong*), printed during the Anglo-Boer War of 1899–1902, accused Rhodes of fomenting the war through "that treacherous duplicity which is an enduring characteristic of British policy in South Africa."⁹⁸ In contrast, June Sharp's photo album includes a postcard portraying a humanitarian Rhodes, showing a bedsheet turned into a noticeboard informing the women and children of Kimberley, which was then under siege by Boer commandos, that they would be sheltered in Rhodes's mine shafts (figure 15). Importantly, the notice is written in English because Dutch-/Afrikaans-speaking women and children had been removed from their

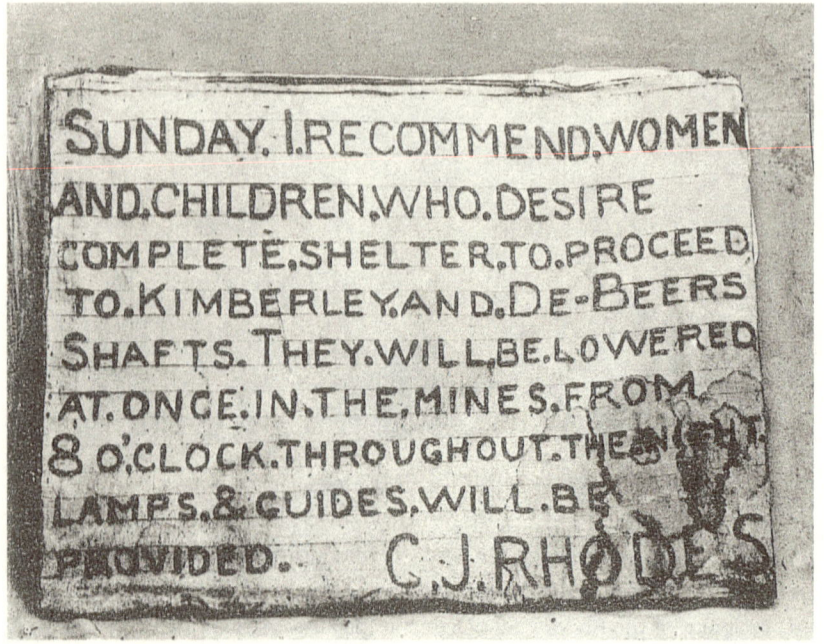

Figure 15. "Photo of the Bed Room Sheet, made into a Sandwich-Board-Notice sent round by Mr. Rhodes near the end of the Siege of Kimberley." June B. Sharp photograph album, Church History Library, Salt Lake City, Utah.

homes and sent to concentration camps as a part of the British war strategy. The card was never sent but demonstrates an image of South Africa its Anglophone business interests wanted foreign visitors to send abroad.

Both English and Afrikaans business interests in South Africa were keen to advertise the country's modernity and resources. Rhodes's De Beer mine organized tours from "courteous American guides," which Franklin Hewlett described as "star attractions" and "well worth the visit."[99] On April 20, 1913, June Sharp sent a postcard to his sister Mary that featured a photograph of a hostel for Black Africans working in a mine (figure 16). Sharp was serving in Kimberley at the time, where mining was the major industry. He wrote under the picture, "I have been in a compound like this where there are about 3,000 natives. It is quite a sight." The scene is not especially picturesque but illustrates once again the corralling of Africa's resources—in this case, human resources—in the name of modernity. Sharp used more than three pages of his journal to describe the operation and collected at least fifteen photographs.[100]

Missionary Alfred J. Gowers Jr. described another visit by missionaries in the February 1912 issue of the *Improvement Era* that reveals the gendered nature of Latter-day Saint missionary discourse about Africa. Gowers framed his report

FIGURE 16. "The De Beers Compound, Kimberley." June B. Sharp photograph album, Church History Library, Salt Lake City, Utah.

of the elders' visit to a Kimberley diamond mine in terms of sourcing diamond jewelry for future fiancées. He described the mines as a masculine world of khaki-suited Black "boys" and "white men" extracting raw materials that were fit for "modern women" only after they had been sent out of Africa to be cut and polished.¹⁰¹ All the reports in the *Improvement Era* recount the experiences of male missionaries for an assumed male readership. In some cases, the only woman who was part of the mission, the mission president's wife, is not named (figure 17). The caption to a photograph of missionaries at a conference in Bloemfontein identifies Emily Jones Hewlett only in relation to her husband: "President Franklin J. Hewlett and wife." Although such anonymizing of women as an appendage of their husbands remains a common practice, the caption's identification of the "elders of the South African mission" ensures Emily Hewlett's exclusion. Despite having been set apart for the mission, she was not an elder. She was also not mentioned in attendance at the meeting in Jeppestown described in the accompanying report from D. Vernon Shurtliff, the clerk of the conference, who traveled with the Hewletts from Belgium to South Africa aboard the SS *Kommodore*.¹⁰² The image of a lone, unnamed woman among a group of men reinforces the exclusion of women from popular ideas of the missionary experience in a modernizing but still exotic land that was perhaps not yet ready for genteel Latter-day Saint women. The *Relief Society Magazine*, which targeted female readers, had many fewer references to both missions

FIGURE 17. "Elders of the South African mission, back row, left to right: William C. Crook, Elmer P. Chipman, C. Byron Whitney, L. A. Nelson, S. Boswell, F. R. Gardner. Middle row: Joseph F. Hintze, President John S. Sagers, President Franklin J. Hewlett and wife; Conference President Gottlieb Blatter. Bottom row: Rufus Beach, D. Vernon Shurtliff, Clifford S Hodgson," *Improvement Era* (April 1912), 562.

and Africa. When Africa was mentioned, it was usually as a symbol of remote distance. One rare instance of Africa being mentioned as a locale for Latter-day Saint proselytizing was in the dialogue of a fictitious story of a widowed mother telling her son she would rather he be sent on a mission to Africa than enlist in the military during the Great War.[103] The idea of Africa was presented to Latter-day Saint women as something so frightening its undesirability was second only to the threat of the battlefield.

The Latter-day Saint version of South Africa remained exotic despite it becoming increasingly tame as a result of the efforts of men like Rhodes, Kruger, and Van Riebeek. Hewlett described a metropolitan Durban, teeming with Europeans: "As you stroll along the bay esplanade you meet Spaniards, Portuguese, Italians, gaily dressed ladies, as if they had just dropped from the shops of Paris."[104] However, South Africans were eager to capitalize on the exotic African stereotype. "We are soon surrounded by Zulus, decked like warriors with horns on their heads and plenty of feathers. They are strongly-built fellows, and are drawing jinrickishas that will seat two average-sized persons" (figure 18). The

FIGURE 18. "Bay Esplanade—Durban. Horned Zulu," *Improvement Era* (August 1912), 886.

local flavor, though, is clearly not for the locals—at least not the Black majority—as Hewlett relates, a "small card informs you that they are for 'Europeans only.'"[105] These men were performing their Africanness, perpetuating caricatures specifically for white tourists.

Caricatures and stereotypes are difficult to stamp out and remained part of the Latter-day Saint image of Africa despite missionary reports of a modern country. In some cases, the missionaries themselves played up the distance of the South African mission from home. Missionary Malcolm L. Robinson wrote to the *Improvement Era*'s editors in 1919 that the magazine was "a most welcome guest to this far distant corner of the earth. . . . This is the most distant branch of the Church in all the world from the Central stakes of Zion."[106] The distance to Africa was not only physical but cultural. An article in the October 1914 *Era* by church leader and University of Utah historian Levi Edgar Young titled "'Mormonism' and the Modern Man" referred to "far off Asia" and "the far wilds of Africa."[107] According to Young, Asia was distant but Africa was distant and wild. In an article intended as "A Study for the Quorums and Classes of the Melchizedek Priesthood," or adult men in the church, another influential Latter-day Saint academic, Joseph M. Tanner, described Africans as superstitious and callous, sacrificing their own children. He wrote that

> various tribes that were nomadic in character often destroyed their children because in moving from place to place they could not care for them. These human sacrifices were generally performed by the men, but

in some of the lowest tribes the mothers joined in this hideous religious rite. Along the west coast of Africa, out of the control of the English, children were destroyed by mothers, and there was a belief among the K—— population of South Africa that unless they laid a lump of earth upon the mouths of their children and thus produced death, the parents would lose their strength.[108]

Similar stories appeared in Protestant missionary periodicals as early as 1844 but were absent from the reports of missionaries with actual experience in Africa.[109] Note how the supposedly barbarous acts are committed "out of the control of the English," implying that, whatever civilizing effects colonialism may be having, like those described by the missionaries, Africa and Africans remained wild and dangerous when left to themselves.

Few Latter-day Saints at the beginning of the twentieth century had direct experience in Africa. Traversing the physical distance from the Mormon population centers in the American West was expensive and time-consuming and very few of them made the trip. This chapter has considered how the Latter-day Saint missionary enterprise in Africa affected perceptions of the continent among church members in the first two decades of the twentieth century, after missionaries returned in 1903. Employing Syed Manzurul Islam's concepts of sedentary and nomadic travel, it has asked whether Latter-day Saint missionaries and members breached the divide between the self and the Other. The chapter has also considered Paul Landau's concept of an "image-Africa" in an Latter-day Saint context. Did the Latter-day Saints have an image of Africa that was altered by the missionary enterprise?

Early twentieth-century conceptions of Africa among Latter-day Saints in Utah were largely caricatures of a "Dark Continent," based on romantic tales of a far-off and dangerous land. In addition to popular images of Africa, Latter-day Saint theology assigned Africans a unique theological Otherness. Missionaries accepted their assignments there with some anxiety. Even after arriving in South Africa, Latter-day Saint missionaries had relatively few meaningful contacts with the majority Black population, frequently noting they did not work with them in their proselytizing efforts. Where contact was prolonged and meaningful—mostly with Coloured rather than Black South Africans—amicable relationships formed. Reports home said little of those relationships but continued to show Black Africans as Other.

More substantive experience in cities and towns reserved for white, especially Anglophone, South Africans demonstrated to the missionaries what they saw as the benefits of the colonial enterprise to tame Africa's wilds and develop the continent's resources. South Africa's towns and cities sported spacious modern buildings, electricity, sewage systems, and paved roads. An expanding network of railroads spirited goods and passengers across the country quickly and efficiently. Exotic animals were not necessarily domesticated but they were caged, and African plants were planted and pruned to form impressive gardens, demonstrating control over the continent. White South Africa was modern and the future of the country.

The missionaries' South Africa was two countries and their travel there was both sedentary and nomadic. One country was Black, where missionaries spent little time. Their brief excursions there fit Islam's definition of sedentary travel, in which they were unchanged by their tourism as their observations and photographs confirmed their expectations of African life. The other country-within-the-country was white South Africa. There the missionaries' ideas of Africa were transformed as they witnessed a country that was modern and wholly different from their expectations. However, the missionaries' reports of a modern Africa were insufficient to alter prevailing stereotypes of the continent. After two decades of continuous missionary labors in Africa, the Latter-day Saint community at large retained its popular image of the "Dark Continent."

CHAPTER 7

Earthquakes, Mudslides, and Hurricanes
Natural Disasters and Humanitarian Aid in Evangelical Missionary Strategy

Lauren F. Turek

The eruption of the Nevado del Ruiz in Colombia started off relatively mildly. At around 3 p.m. on November 13, 1985, a series of minor explosions in the Arenas crater sent up steam and small plumes of ash that drifted down onto the towns that lay to the northeast of the 17,500-foot-tall volcano. Scientists and local officials had been monitoring the volcano since late 1984, when they first observed an uptick in seismic and volcanic activity, and had developed an emergency response plan and a hazard map to prepare for an eventual eruption.[1] Shortly after the November 13 eruption began, reports went out to local civil defense and Red Cross offices, and the Regional Emergency Committee gathered for a prescheduled meeting. The ashfall tapered off within a few hours, however, and officials decided not to issue calls to evacuate at-risk towns.[2]

Yet later that evening, the eruption intensified. At 9:08 p.m., a violent explosion sent magma spewing into the air "in a jetting column of hot pumice fragments and ash."[3] According to reports and studies conducted after the eruption, the "hot ash rapidly accumulated on the volcano's snowy summit and its five glaciers to depths as great as 20 feet, melting the snow and ice."[4] The result was catastrophic. Meltwater and ash coursed down the sides of the volcano, combining with "soil, rocks, and trees" to generate devastating mudslides known as "lahars," some of which moved "at speeds of 35 kilometers per hour," according to scientists' estimates.[5] Worse yet, two of the lahars rushed into the Lagunillas River, obliterating a natural dam near the town of Armero.[6] Attempts to issue evacuation orders either failed to go through due to downed communications networks or simply came too late for people to flee; indeed, many victims were sleeping when the mudslides inundated their towns.[7] The suffering was immense. Floodwaters and mud buried about 90 percent of Armero, as well as significant parts of Chinchiná and other nearby towns.[8] Survivors described a scalding "river of mud and rocks ... crashing through the doors and windows" of their homes, sweeping away family members and causing devastating injuries.[9] Some twenty-three thousand people perished in the tragedy, with thousands more injured and many thousands of homes destroyed.

The world responded to the disaster—and to Colombia's appeals for help—with an outpouring of aid. In addition to the assistance that the US Agency for International Development (USAID), the UN Disaster Relief Organization, and the Red Cross provided, religious groups sent funds, antibiotics, clothing, tools, and other needed supplies to aid those suffering in the affected region.[10] The day after the Nevado del Ruiz erupted, the Southern Baptist Convention (SBC) Foreign Mission Board provided an initial $10,000 in extra funding for its missionaries in Colombia to use as they joined in with Red Cross relief efforts.[11] In the months that followed, Southern Baptist missionaries and their local Baptist brethren visited victims, helped the Red Cross distribute medications and provide medical care, and established a Center of Hope to provide longer-term care to survivors.[12] Members of the Association of Evangelical Relief and Development Organizations, which included World Vision, World Relief, Food for the Hungry, and Medical Assistance Programs (MAP) International, also mobilized quickly with coordinated efforts to provide aid.[13] Unlike secular relief organizations, however, evangelical groups sought to provide spiritual as well as material aid to the victims and tended to view the Nevado del Ruiz eruption and similar natural disasters as opportunities to extend their evangelistic reach throughout the world.

That Christian groups stepped in immediately after the Ruiz tragedy to help ease the suffering of the victims is not surprising. The Bible commands Christians to feed the hungry, care for the sick, and show mercy to the afflicted.[14] Scholars have written extensively on the long history of Christian charity, exploring its biblical roots and varied motivations, as well as the emergence of dedicated Christian humanitarian organizations in Europe and the United States in the nineteenth century.[15] Nor is it surprising that evangelical Christians, with their commitment to evangelism, would seek to share their faith with those that they aided, as a number of recent works on evangelical humanitarianism reveal.[16] Nonetheless, the explicit links that evangelical groups drew between the provision of disaster relief and the fulfillment of their evangelistic aims sheds considerable light on how missionary strategy evolved in the late twentieth century in response to the perceived "crisis of missions" of the 1960s and 1970s.[17]

This chapter will explore the language of missionary opportunity that pervaded discussions among Baptists, Pentecostals, and other evangelicals about natural disasters and disaster relief efforts abroad. Denominational mission strategy documents that addressed disaster relief, along with news articles on the US evangelical response to victims of hurricanes, earthquakes, mudslides, and floods in other countries, reveal that although US evangelicals did evince a commitment to certain forms of social action, evangelism remained a primary focus of their foreign engagement. In the case of the Nevado del Ruiz eruption, articles in the *Baptist Press* included interviews with several missionaries in Colombia who reported that "disaster relief 'opens doors that would never be opened in any other way,'" offering them "direct contact with people in need, to whom we can give ... a direct witness of God's mercy."[18] To wit, Baptist missionaries in Colombia gained enough new followers by evangelizing among the recuperating victims to found at least two new congregations near the towns affected by the volcano.[19] This was by no means unique to the Ruiz disaster. As such, examining how evangelicals blurred the lines between their disaster relief efforts and their missionary objectives provides additional insight into how and why evangelicalism expanded so dramatically in parts of Latin America, Africa, and Asia in the late twentieth century.[20] It also illuminates how the heated debates over missionary work that emerged in the 1960s and 1970s shaped the strategic planning of US evangelical denominations and humanitarian aid organizations and thus US foreign relations more broadly.

Evangelical efforts to spread the Christian faith throughout the world intensified in the 1970s. Significant population growth in the Global South contributed to a sense of anxiety among evangelicals that their extant foreign missionary work could not keep up, which might imperil their efforts to achieve the Great Commission.[21] Furthermore, the movements for decolonization and anticolonial nationalism that emerged in Africa, Asia, and elsewhere in the Global South after World War II had inspired vigorous critiques of Christian missionary work for its role in propagating cultural imperialism and colonialism.[22] During the 1960s, many US and European evangelicals had watched with increasing alarm as mainline Protestant denominations responded to these critiques by curtailing their overseas missionary work and prioritizing social justice over "traditional" evangelism.[23] Seeking to counter this trend, US evangelicals poured considerable resources into writing about the necessity of foreign missionary work and researching how they might make cross-cultural evangelism more effective.

They shared their perspectives and research at international conferences, including at the International Congress on World Evangelization that the Billy Graham Evangelistic Association organized in 1974.[24] At these conferences, US evangelicals encountered the voices of their brethren from the Global South, many of whom advocated for indigenous rather than foreign evangelism, local autonomy for their churches, and a greater emphasis on attending to the social, economic, and political injustices in the world that hindered evangelism.[25] Despite the spirited debate that these perspectives evoked, most US and European evangelicals continued to view evangelism as the chief objective of the church. Social action occupied a subsidiary position, accepted as "part of [the] Christian duty" but not more important than that most urgent task of spreading the gospel to the estimated two billion people on earth who had yet to hear it.[26]

The perception that demographic and political change posed a challenge to their foreign missions programs led many evangelical denominations in the United States to launch strategic planning initiatives to update their approach to missionary work. In 1975, the SBC Foreign Mission Board called on its members "to project plans for the next twenty-five years" and, after receiving "a veritable flood" of proposals, held a series of conferences to discuss the ideas that they generated.[27] Through these meetings, the SBC Foreign Mission Board developed a new program called the "Bold Mission Thrust," which aimed to greatly expand the reach and efficiency of Baptist missions.[28] In addition to recommending significant increases in the number of mission fields, missionaries, local volunteers, and overseas churches, planning documents highlighted "accentuated attention to human need" and "vigorous, appropriate, and prompt responses to ... disasters" as essential to achieving the "great over-arching objective" of sharing the gospel with everyone on earth.[29] These latter two goals appeared at the end of an enumerated list of "bold new thrusts in missions" that the denomination aimed to undertake, trailing behind the more explicitly evangelistic goals.[30] Yet their inclusion on the list suggested that, in the context of the crisis of missions, Baptists viewed benevolent and social ministries such as disaster relief primarily as tools for evangelism.[31]

The language that the SBC Foreign Mission Board used throughout the strategic planning documents bears this out. In "Foreign Missions Looks Toward 2000 A.D.," the 1976 report that outlined the "Bold Mission Thrust" program, the board offered evangelistic justifications to support its call to expand compassionate ministries. It referenced and reaffirmed a program statement on health care that the SBC adopted in 1966, which asserted that providing "medical assistance to people in foreign countries" operated "as an expression of Christian love, and as a means of witness in order that they might be brought to

God through Jesus Christ."[32] The report also noted that for the purposes of the "Bold Mission Thrust," the SBC should evaluate foreign medical care in part based on its "spiritual effectiveness and results," which is to say, its efficacy in proselytizing to those receiving care from Baptist medical missions.[33] Likewise, the board asserted that its long-range planning for providing relief during "hurricanes, floods, droughts, volcanoes, crop failures, earthquakes, epidemics," and other disasters would emphasize evangelism.[34] Accordingly, the board stated that it would develop its natural disaster response programs in a manner *"consistent* with the biblical imperative of the Great Commission (Matt. 28) and the great culmination (Matt. 25)," so as to be *"complementary* to and *supportive* of our role in evangelism and church development, and *responsive* to the needs of the world and the concern of our people."[35] In referencing Matthew 25, the board certainly underscored the biblical basis for providing disaster relief.[36] Nevertheless, by citing Matthew 25 *after* Matthew 28—and by similarly discussing evangelism and church development *before* human need—the board also again elevated the evangelistic task to a position of primacy and operationalized compassionate service as a tool for achieving it.

This hierarchy of goals influenced how Baptists discussed the disaster relief efforts they engaged in during the late 1970s and beyond. Natural disasters provided new and seemingly divine openings to pursue the "Bold Mission Thrust," as missionaries and disaster relief volunteers could offer "direct, intense, personal evangelism" at moments of crisis that might make those they met especially receptive to the message.[37] For this reason, evangelicals came to see disaster relief as a reliable conduit for witness, one that many victims and local evangelicals alike seemed to welcome. For example, after an earthquake and tidal wave devastated his city, one Filipino Baptist pastor praised the aid the SBC sent, calling it "a very good Baptist testimony."[38] This receptive attitude proved encouraging to SBC missionaries there, one of whom reported that he looked forward to establishing "extensive and prolonged ministries among the people" affected by the disaster.[39]

A language of opportunity pervaded the reports and interviews that Baptists shared in denominational newsletters and other media about their experiences providing assistance after natural disasters.[40] After a hurricane ravaged the Caribbean island of Dominica in 1979, the pastor of a Baptist church in Dallas that raised money and sent a team of missionaries to help repair homes there described the work as "bold mission in action" and a key opportunity to "reach the world for Christ."[41] Southern Baptist doctors who rushed to provide care after an earthquake destroyed large swaths of Guatemala City stated that they felt "grateful that God had given them many opportunities to minister in his name."[42] Each injured Guatemalan that they encountered represented a potential soul that they might win to Christ. Building homes and a new medical center would "be the springboard for a Baptist witness," another article proclaimed.⁴³ Similarly, when an earthquake struck Ecuador in 1987, Southern Baptist missionaries and their Ecuadorian brethren amassed thirty tons of provisions for the victims and touted their "plan to use food distribution as a way to share the gospel."⁴⁴ Talking about disaster relief as an evangelistic opportunity emerged as a consistent trope in denominational newsletters in the mid-1970s, and Baptist leaders in the United States and abroad, as well as Baptist missionaries, frequently emphasized how disaster relief contributed to their efforts to achieve the Great Commission.

Indeed, many newsletter articles about natural disasters made explicit note of how many new churches evangelicals established and how many people evangelicals "saved" in the course of providing disaster relief. In 1982, the SBC newsletter *Baptist Press* reported that "the same hurricane that battered hundreds of homes and killed dozens of people blew open doors of opportunity for Baptists in the west coast town of Los Mochis, Mexico."⁴⁵ Praising US and Mexican Baptists for their disaster relief efforts, the article noted that because of their involvement, "Baptists have been granted new opportunities to share their faith," proudly celebrating the number of souls won to Christ.⁴⁶ The *Baptist Press* reported with similarly glowing language after Baptists in Mexico announced that they would use a pair of devastating earthquakes in 1985 to launch a church-planting project that aimed to establish fifty new churches in Mexico City within a year.⁴⁷ Baptists also rejoiced to learn that postearthquake revivals in El Salvador "won 3,925 new believers to Jesus Christ."⁴⁸ After an earthquake leveled Kobe, Japan, the Billy Graham Evangelistic Association (BGEA) worked with city leaders to clear "an entire city block" of collapsed buildings to make room for a huge screen onto which they could project a Billy Graham crusade to offer the people of Japan salvation.⁴⁹ Including the suffering people of Kobe, the BGEA anticipated that the crusade would reach an audience of one billion people worldwide.⁵⁰

Baptists were not alone in viewing natural disasters as opportunities for Christian witness. In response to the cataclysmic 7.5 Mw earthquake that struck Guatemala before dawn on February 4, 1976, killing over twenty-three thousand people and causing serious injury to another seventy-six thousand, Christian relief agencies mobilized immediately to provide medical care, food, and supplies for rebuilding. The Division of Foreign Missions and the Mobilization and Placement Service of the Assemblies of God, a Pentecostal denomination, called for volunteers to travel to Guatemala to assist in rebuilding churches, Bible schools, and other structures.⁵¹ In their newsletters, members of the Assemblies of God emphasized the role that they believed Christian salvation and faith itself played in supporting the suffering people of Guatemala. One missionary claimed that, "as we visited one stricken village after another, we saw Christians clinging to the promises of God and being comforted" despite the death and destruction that surrounded them.[52]

Pentecostals shared with Baptists the sense that natural disasters offered opportunities for spiritual renewal and adjusted their missionary strategy accordingly. The Assemblies of God devoted months to developing new evangelistic programs to complement their disaster relief efforts in Guatemala; in November 1977, they launched "Invasion '77," a series of "200 Good News Crusades" throughout Guatemala.[53] The program represented an effort to expand the denomination beyond rebuilding the original 131 Assemblies of God churches in Guatemala. The revivals would be led by US and Guatemalan evangelists, and the crusades had a stated goal of planting at least eighty new churches throughout Guatemala.[54] Invasion '77 proved enormously successful, in part because core aspects of the Pentecostal faith proved attractive to Guatemalans suffering in the aftermath of the earthquake. Theologian Néstor Medina argues that not only did evangelical churches provide more efficient disaster assistance than Catholic churches after the earthquake but, additionally, "Pentecostalism helped people rebuild their lives and make sense of their reality through apocalyptic lenses. The Pentecostal message of the imminent coming of the Lord, war, suffering, and earthquakes as signs of the end times contributed greatly to people flocking to Pentecostal churches" in the months and years after the earthquake.[55] Medina and others view Pentecostal evangelism after the earthquake as a key contributor to the tremendous growth of evangelicalism in Guatemala after 1976.[56] Relief work after the earthquake provided the opening for that evangelism.

The relationship between disaster relief and evangelistic opportunity that Baptist and Pentecostal denominations identified as they worked to navigate the crisis of missions also crept into the language that evangelical humanitarian nongovernmental organizations (NGOs) used when discussing their missions. These agencies, which had exploded in number after World War II and included World Vision, the World Relief Commission of the National Association of Evangelicals, Food for the Hungry, MAP International, and many more, each had "distinct philosophies of ministry" that shaped their approach to Christian social action.[57] Although these agencies tended to be nondenominational or multidenominational and ostensibly focused primarily on providing disaster relief, medical care, and other humanitarian assistance, they were also at their core faith-based organizations. Some, such as the World Relief Commission, explicitly touted evangelism as "a high priority" goal of their humanitarian missions.[58] Others, especially those like World Vision that received funding from

USAID and other government agencies, maintained that they did not proselytize while providing aid.[59]

Yet even those organizations that eschewed direct proselytism made it clear that they viewed their relief work as a form of Christian witness. In a 1975 interview with *Christianity Today*, World Vision President Dr. W. Stanley Mooneyham asserted that while his organization's work did not necessarily have a *"direct evangelistic connection"*—after all, he remarked, "we don't stamp 'Jesus Saves' on every vitamin pill"—he still saw humanitarian aid as a means "to demonstrate Christian love in tangible ways."[60] This perspective, which many of the evangelical staff members, volunteers, and donors of these NGOs shared, blurred the lines between purely evangelistic and purely humanitarian work.

In the context of the debates over the crisis of missions and the proper place of evangelism and social action within the church that bubbled up in the 1970s, this blurring is significant, particularly given Mooneyham's insistence that "in our work we put evangelism first and last."[61] US-based evangelical NGOs did not operate in a vacuum. The critiques that evangelicals from the Global South such as C. René Padilla leveled against their US counterparts for focusing too much on tallying up saved souls rather than on fostering forms of "evangelism . . . oriented toward breaking man's slavery in the world" shaped how relief agencies framed their objectives.[62] The preface to Mooneyham's interview alluded to the power and sting of those critiques, noting that "many Christians are being sensitized to their responsibility to engage in compassionate ministries" to alleviate global suffering, poverty, and inequality.[63] Even as Mooneyham argued that evangelism and social action were "not synonymous," he also made clear that he believed that neglecting either biblical responsibility would damage the church and its teachings and "make its message less credible" to those whom evangelicals hoped to reach.[64] In other words, relief work was instrumental to conveying the appeal, legitimacy, and value of Christianity to the unevangelized. Mooneyham took pains to stress that his agency did not "provide help to suffering people only because they are potential evangelistic statistics" but in the same breath celebrated the opportunity that relief work provided to share his faith.[65] That the leaders of evangelical relief agencies found it difficult to discuss social action without also referencing and elevating evangelism indicates that, on a fundamental level and despite official claims to the contrary, they viewed humanitarian aid as a tool for sharing Christian witness first and foremost.

Although clearly sensitive to critiques of foreign missionary work from evangelicals in the Global South, members of evangelical NGOs nonetheless often used a language of opportunity when discussing the humanitarian assistance they provided in crisis scenarios. In a special report about the work of the World Relief Commission (WRC), Lillian Graffam—the wife of WRC Executive Vice

President Everett S. Graffam—argued that evangelicals should view humanitarian aid as integral to evangelism. In addition to visually representing their connection by referring to the two aims as "relief/evangelism" throughout her report, she also made the case that the aid that agencies like the WRC provided to those suffering from natural disasters gave missionaries on the ground "a tangible way of saying 'God loves you.' . . . Often when the missionary can offer a 'bowl' in one hand he finds a receptive heart to the Bible in the other."[66] She supported this assertion by explaining that the speedy delivery of WRC funding and supplies to Nicaragua after an earthquake in 1972 had allowed Baptist, Pentecostal, and other "relief/evangelism teams" there to attend to the suffering populace, which was then primed for evangelism.[67] According to Graffam, "this outreach resulted in considerable church growth" in Nicaragua.[68] Similarly, in an article discussing WRC support to relief after the 1976 earthquake in Guatemala, Graffam noted that "equally important with the caring for the physical needs is making sure the people have an opportunity to hear about salvation in Christ, the one in whose name the help is being given."[69] Such statements revealed that overcoming the crisis of missions and working toward the Great Commission remained an overriding objective for evangelicals and evangelical agencies that provided disaster relief.

Indeed, concern about the crisis of missions and its threat to global evangelistic goals emerged in a range of reports and articles about disaster relief during the 1970s and 1980s. A 1984 *Christianity Today* article about the work of World Vision and the WRC in famine-stricken countries in Africa stressed that these agencies worked with "local churches, missions, and national evangelical fellowships" and involved local villagers in aid and development projects where possible.[70] Arguing that the involvement of locals in these projects softened attitudes toward outside missionaries and led to "the formation of churches," the author gave the example of a Christian relief project in Burkina Faso that influenced villagers to stop "resisting the efforts of the evangelist" who was stationed there.[71] The article praised the role the relief workers played in laying the groundwork for evangelistic success, noting that "today, the village's Protestant church has more than 100 members."[72] Likewise, in her report about the WRC, Lillian Graffam touted the role that "national (native) Christians" played as partners in helping US evangelical agencies administer relief and thus in evangelizing their brethren.[73] This emphasis on Christian "nationals" provided a response to criticisms about foreign missionary work from Global South evangelicals, yet also underscored evangelicals' tactical approach to thinking about evangelism: because "nationals" could witness without the "culture clash" that US evangelicals might experience, they could evangelize more effectively.[74] As with Mooneyham's essay, this language alluded to statements from evangelical leaders such as

C. René Padilla, who condemned Western foreign missionary work as cultural imperialism, as well as to Padilla's US critics who hoped a more "culturally sensitive" approach to evangelism would allow evangelicals throughout the world to dedicate themselves to their primary aim of achieving the Great Commission.[75]

Natural disasters presented an ideal opportunity for US evangelicals to demonstrate what they saw as the continued need for their involvement in the Global South despite critiques about cultural imperialism, as their churches, missionary agencies, and humanitarian organizations had the resources to respond quickly and efficiently to suffering in poorer countries. World Vision and others could, for example, speed millions of dollars to local churches serving the victims of drought in Zaire, relief work that evangelicals viewed as contributing to a "spiritual awakening" and revival of Christianity in Central Africa in the late 1970s.[76] Financial resources were just the start. In 1975, the WRC partnered with missionary organizations including the Missionary Aviation Fellowship (MAF) and the Wycliffe Bible Translators Jungle Aviation and Radio Service (JAARS) to found a Relief Air Force. This venture gave the WRC access to MAF and JAARS "aircraft and personnel" to ensure their response time to natural disasters would be as quick as possible.[77] With a range of different aircraft at their disposal, these groups could "fly into the disaster area to provide on-the-spot damage surveys, ferry food, relief supplies, medicines, and personnel," while also reporting back to the WRC and "the general evangelical public," who could then respond with donations to those in need. As advertising brochures for the Mission Aviation Fellowship indicated, providing such largesse at such speed facilitated their core goal of "giving *every person* a valid opportunity to accept Jesus Christ."[78] Such brochures and articles often referenced the number of individuals saved or churches planted along with statistics about the number of people served after the disaster and pledged ongoing support to those working in the region and to new churches so they could flourish and lead to organic Christian growth abroad.[79]

The advantageous relationship that evangelical Christians saw between disaster relief and evangelism was not an exclusive phenomenon of the 1970s and 1980s, nor were evangelical Christians alone in linking relief work with their evangelistic mission. Indeed, as other authors in this book note, missionaries have long viewed moments of social disruption, whether in the form of a natural disaster, economic crisis, or political upheaval, as openings for evangelism. Chapter 3 by Devrim Ümit, for example, addresses the unraveling of the Ottoman Empire and the American Civil War in the late nineteenth century as moments of tumult that influenced US missionary interests in Ottoman Turkey as well as the receptivity of people living in the Ottoman Empire to missionary Christianity. Late twentieth-century evangelicals were also not alone in acknowledging the practicality of coordinating with local Christians and working through local organizations, particularly in the context of critiques about US or Western missionary cultural imperialism. As Melissa Wei-Tsing Inouye notes in chapter 9, even at the turn of the twentieth century, Chinese Christians and British Protestant missionaries operating in China knew it was critical to convey the value of their faith to those they evangelized if they were to succeed in their mission. That task required collaboration between locals and foreign missionaries, as Chinese Christians played an essential role in legitimizing the faith for those who had yet to be converted, while the tools or "cultural technologies" that foreign missionaries provided to Chinese Christians helped demonstrate the value of conversion. In more recent times, members of the Church of Jesus Christ of Latter-day Saints have reflected on the relationship between humanitarian work and Christian witness. Some, such as James Mason, have sounded cautionary notes about the risk of commingling relief with evangelism, cautioning that relief might lead to conversions out of a desire for help rather than a true commitment to the faith.[80] Others, such as Garry Flake, note that providing humanitarian aid during natural disasters "demonstrate[s] a gospel of love and a caring attitude for those in need throughout the world," which helps to foster understanding about the Latter-day Saint Church throughout the world.[81]

Still, the crisis of missions that inspired evangelical soul-searching and a renewed energy for missionary work in the mid-1970s did bring fresh attention to the possibilities that humanitarian aid held for achieving broader evangelistic aims. Offering assistance to those suffering after a hurricane, volcano, earthquake, famine, or flood allowed evangelicals to witness indirectly—by serving as a living example of the "goodness" of the Christian faith—and directly, through proselytism as they helped or work with individuals. That evangelicals talked consistently and publicly about disaster relief using a language of evangelistic opportunity makes clear that they viewed the biblical command to share the gospel with everyone in the world as an urgent, immediate, and overwhelming necessity. This sense of millennial urgency undergirded their broader evangelistic strategy in the 1970s and 1980s but also influenced the goals and organization of their humanitarian aid agencies and programs. As evangelical humanitarian aid organizations became increasingly central to the distribution of relief (including USAID assistance) worldwide in the 1990s and 2000s, this focus opened these groups up to criticism for seeming to require recipients of humanitarian aid to submit to proselytism. Nevertheless, seizing the opportunity that natural disasters presented to share the gospel proved incredibly effective for evangelical denominations, which grew exponentially in Latin America, Asia, and Africa in the last quarter of the twentieth century.

CHAPTER 8

Inventing Rupture in India and America
Adivāsi Converts, Hindu Nationalists, and American RLDS Missionaries, 1966–1996

David J. Howlett

In 1966, thirty-year-old Limpan Raika became a Christian. Originally from a small Sora tribal village in the hill country of south-central Orissa (now called Odisha), India, Raika moved to another Sora village that had recently converted to Christianity en masse. As Raika related to me in a 2014 interview, the contrast between his home village, where people practiced a traditional tribal religion, and his new village, where people practiced a form of Christianity, proved compelling. In his old village, he noted, "People are worshipping and giving offering like cow and water buffalo. All those things are become poverty to the people, but when I could see this village, they are not offering water buffalo and cow, and then the Christian life is very much an attraction, like changing their life." Raika joined the new religion and within a year became a lay teacher who evangelized other villages. He shared that his success in evangelism mostly came through the appeal of his new practices: "Like I forsake drinking alcohol, or the best thing is I am wearing nice clothes, or I have forsaken idol worship. Those things, I have become example, and they saw me, and then they became Christian."[1]

Raika's new practices seemed to make a striking break with common social or ritual practices that had structured daily life and identity among Soras. Drinking circles that had once been places for daily conviviality were now disrupted. Costly sacrifices that had been crucial to frequent communication between the living and the dead were now ended. And earth-toned clothes that marked Sora as different from their neighbors in the valley were exchanged for brightly colored saris for women and shirts and slacks for men. What happened through Raika's evangelism was not an isolated occurrence. Within thirty years, hundreds of Sora lay teachers were preaching in similarly transformed Sora villages that had joined a mission within a denomination whose full name they rarely used, the East India Mission of the Reorganized Church of Jesus Christ of Latter Day Saints (RLDS), or East India Mission, as most Soras called the denomination as a whole.[2]

At first glance, Limpan Raika's story seems shot through with moments of "rupture," a term with particular weight in cultural anthropology. In some sectors of this academic discipline, "rupture" is in vogue as a conceptual tool to characterize sharp temporal breaks found in phenomena as diverse as responses to environmental catastrophe, spectacles of terror, and populist politics.[3] First and foremost, though, the concept of rupture has shaped studies of religious conversion and, in particular, studies of religious conversion among late twentieth-century Indigenous peoples. In much of the current literature, scholars emphasize that, as Indigenous peoples confront the social processes of globalization, they may convert to a new religion en masse and create sharp ruptures from their previous identities.[4] According to these scholars, rupture takes shape in the narratives that people tell about their conversions, as well as in the rituals that converts practice. Joel Robbins in particular has argued for the merits of thinking about globalization and conversion from the perspective of rupture, as opposed to emphasizing processes of cultural continuity, as anthropologists have been wont to do in the past. In one influential essay about Pentecostal conversion among the Urapmin in Papua, New Guinea, Robbins mused, "Looking at Pentecostal discourses and rituals from the perspective of discontinuity allows us to highlight aspects of their content that have often been overlooked or dismissed as unimportant" by the vast majority of scholars.[5] That is, it allows us to see aspects of their content dismissed by scholars until 2003 when Robbins published these words. At the time I drafted this chapter, Robbins's essay just quoted, his subsequent book, and his related essay had together been cited an eye-popping two thousand times.

While this chapter uses "rupture" as a meaningful term to think about conversion, I take a slightly different focus to what most scholars have done thus far. Here, I do not take rupture as only an observational fact about a social process, as simply a useful academic category of analysis, or as primarily an analytic corrective to arguments about cultural continuity. Instead, I focus upon how rupture is "invented" by particular historical actors for political and public ends and endowed with contested valences by these same historical actors. In other words, I want to think about why some things are coded as rupture and other things are not, as well as tease out the work that this does for various historical actors with ideological projects that they want to promote. Robbins himself has recently gestured toward the merits of such a perspective, citing a study of how "revolution" was invented in what we now call the French Revolution, though he does not follow up this suggestion by applying it to his own past ethnographic work.[6]

My case study investigates the "invention of rupture" by three stakeholder communities in the late twentieth-century Indian state of Orissa: (1) the onetime animistic *adivāsis* ("Indigenous peoples"), specifically the Sora people, who converted to Christianity; (2) elite Hindu nationalists connected to a political pressure group (the Vishwa Hindu Parishad); and (3) American RLDS missionary administrators who, on yearly tours of church congregations in Asia, visited the congregations and conferences of the newly converted adivāsis. The juxtaposition of these three groups illustrates the very different valences that may be given to the ruptures of conversion. As will be seen, for the Soras in Orissa, conversion represented a resonant rupture, or a rupture that replicated older cultural forms even as it denied any connection to them. For the Hindu nationalists in Orissa, conversion represented a malignant rupture, or a rupture that maliciously disrupted communal harmony and had the potential to infect the nation as a whole. And, for the American RLDS administrators, tribal conversion created a vicarious rupture, or a secondhand rupture that they experienced through the Soras, and, subsequently, aided in the American leaders' attempts to create dramatic, liberalizing changes within their own largely American church. How Christian adivāsis, Hindu nationalists, and liberalizing American RLDS officials constructed rupture told something of their own aspirations, as well as their position of power relative to other interest groups in Orissa.

Beyond offering a study of the valences of conversion, and, thus, detailing the cultural work of rupture, this chapter offers one more intervention, albeit in passing. Namely, in the section on American RLDS missionary administrators, this chapter details how they adopted ecumenical Protestant notions of indigenization in missions and adapted this orientation to their missions in Soraland and beyond. As such, this section reveals the first major attempt by any Mormon denomination to articulate a formal missiology, as well as showing a Mormon group in dialogue with the wider ecumenical Protestant world in the 1960s. If there is a "missing missiology" in the Latter-day Saint Church's missionary tradition, as David Golding points out in chapter 10 of this book, it is patently evident in the RLDS tradition. As will be seen, RLDS indigenization became church policy even as the first missionaries arrived in Soraland in 1966, resulting in a Sora RLDS Church that looked very little like the American RLDS Church in the Midwest in terms of beliefs, priesthood offices, and local church structures. This stood in stark contrast to the Latter-day Saint Church's policy of "correlation" in the same era, a policy that exported Utah-based beliefs, practices, and vocabulary to urban, middle-class Indians who were already Christians (not poor, rural, animist adivāsis, as in the case of the RLDS).[7] A fuller exploration of RLDS missiology and the lack of Latter-day Saint missiology goes far beyond the scope of this chapter. I simply gesture to it here (a rupture in my overall narrative) and return now to a more pertinent story: how Soras came to characterize their Christian conversions in a way that might best be typified as a resonant rupture.

Christian Soras and Resonant Ruptures

The Sora are part of a larger group of people classified by the Indian government as "Scheduled Tribes" and more recently identified by various rights groups as adivāsis, or "Indigenous peoples."[8] Today, even with economic opportunities available in large cities, many Soras live in the small agricultural villages in the so-called tribal belt in Odisha. Soras number perhaps 300,000 and are divided into further groupings, including the Lanjia Sora, a group that resides in the rural hill country of the Eastern Ghats.[9] Since the mid-twentieth century, Lanjia Sora have largely turned away from older animistic forms of worship and embraced some form of Christianity, with a very small number practicing a form of Hinduism.[10]

The Christianization of the Sora has been documented by two well-known scholars. The first, the eccentric former missionary, tribal political advocate, and amateur anthropologist Verrier Elwin, wrote a rambling study of the Sora in the mid-twentieth century. The second, a Cambridge anthropologist, Piers Vitebsky, conducted intermittent fieldwork with the Sora across four decades and wrote two extraordinary monographs that trace the contours of traditional Sora religion and its transformation into Baptist Christianity from the 1970s to the present.[11] While Elwin's book on Sora religion may be the most influential study of an Indian tribal religion ever published, Vitebsky's much more nuanced and thoroughly researched ethnographies provide fine-grained attention to the transformations Soras underwent in an age of globalization.

Fortuitously for my own research, the Lanjia Soras whom Vitebsky studied lived only forty kilometers from the Lanjia Soras who became RLDS members in the 1960s. The traditional religion of these Soras bore some resemblances to the village Hinduism of the plains of Odisha. Yet, as Vitebsky notes, "If having gods is a definitional criterion of being Hindu, then Sora animists are something else."[12] Instead of gods, Soras had ancestors who evolved into different forms of personhood after death. Immediately after death, these ancestors dwelled with a group of other ancestors in natural forms, like streams or rock formations. In this form, the ancestors were dangerous and would feed upon the living, afflicting them with disease if the living happened to come into contact with them. To sate the appetites of these ancestors, Soras made elaborate sacrifices of water buffaloes, pigs, and chickens. Eventually, these same ancestors evolved into new, less antagonistic forms that reciprocally nourished the crops of the Sora. Ultimately, the ancestors lost all personhood in their final form as butterflies, the last death in Sora cosmology.[13]

Ritual life in a Sora village revolved around conversations and contact with the dead through ritual specialists, *kurans*, who vocalized the dead's feelings and requests. In a series of festivals around the first death transitions, Sora families went into deep debt to Pano-caste middlemen from the valleys who made high-interest loans and procured water buffaloes from the lowlands. Sora families then sacrificed these water buffaloes, a ritual undertaking that went far beyond the quotidian sacrifices of pigs or chickens that could occur on a more regular basis. As an upshot of these practices, Soras in the hills were connected to mostly Hindu people in the valleys through intergenerational debt bondage.[14] Christianity rearranged all of these relationships.

In the mid-1960s, scheduled caste Baptist missionaries from Andhra Pradesh who had recently affiliated with the US-based RLDS Church began to evangelize Sora villages. With a small cadre of Sora converts turned lay missionaries, these missionaries helped direct an extraordinarily successful missionary endeavor that created village congregations affiliated with the newly created East India Mission of the RLDS Church. By the 1970s, more than a dozen Sora village congregations had emerged, and growth continued steadily until more than a hundred Sora village congregations had affiliated with the East India Mission by the early 2000s. While it remains outside of the parameters of this chapter to detail this expansion of the Sora RLDS Church, a brief summary of some of its conversion rituals helps address how Soras constructed rupture as an identity feature.

Vitebsky argues that the Sora Baptist pastors he encountered in his fieldwork "made an aggressive 'investment in discontinuity'" as they established Christianity in Sora villages.[15] Discontinuity in Sora Christianization also characterized Soras who affiliated with the RLDS Church. In fact, RLDS Sora converts engaged in what Robbins typified as "rituals of rupture," or rituals that marked off the converts from their former identities.[16] For example, Sora RLDS missionaries, as well as the Indian RLDS missionaries from Andhra Pradesh, required new converts to engage in literal acts of iconoclasm. Traditional Soras kept pots in their homes to trap the *sonums*, or spirits, of recently dead relatives who might assault them if allowed to wander.[17] New converts would take these same pots out of their homes, and, in front of the entire village, break them on the ground, thus signaling that they had rejected the efficacy of traditional Sora practices to protect them.[18] Funerary ritual specialists and traditional healers, *kurans*, had square pictures on their home's walls where their *sonum* spouse would live when he or she visited the home of the living healer. The new converts destroyed these, too.[19] As a marker of a new identity, these rituals were as important in Sora conversions as was baptism.

Beyond these literal acts of iconoclasm, Sora converts told themselves and others their conversion narratives, stories that were marked with the language of rupture and sharp change. Most often, Sora conversion stories followed a narrative arc of being in poverty or practicing false ways and then finding peace and happiness in the Holy Spirit. "Everything was changed in our lives. . . . If we had not become Christian [in the 1960s] we would have remained men who are making witchcraft," remarked the elderly Baidi Mandal to me in a 2014 interview.[20] Note though, that, as anthropologist Birgit Meyer argues, "rupture necessarily implies some kind of discursive continuity, if only because 'being against' always entails some degree of 'being with.'"[21] Mandal's memory of her family's former practices as witchcraft still gives them an odd extended life. Rupture, then, may deliver to its converts an afterlife for earlier forms of life.

This last point can be seen in sharper relief if we take a longer view of Sora conversions and the resulting social relationships. In a separate article, I offer an extended argument on how conversions deterritorialized and then reterritorialized Sora relationships between their place in the hills and the state in the Hindu valleys.[22] This argument is a riff upon James C. Scott's classic and controversial *The Art of Not Being Governed*, a work that theorizes about highland peoples' attempted evasions of the state in Southeast Asia, leading to zones of lowland states and hill nonstates. Vitebsky sees Scott's hill and valley framework as partially applicable for the Sora in South Asia, at least until the 1940s. After that era, the nation-state, according to Vitebsky and Scott, metaphorically flattened the hills of South and Southeast Asia.[23] In contrast, I have argued that, in the global 1960s and 1970s, Sora conversions created separation between themselves and the Hindu nation-state in Orissa, as well as separation between themselves and the largely American-controlled RLDS denomination headquartered in the American Midwest. In other words, the hills and the valleys, patterns for Sora relationships with others, had an unexpected afterlife in the postindependence era.

This separation between the Sora and their putative others was achieved in manifold ways. For more than fifty years (1966–2018), Sora pastors successfully resisted American RLDS administrators who wanted the Sora-led Baptist-inspired church structure of the RLDS East India Mission to mirror American RLDS church structures and priesthood offices.[24] Furthermore, older client-patron relationships between the Soras in the hills and the Hindus in the valleys became transposed onto relationships within the global RLDS Church. In the preconversion era, illiterate hill Soras mediated their relationships with elite Hindus in the valleys through literate Pano-caste traders who sold Sora goods, drew up Sora deeds, and procured high-interest loans for Soras. In the postconversion era, literate Soras no longer needed Pano-caste traders. However, within the space of the RLDS denomination, Soras reestablished these structural relationships in ways that more directly benefited themselves, but with new intermediaries and new patrons. Elite English-speaking Sora pastors took the place of the Pano-caste traders. These English-speaking Sora pastors mediated between Sora congregants (who only spoke Sora) and American RLDS administrators (who only spoke English). Initially, elite Sora pastors mediated information, church discipline, and rituals. By 1990, these Sora pastors mediated development funds from the American RLDS Church, too.

In select ways, RLDS Soras constructed a new realm for hill and valley separations within the auspices of the global RLDS Church. This exemplifies what Vibha Joshi in her study of Baptist Nagaland calls "patchy continuity," or, more helpfully, what Kimberly Jenkins Marshall in her study of Navajo Pentecostals calls "resonant ruptures," or ruptures that gain their power through their resonance with previous cultural forms, even in the face of "dramatic denial of this continuity" by the enactors of these ruptures.[25] Through these acts of resonant rupture, RLDS Soras disengaged with older exploitative relationships and delivered a limited amount of sovereignty for themselves by reconstructing older patterns for social boundaries.

As Soras converted to Christianity in this era, they also began to more directly join in with the political processes of the democratic Indian nation-state. Sora acts of rupture, part of a larger conversion movement among tribals, gained the attention of political actors beyond local Sora villages, too. In the process, what Soras characterized as liberating ruptures were recharacterized by others as harmful ruptures. Hindu nationalists, in particular, constructed mass conversions to Christianity as malignant ruptures that denationalized tribal peoples. Orissa, the home state of the Soras and many other tribal peoples, became part of the front lines for a decades-long political struggle to define the boundaries of belonging and acceptable religious practice within the postindependence Indian nation-state. It is to this story that I now turn.

Hindu Nationalists and Malignant Ruptures

Constructing Christian conversion as a malignant rupture has a much longer genealogy than actions dated to the 1960s. This includes anticonversion measures passed by a number of the Indian princely states in the 1930s, as well as influential anticonversion arguments articulated by Gandhi himself during the drive toward Indian independence.[26] By the first decade of the postindependence era, secular nationalists and Hindu nationalists alike were critiquing Christian conversion as a menace to India's sovereignty. For secular nationalists like Jawaharlal Nehru, Christian conversion threatened to create separatist states, raised the possibility of continued foreign influence by imperial and nonstate actors, and could undo the sovereign ambitions of Indian nationalists for a united India.[27] Conservative Hindu elites might share these same concerns, though, unlike Nehru, they saw Christian conversion as threatening *Hindu Rashtra*, their conception of India as primarily a Hindu nation-state rather than a united secular state. In the former princely states, Christian conversion, particularly conversion of lower castes and tribal peoples, threatened to undo a Hindu-dominated social order predicated on caste distinctions. Furthermore, Christian conversion menacingly raised the specter of radical land reforms.

This last point has direct relevance to conversions involving Soras. Through colonial revenue-gathering policies, many tribal peoples had been dispossessed of lands and become tenants to high-caste Hindu elites. After Christian conversion, some tribal groups, like Munda Lutherans in the 1930s, demanded new rent arrangements or challenged landlords for deeds in courts. While not all tribal Christians mirrored the liberationist politics of the Munda Lutherans, the possibility that they would worried local Hindu elites who benefited from the continued tenant-landlord system.[28] The Sora people that I have highlighted in this chapter experienced what Vitebsky characterized as unremitting humiliation and economic oppression from these feudal relationships both before and immediately after independence.[29] Local landlords had powerful reasons to oppose the possibility of Sora social and economic mobility. For these landlords, Christian conversion represented all that they feared might happen in postindependence India—continued foreign control and a radical reworking of the local social hierarchy.

Nevertheless, in 1947, delegates to the Indian Constituent Assembly codified the right of individuals to not just practice religion freely but also to propagate their religion. These rights were enshrined in Article 25(1) of the Indian Constitution. Still, the right to propagate one's religion provoked heated arguments within the Constituent Assembly Debates that approved the constitution.[30]

Sustained critiques of the right to propagate one's religion were distilled in a landmark 1956 report, the Niyogi Committee Report on Christian Missionary Activities, issued by a committee commissioned by the newly formed state of Madhya Pradesh. The committee itself had been formed to investigate Hindu claims of Christian missionary abuses in tribal areas. While the Niyogi Committee Report has been analyzed at length by any number of scholars, I want to highlight a few points relevant to this chapter.

First, the authors of the Niyogi Committee Report presumed a paternalistic relationship between the state and tribal peoples, going so far as to suggest that tribal peoples could not make responsible choices for themselves due to their "undeveloped minds." Second, following arguments articulated by Gandhi in the 1930s, the authors argued that conversion had to be for "spiritual" reasons as opposed to any material rationale. Finally, as religious studies scholar Ronald Neufeldt summarizes, the Niyogi Committee Report writers assumed that "the tribals were Hindu" and that Christian conversion "had the effect of turning these simple-minded tribals against Hindus and therefore against loyalty to the nation."[31] In other words, Christian conversion made a radical social, cultural, and political break with the tribals' past.

After the controversial Niyogi Committee Report, Orissa became the first state to pass an anticonversion law, titled the Orissa Freedom of Religion Act (1967). The authors of this act succinctly summarized the aims of the act as follows:

> Conversion in its very process involves an act of undermining another faith. The process becomes all the more objectionable when this is brought about by recourse to methods like force, fraud, material inducement and exploitation of one's poverty, simplicity and ignorance. Conversion or attempts to conversion in the above manner besides creating various maladjustments in social life, also give rise to the problem of law and order. It is therefore, of importance to provide for measures to check such activities which also directly impinge on the freedom of religion.[32]

Crucially, the authors saw conversion as necessarily subversive toward surrounding (majoritarian) communities and framed conversion as an issue of not just "freedom of religion" but "law and order."

By the early 1970s, Christians in Orissa challenged the anticonversion law in court, arguing that it contravened the "right to propagate" one's religion, as protected in the Indian Constitution. The High Court of Orissa issued a mixed finding, stating that the so-called depressed classes, of whom tribals were one, needed protection from conversion, as they were deemed by the court, in sociologist Goldie Osuri's summary, to be "incapable of rational judgment or to exercise freedom of conscience in relation to religious belief."[33] However, the court ultimately struck down the Orissa law as it found the power to regulate religion lay with the union government rather than the state government; therefore, the Orissa state legislature had exceeded its power by enacting the law. This decision lasted until 1977 when the Supreme Court of India validated an anti-conversion law passed in the state of Madhya Pradesh (1968). The court ruled that the Madhya Pradesh law related primarily to public order rather than religion. With this legal rationale, the Orissa law was also reinstated, and, by 1989, greatly strengthened by an act minutely delineating the bureaucratic processes for establishing a valid conversion, processes that included a lengthy interview with local police and forms filed at least sixty days in advance of a conversion.[34] Such a juridical framework defined conversion as a highly disruptive social force that undermined public order and could therefore be justly regulated by the state through bureaucratic means, as well as through the threat of force.

Elite *Hindutva* (literally "Hindu-ness") activists did not simply use laws, courts, and law enforcement procedures to restrict Christian conversion. They also engaged in "missions" themselves. In 1966, the young Swami Lakshmanananda Saraswati and another Hindu activist entered the Kandha tribal-majority Phulbani district of Orissa, a district now encompassed by the Kandhamal district and near the district where Soras began to convert to the RLDS Church in the same year. Saraswati and his coworker were sent by the newly organized Vishwa Hindu Parishad (VHP), a religious organization and political pressure group affiliated with the militant right-wing Rashtriya Swayamsevak Sangh (RSS) and its political party, the Bharatiya Janata Party. Funded by the VHP and wealthy Hindus who lived on the Orissa coast, Saraswati established an inland base of operations that, in many ways, emulated the structures and tactics of Christian missions in the region. By 1969, Saraswati had established an ashram and school for tribal children, deep within the Kandha-majority region. In addition, he waged a relatively successful prohibition campaign and organized yearly Hindu religious conferences for tribals, all with the aim of Hinduizing the Kandhas.[35] Thus, during the global 1960s and 1970s, Hindu and Christian missionaries both moved into the heavily tribal region of Orissa, the former with the backing of rising political elites within Orissa and the latter with the tepid backing of an American church.

Such missionary movements had long-range political consequences for the largely tribal residents of the districts, too. Saraswati had great success among the Kandhas or Kui of Kandhamal, and, according to anthropologist Pinky Hota, became "a powerful and iconic leader who was widely regarded to be the chief architect of the Hindu reclamation of Kandhamal."[36] While Sora RLDS missionaries assiduously avoided politics, their church spread to encompass more than a hundred Sora villages in the regions adjacent to Kandhamal, and local politicians, school teachers, and powerful pastors all emerged from the resulting network. By the early 1980s, Sora RLDS missionaries themselves evangelized Kandhas in neighboring areas, creating a small Christian minority within this tribe that Saraswati had claimed for Hinduism.[37]

As numerous scholars have pointed out, Hindutva political officials assiduously avoided defining Hindu missions to tribals as missions per se or the Hinduization of tribals as conversions. Instead, Hindutva activists denominated their forays into tribal areas as *ghar wapsi*—or "returning home"—campaigns. As political scientist Laura Dudley Jenkins notes, the valences conjured by "homecoming implies that they [Hinduized tribals] are not converting at all but simply returning to their original and primary identity."[38] This rhetoric was maintained despite the fact that Hindutva activists like Saraswati borrowed the methods and means of Christian missionaries to change the practices, beliefs, and affiliations of tribal peoples.[39] Within a Hindutva formulation, "homecomings" reincorporated tribals into an essentialized Hindu society, promoted social harmony, and avoided the ruptures of Christian conversion. The practical upshot of this was that Hindu converts "elude[d] scrutiny under the freedom of religion laws used to report, question, and investigate converts to minority religions," while Christian converts could be legally regulated.[40]

A violent coda sadly marks the story just narrated. In December 2007 and August 2008, anti-Christian riots broke out in the Kandhamal district. As religious studies scholar Chad Bauman notes, the riot on December 24, 2007, was provoked after an "altercation between Christians and the aging Swami Lakshmananda Saraswati . . . in which the swami claimed to have been injured. Many rioters framed their violence against Christians as a response to that altercation." The August 2008 riot was sparked when Naxalites (Maoist insurgents) assassinated Saraswati in his Kandhamal ashram. Hindutva-led retribution, largely committed by Hinduized Kandhas against Christian Pandas (a Dalit group), resulted in the worst incidents of Hindu-on-Christian violence in the postindependence era. The two riots, notes Bauman, resulted in "more than fifty deaths, dozens of cases of sexual assault and rape, the destruction of thousands of homes, and the temporary or permanent displacement of over five thousand refugees."[41] Most Sora and Kandha (Kui) Community of Christ members, living in relatively rural mountain villages, escaped this violence, though at least one Sora Community of Christ church was set on fire and its pastor beaten. Typifying Christian conversions as malignant ruptures, then, has helped generate violent intercommunal conflicts in Odisha in the recent past.

RLDS American Missionaries and Vicarious Ruptures

A third group is part of this story: the American RLDS missionaries and administrators who supervised the East India Mission. They have been conspicuously absent in most of the narrative in this chapter. This is in part because American RLDS missionaries often had limited contact with adivāsi converts in Orissa. The American-based RLDS Church entered India in the 1960s, a time when most missionary groups were turning over missions to indigenous leaders, and RLDS administrators self-consciously embraced a missiology of indigenization. As such, they relied on adivāsi evangelists and other Indian evangelists to do the major work of proselytizing, organizing, and running the church and its mission houses, schools, clinics, and village congregations. American missionaries were actually middle-aged church administrators, apostles and seventies, who made multiweek visits to rural Orissa, year after year, where they might preach, baptize, confirm new members, and preside over conferences. Their role might be better typified as that of a visiting dignitary rather than a long-term missionary.

Nonetheless, these missionary administrators, as I will call them, saw the conversion of the Soras as a moment of rupture. Yet, unlike the "resonant rupture" that characterized the Sora accounts of their conversion, or the "malignant rupture" that Hindu nationalists saw in Sora conversions, RLDS administrators viewed Sora conversions as what I will typify as a "vicarious rupture," or a secondhand rupture the missionaries experienced through the Soras that led the missionaries to advocate for radical reforms within the American RLDS Church. In articles for the RLDS Church's official magazines and legislation passed at the church's biennial World Conference, RLDS missionary administrators maintained that Sora conversions were an important force in the transformation of their parochial, Midwestern American, Mormon-like church into a cosmopolitan, ecumenical, global church. As such, missionary administrators were part of what some scholars have termed the "RLDS Reformation" or the "RLDS Vatican II," and they participated in a phenomenon similar to what historian David Hollinger has documented for early twentieth-century mainline Protestants—a boomerang effect whereby they left the United States to change Asia but returned from their missions to change the United States instead.[42] In this case, RLDS missionary administrators decisively changed the American RLDS Church.

For RLDS leaders, a crucial prerequisite to the experience of vicarious rupture was a formal missiology of indigenization. RLDS church leaders began to articulate a missiology of indigenization in the late 1950s, years before their missions to India. At a 1957 RLDS conference at Graceland College in Iowa, leaders gathered to hear papers on how the church should pursue missions in Asia. Conference organizers posed the question, "Can there be an indigenous Latter Day Saintism in Hawaii, Korea, and Japan?" The answers that conference-goers received were surely a bit jarring to RLDS traditionalists. There could be an indigenous Latter Day Saintism, but, as Japanese convert (and future apostle) Kisuke Sekine argued in his paper, "people in Japan today do not need a translation of the Book of Mormon, or Doctrine and Covenants" but instead "spiritual companions in the search for eternal truth."[43] This was a spare version of the restored gospel most RLDS members taught and portended the questioning of traditional beliefs that church leaders would broach more openly in the 1960s.

Between 1960 and 1970, RLDS Apostle Charles Neff oversaw the church's growth in Asia, including India. In 1960, he moved to Japan and worked alongside other American missionaries, such as Methodists and Adventists, as well as worshipping with the tiny group of RLDS Japanese nationals. Neff's dispatches to the American headquarters continually questioned the relevance of the traditional RLDS message for Japanese people and peoples in Asia more generally.[44] By the time he returned to live in the US in 1962, he was a convert to the concept of indigenization and worked to make this the official policy of RLDS missions.

In 1966, Neff and two other apostles presented a document to the RLDS World Conference titled "Statement on Objectives for the Church," a concise five-point set of objectives approved by the First Presidency and Council of Twelve Apostles. Point 2, titled "Deepen the effectiveness of worship within the church," explained that this general goal "must be expressed through forms of worship which are indigenous to the cultural patterns of the worshipers." The authors wrote that "the church in every nation must be self-supporting in leadership and finance" and that, as the church grew, there would be a change in "the administrative relationship to local units," all in the service of a goal to "decentralize the administration of the church."[45] These goals mirrored missiological trends within liberal Protestantism more generally, including the nineteenth-century "three-self plan" of Rufus Anderson and Henry Venn that became normative for post–World War II ecumenical Protestants.[46] The three-self plan advocated that mission churches should be self-governing, self-funded, and self-propagating. While Neff never cited Anderson, Venn, or later Protestant indigenizers, he had thoroughly inculcated their ethos.

Over the course of the 1960s and 1970s, Neff and other RLDS missionary administrators used the example of adivāsi conversion to argue for the indigenization of the RLDS message. Newly returned from his second month-long trip to rural Sora tribal areas, Neff authored a 1967 article that forcefully made this point. "One of the most interesting challenges before the church in this stage of its development is planting the Restoration gospel in non-Christian lands and cultures," wrote Neff. "The opening of the work in certain countries of the Orient in 1960, and expanding to Africa and India more recently, has caused us to face up, as never before, to this challenge." These new developments, Neff asserted, made it necessary to adapt the message that was shared abroad. "A lesson in church history would not be meaningful to the undernourished, sick, and illiterate Sora tribesman in India," Neff opined. "Providing answers to questions that people aren't asking anymore," he continued, "is a serious problem with Latter Day Saints everywhere."[47] The church, therefore, needed to be culturally relevant in whatever place it grew.

As Neff argued that Midwestern Mormonism was not relevant for adivāsis, he also meant that this same Midwestern Mormonism was no longer relevant for Americans either. Reformers like Neff questioned the relevancy of the doctrine of the RLDS Church as the one true church and the use of the Book of Mormon as a universal text within the church. The reformers, too, were not lone voices in the wilderness. They counted among their group the majority of the apostles, both counselors in the First Presidency, church religious education employees, most of the full-time missionaries in Asia, and the editors of the church's magazines. These individuals pursued graduate education at mainline Protestant seminaries and sponsored seminars for RLDS church leaders where theological and historical issues could be openly explored and questioned. In sum, a cadre of RLDS leaders like Neff catalyzed a process that one sociologist of religion has characterized as the "re-Protestantization" of the RLDS Church.[48]

Elsewhere, historians have detailed how a late 1960s and early 1970s controversy over the baptism of several polygamist Soras helped deepen an emerging schism within the American RLDS Church between self-styled fundamentalists and liberals like Neff.[49] Here, I will briefly summarize the controversy and highlight a few relevant points. While on his second trip to Orissa in 1966, Charles Neff baptized a group of Sora converts. During the ceremony, a Sora man, identified by Neff's translator as a polygamist, walked into the water and also requested baptism. Neff, not knowing what to do, refused the request and realized there needed to be an official policy on the baptism of polygamists, as polygamy was common among Sora village elites. Neff knew that nineteenth-century American RLDS members had formed their identity around the fact that they were the Latter Day Saints who did not practice polygamy, unlike their ecclesiastical cousins in Utah (members of the Latter-day Saint Church), and many of Neff's coreligionists still saw that fact as an important part of RLDS identity. When Neff returned home from his trip, he brought the Sora policy matter to his colleagues on the Council of Twelve Apostles. After consulting multiple Christian denominations, anthropological texts on Sora polygamy, and local Sora leaders in Orissa, the RLDS Council of Twelve Apostles approved a policy in 1967 that allowed for Sora polygamists (men and women) to be baptized but forbade the addition of more wives into a family after baptism. News of this apostolic policy began to circulate among American church members and the policy was protested, as well as supported, at local church gatherings and conferences over the next few years.

Finally, the controversy came to a head at the 1972 RLDS World Conference in competing resolutions to affirm or disbar the apostolic policy. At stake was whether the traditional RLDS message needed to be adapted to local circumstances or whether it, always and everywhere, transcended them. For example, one resolution in favor of the apostolic policy stated that the church was called to "proclaim and extend the love of God in Christ to persons in pluralistic societies and among differing and changing life-styles throughout the world" and that "the variety of cultural heritages brings richness and depth to an understanding of the gospel." A global church, in other words, needed to adapt itself to local circumstances, and the church as a whole would learn from this experience. A competing resolution affirmed the opposite. Titled "Baptisms in Primitive Cultures," it affirmed that the "doctrine of Jesus Christ has universal value and application" and quoted scriptural prooftext after prooftext for why polygamy was always wrong and why, therefore, church membership by Sora polygamists was out of the question.[50]

The conference was set to vote on these resolutions when the First Presidency intervened. RLDS Prophet W. Wallace Smith issued a revelation that endorsed the apostolic policy in rather tepid language. It stated, "Monogamy is the basic principle on which Christian married life is built. Yet, as I have said before, there are also those who are not of this fold to whom the saving grace of the gospel must go. When this is done the church must be willing to bear the burden of their sin, nurturing them in the faith, accepting that degree of repentance which it is possible for them to achieve, looking forward to the day when through patience and love they can be free as a people from the sins of the years of their ignorance."[51] Following conference procedure, the revelation was debated and passed by the conference to be added to the church's Doctrine and Covenants, though not without considerable opposition from many delegates.

Opponents to the baptism of Sora polygamists saw a dangerous move toward cultural relativism in the now canonized church policy. Fundamentalists, like the independent publisher Richard Price, loudly proclaimed, "Members of the Church of Jesus Christ had fought polygamy with fervor for over one hundred years. . . . But to the surprise of all the Restorationists [RLDS conservatives], the

New Positionists [RLDS liberals] throughout the Church took up the cry that to deprive the Soras of polygamy would be wrong—the American saints were only trying to force 'American culture' upon them. The New Positionists apparently do not know that monogamy is God's culture, not America's."[52] Fundamentalists saw the Sora policy as part of a larger project that would relativize traditional RLDS beliefs and make them expendable as liberals like Neff pushed for further reforms within the emerging "World Church," the shorthand name for the RLDS Church used by its leaders.

Influenced by currents in cultural anthropology of the same era, liberalizing RLDS leaders did in fact advocate for a kind of cultural relativism when considering changes within the church, and nowhere was this more evident than in two articles about the "Sora worldview" and the "American worldview" published in the official RLDS magazine in 1974. In the first, RLDS editors quoted a section from a cultural anthropology textbook that explained the "Sora worldview," a view that "provides explanations for the great questions of life: 'Why do some men fall ill and not others?' 'Why do men die?' 'Why is the world the way it is?'"[53] The article continued by offering a functionalist explanation for Sora animal sacrifice, an ironic inclusion as most Christian Soras cited costly animal sacrifices as the very reason they had turned from traditional practices to Christianity. Nonetheless, the inclusion of the article signaled that the editors thought that traditional Sora forms of life stood on par with forms of life nearer to their Anglophone readers and thereby relativized the claims of the nearer form to any form of cultural supremacy.

The second article, also drawn from a cultural anthropology textbook, offered a trenchant critique of what it claimed was a more or less coherent "'rational-mechanistic' viewpoint" taken by Americans "that assumes that living conditions are improvable—materially, biologically, and socially.... Americans 'make war' on poverty, 'stamp out' disease, 'wipe out' illiteracy, and embark on the 'conquest' of space, as their forbears conquered the wilderness." Americans acted a certain way because they thought the world worked in a certain way, and those actions were relative to a certain time and culture, asserted the article. By publishing this excerpt in the official RLDS magazine, American RLDS leaders not so subtly pushed back against those who asserted that RLDS traditionalist beliefs and practices were free of cultural constraints. In effect, the editors asserted that all beliefs manifested localized concerns.[54]

As the 1970s turned into the 1980s, liberal American RLDS leaders and their allies among the membership believed that they had entered an exciting period of temporal disjuncture in the life of their church. When the RLDS First Presidency introduced the most contentious reformations of this period, a revelation in 1984 that called for the ordination of women and a temple in Independence,

Missouri, dedicated to world peace, they justified these changes, in part, with the language of rupture. Two months before publicizing the revelation, the First Presidency published an article on the "nature of revelation" that asserted that all new revelation "is disjunctive with the past—not merely a restatement of former revelation." As such, it "brings new insights to the Church and points us in new directions."[55] Alan Tyree, a longtime missionary to French Polynesia and member of the First Presidency, penned these lines, though they were endorsed by the entire First Presidency. Notably, this included Howard "Bud" Sheehy, who had been the apostolic supervisor for the East India Mission from 1970 to 1978, and Wallace B. Smith, who had visited Orissa on several occasions during his tenure as RLDS prophet-president.

The phrase "disjunctive revelation" became especially controversial with RLDS conservatives who saw the concept as contrary to their idea of an eternal, unchanging restored gospel. As historian William D. Russell explains, "Disjunctive revelation became a byword, an epithet for many conservative Saints. . . . [Disjunctive revelation] symbolized how far down the road toward spiritual darkness and apostasy that Church leaders had traveled." In the ensuing controversy, more than 20 percent of church members left the RLDS Church and founded independent conservative congregations called Restoration Branches. Decades later, some of these Restorationists still cited disjunctive revelation as one of the signs of RLDS apostasy.[56]

Twelve years after the 1984 controversy, the new RLDS prophet-president W. Grant McMurray was interviewed by the church's magazine about a recent trip he had taken to dedicate new Sora RLDS chapels in Orissa. McMurray used the occasion to reflect upon church mission as a whole over the past thirty years. Like Neff had thirty years before, he posited that the church's expansion into places like Orissa "pressed us to examine the most foundational, universal principles of the faith." Before this era of expansion, the RLDS "had been rather parochial in its outlook," ventured McMurray. "Our emphasis was strongly related to a desire to stress how we were different from the mainline Christians denominations and from the Utah Mormons." However, through missions in Asia, "we unexpectedly found ourselves in cultures where those were extremely insignificant questions. Instead, what we had to do was to positively articulate the central principles of the Christian faith, rather than to dwell on the differences."[57] For McMurray and American RLDS members who remained within his fold, Sora conversions had challenged them to change the core of their faith. Whether Sora conversions or another set of factors served as a catalyst for this process is beside the point here. RLDS leaders and liberal members, as well as the conservative members who left the church, typified Sora conversions in particular ways that required action on the part of those who witnessed these conversions from afar. For liberals, this meant a large-scale reform of their denomination along what they saw as more cosmopolitan lines. For conservatives, this meant seceding from their denomination's formal structure due to these same reforms, a reaction to the liberal RLDS reaction to Sora conversion. Thus, Sora conversions created vicarious ruptures for American RLDS members.

Rupture as Meaning, Action, and Social Construction

In this chapter, I have explored three valences of rupture that historical actors with particular interests used to characterize the conversion of Soras in the 1960s and beyond. Of course, the categories I have deployed—resonant rupture, malignant rupture, and vicarious rupture—are simply ideal types that I have created or adapted to make sense of the varied ways people characterize sharp, temporal discontinuities. In doing so, I have attempted to make several larger points that I hope can inform scholars with little interest in the RLDS, adivāsi conversions, or Hindutva political mobilization. Namely, I have shown how rupture can be shot through with liberating, pejorative, or sympathetic meanings. However, two final points should be made that go beyond the "meanings" of rupture to get at what it does and how it comes to be.

First, when historical subjects in this chapter coded their own actions or the actions of others as rupture, they were not simply giving language to disruptive changes that they had experienced or had happened to others. They were also making an ideological intervention to create those disruptive changes, with manifold social, political, and economic consequences. In short, speech has a performative element to it, and speech acts may create or destroy sociopolitical relationships. Second, in a related vein, while it has become axiomatic among some scholars to talk about how continuity is an ideological construct, we might usefully observe that rupture, as well, is a politically fraught social construction.[58]

CHAPTER 9

Technological Christianity
Transferring Processes, Forms, and Organizational Tools within Global Missionary Encounters

Melissa Wei-Tsing Inouye

In February 1942, the Gestapo finally arrested Helmuth Hübener, a sixteen-year-old who had been distributing anti-Nazi flyers with titles such as "Hitler, the Murderer," "They Are Not Telling You Everything," and "The Voice of Conscience" in the streets of Hamburg since August 1941.[1] The flyers came in small and large sizes and had been typed on two different kinds of typewriters, using carbon paper. Summarizing the subversive content of British shortwave radio broadcasts, the flyers appeared in mailboxes, hallways, a telephone booth, and the street.[2] Under torture, Helmuth admitted that two of his friends, boys from church named Rudi and Karl-Heinz, had known about his flyers, but he maintained that he was primarily responsible and had received no help from adults. Helmuth's half brother Hans recalled, "The Gestapo could not imagine that a 16-year-old, alone, by himself, carried out this scheme and composed these clever flyers without adult help. They believed he was a member of a large adult resistance organization."[3]

Government agents interrogated members of the St. Georg congregation of the Church of Jesus Christ of Latter-day Saints. They found that Helmuth had obtained both typewriters in the course of his work as a volunteer clerk for the congregation. But he had had no adult help. "They thought there must have been a large ring which they could now break up," remembered Karl-Heinz Schnibbe. "But there were no adults instigating us."[4]

Helmuth Hübener went down in history as the youngest person, at the age of seventeen, to be condemned to death by the infamous Nazi People's Court. In Germany his precocious resistance has been noted in public memorials, streets, and juvenile facilities.[5] He was a singularly courageous and capable person. But he also had help, of a certain kind: his membership in the Church of Jesus Christ of Latter-day Saints.

Hübener's upbringing within his church gave him access to, and knowledge of, certain "cultural technologies"—or, as John Durham Peters elegantly puts it, "elemental techniques that organize time, space, and power."[6] A "material technology" like a plow is a physical device that accomplishes the task of turning the soil. A "scientific technology" like gene editing is a set of techniques that accomplishes the task of altering DNA. A "cultural technology," for the purposes of this chapter, is a device or technique that accomplishes tasks in the realms of human association and organization.

Originally in German language scholarship *Kulturtechnik* (cultural technique) referred to the work of agricultural cultivation, such as plowing or fertilizing or spreading manure. Over time it came to also include competence with certain new forms of media, such as knowing how to use the remote control of a television. Eventually the semantic boundaries of *Kulturtechnik* further blurred to encompass all processes or objects that broke new ground in human experience, crossing boundaries and contexts.[7] For example, in a revolutionary context, the beautiful trees and elegant cobblestones lining Paris's streets became material for a barricade. The barricade was not only a physical creation with a useful function of blocking the way of the troops, it also demarcated friends and foes, social strata and political opinions. It was also a sort of ritualized event. In the process of being assembled, the barricade created hybrid collectives, contributed to formation of a revolutionary identity, and produced a happy din of sensory activity as the street, like the old, entrenched order, was broken up and reformed into a sign of revolutionary life.[8] Cultural technologies, therefore, encompass physical things like plows and barricades and also actions such as the polite cough and intangible structures such as organizational forms. The most interesting kinds of cultural technologies, from my point of view, are those invisibly embedded within everyday life, habits, and ways of thinking about things.

Elsewhere I have written about cultural technologies in the context of European missionary societies in twentieth-century China. Much has been written about the way missionaries imported into China new ideological paradigms (such as Christianity and rationalistic modernity) and new material and scientific technologies (such as high-speed printing presses and cataract surgery). Through their church governments, weekday Bible study groups, phonetic scripts to promote literacy, liturgies, and hymn-singing practices, missionaries also introduced cultural technologies.[9] Just as rationalistic discourse could be used to denounce Christianity and printing presses could be used to print secular journals, cultural technologies could also overflow religious boundaries and find other handy applications.

As a Latter-day Saint, Helmuth Hübener had access to a wide range of cultural technologies that amplified his work of resistance. To be clear, this same suite of tools was used by other local Latter-day Saints to support the Nazi cause. But this is precisely the point. Anyone can use a printing press or a typewriter to say whatever they like. What were the cultural technologies within the St. Georg Branch in Hamburg? The Latter-day Saint faith began in 1830 with a seminal publication, the Book of Mormon. Within twelve years it had reached Germany, carried by the American missionary Orson Hyde, who wrote and distributed a pamphlet, "A Cry from the Wilderness" (1842). The faith had an ethos of publishing, an irrepressible broadcast mentality. Within the local congregation, lay ecclesiastical structures created a close-knit community where members were always volunteering to fill public-facing roles as leaders, teachers, preachers, and missionaries. The St. Georg congregation was a node in an international network connecting German members, foreign missionaries, German émigrés in Utah, and church leaders in Salt Lake City. "From the beginning, Mormonism was figured as a global communications and transportation network," John Durham Peters has noted.[10]

In addition to absorbing this penchant for public persuasion and the international network that arose from it, Helmuth had been trained from childhood with a particular skillset. He had learned to evangelize to strangers and to preach sermons to the entire congregation. In the church's youth programs, starting almost as soon as children could talk, he learned to interact as part of a group and developed deep friendships. He had a strong identity as a member of a worldwide religious movement whose loyalties and values transcended nationalistic ideologies. As a member of a much maligned, insular faith, he had access to privacy and a high tolerance for social disapproval. His responsibilities within the church's lay organizational structures gave him access—unusual for a person of his age—to correspondence, records, and equipment (the typewriters). Directing his two Latter-day Saint friends, Rudi and Karl-Heinz, much like the head of an Latter-day Saint presidency (structured with a president and two counselors, duplicated at multiple levels within an Latter-day Saint congregation), Helmuth was able to stay undetected for months. Only when he began to widen the circle beyond the Latter-day Saint cocoon of privacy was he exposed.

In sum, one of the reasons Helmuth's teenage activities looked to the Gestapo like a ring of sophisticated adult operatives was that Helmuth had access to a number of community structures, pathways for action, and habits of association that amplified his efforts: a community with an ethos of publication and evangelization, a private yet international network, and extensive experience in leadership and communication. Through his religious participation, he had an (abstract) truth-seeking ideology and a (material) typewriter. The cultural technologies occupied the space between these two abstract and material assets: the structure and orientation of the local congregation, the extent and coherence of the international network, the organizational and educational programs for Latter-day Saint youth. Although in his pamphlets distributed in the streets and defiant defense before the tribunal judge, Helmuth never invoked Latter-day Saint teachings, his actions bore the signature of the technologies—the techniques—of his religious culture.

And, significantly, even as a teenager with no official hierarchical authority, these cultural resources were fully his own. Neither Arthur Zander, the Nazi Party member who led the St. Georg Branch, nor the American hierarchs who administered the church from Salt Lake City would have sanctioned Helmuth's resistance. He mastered the church's cultural technologies, originally intended to expand the borders of the religious kingdom centered in Salt Lake, and then applied them to his own project against Hitler.

Religion as Cultural Technology

This chapter discusses cultural technologies in the context of global Christian mission encounters, with a specific focus on charismatic practices and organizational structures. I am interested in how cultural forms or tools are developed, transmitted, appropriated, and adapted in the dynamic, liminal mission space. In particular, I am interested in cultural technologies that escaped their original religious context and proliferated in new spheres.

I argue that the transmission of cultural technologies is just as significant as the transmission of "beliefs" or "precepts" that missionaries often saw at the center of their project. Perhaps we should begin to view particular rites, practices, and organizational forms in the same way we view the printing presses, cameras, and cataract surgery procedures that also spread as part of the mission encounter. Cultural forms, easily separated from their originating context, necessarily spread not only throughout a particular Christian denominational strain but far beyond. Elsewhere I have proposed an emphasis on cultural technologies as a counterbalance to the focus on "cultural imperialism" that has long been part of conversations about global Christian mission.[11] Here I would like to do something slightly different, which is to use a comparative approach to illustrate the many ways in which cultural forms arising from global Christian mission encounters blur existing boundaries and take on a life of their own.

This chapter compares cultural technologies within the London Missionary Society, the True Jesus Church, and the Church of Jesus Christ of Latter-day Saints in the nineteenth and twentieth centuries and shows how these technologies, while completely distinctive to a particular religious movement's ethos, history, and native resources, could also be completely portable, unfolding in new contexts quite unimagined (and sometimes undesired) by those who had introduced them. In the case of the London Missionary Society, missionary-introduced technologies to facilitate church governance and Bible reading enabled native Christians to start their own churches and even bolstered the efforts of completely secular organizations such as the Chinese Communist Party. In the case of the Church of Jesus Christ of Latter-day Saints, as we have seen, organizational structures and youth programming imported from the United States allowed a teenager in Germany to launch a risky resistance to the Nazi government.

Religious rites, practices, and organizational structures are all cultural technologies, from a Catholic High Mass to the tying of a white *shimenawa* rope around a sacred tree to a Vacation Bible School. In the minds of believers, such religious processes and forms accomplish things (such as sacred connection, recognition of the immanence of the divine, or cheap and morally productive summer childcare) that would not otherwise be possible.

In historical conversations, missionary movements such as the London Missionary Society, True Jesus Church, and Church of Jesus Christ of Latter-day Saints, though they go about mission work in very different ways, are often discussed in terms of either their abstract ideologies or their material infrastructure. Christianity's ideological resources included not only the doctrines and messages about Christ's gospel ("good news") but also stories from the Bible, the words and phrases of prayer, and so on. On the opposite end of the spectrum of missionary imports, particularly in the nineteenth and early twentieth centuries, we find scientific or material technologies that had independent secular applications, such as cataract surgery or printing technologies.[12] Such technologies had not been invented for the purpose of Christian missions but were general tools for a variety of applications.

In between these two poles of purely ideological and purely material technologies were a host of cultural technologies reordering time and space, more tangible than a doctrinal precept but not material like a nuts-and-bolts printing press. These in-between resources included rituals, worship practices, linguistic tools, literary forms, pedagogical devices, and collective procedures, all designed to facilitate the purpose of Christian evangelization and salvation. Recent scholarship has shown the many ways in which missionaries initially deployed these cultural technologies, which include Christian rites such as baptism and confession, customs such as taking Christian names, group hymn-singing and Bible study, new alphabets, scripts, and texts to facilitate Bible reading, structures of church government, and so on.[13]

To provide examples from this book, Devrim Ümit (chapter 3) and Lauren F. Turek (chapter 7) have both highlighted humanitarian disaster response as a way for Christian organizations in the distant and recent past to deliver evangelism to areas that are usually hard to penetrate. Chapter 6 by Jeffrey G. Cannon on Latter-day Saint imagery of Africa showed the effectiveness of images in engaging audiences of donors by creating distance. As in electrical circuits, or hot and cold weather fronts, a difference or differential in power and capacity creates dynamic movement, flow from one set of potentials to the other.

In sum, the concept of cultural technologies emphasizes the dynamic, transformative, and conveniently transferable elements of culture. Some German media scholars have gone so far as to suggest that cultural objects, ostensibly at the beck and call of a human user, are actually the subjects dictating to human users, who become the objects (in the case of material technologies, cars, smartphones, and Minecraft come to mind).[14]

The power of all technologies, including cultural technologies, to escape control is important to keep in mind when studying the kind of cultural exchange that occurs in the context of global Christian mission. Within the community of scholars who study Christian missions it is also widely accepted that cultural transformation or cross-pollination can be driven by problematic motives or assumptions, such as in the case of the many Christian missions in the modern era with a colonizing mindset or racialist hierarchical structure. In many cases Western missionaries aspired to cultural hegemony, which often included the erasure of indigenous traditions and religious practices. Nevertheless, as I have argued elsewhere, what the missionaries aspired to do or even reported they were doing should never be equated with what they actually did or how others experienced or appropriated their work.[15] In many places around the world, only a few people converted and joined the missionaries' denominational club. But runaway conversions or not, the space of the mission exchange was a fertile environment for groups of people to cultivate new devices, forms, and tools (technologies). The space of culture was a space of creation and innovation. Through the mission exchange, and within its many dimensions, cultural technologies opened up new possibilities.

The London Missionary Society's Organizational and Biblical Culture

The London Missionary Society (LMS) was the first transnational Protestant institution to send a missionary to China (Robert Morrison in 1807). While the LMS was largely unsuccessful for over a hundred years of Protestant mission in China—due in part to the lack of a critical mass of converts, of course—between 1900 and 1930 missionaries and local church leaders finally did establish modes of organization that were well suited to the native environment and also novel in a way that facilitated their spread. Just as a new device or gadget flops or flourishes depending on whether large numbers of people can find it useful in their lives, the missionaries and their Chinese collaborators jointly devised new ways of "doing" community in China, often based on similar exchanges in other mission spaces all over the world, from the South Pacific to South Africa.

In early twentieth-century China, technologies of organization found numerous applications and adapters. This period of time was a time of breakneck social and political reorganization (and disintegration). In the administrative vacuum left by the decline and eventual fall of the Qing, the failure of a functioning parliamentary democracy in the first years of the republic, and the regional fighting of the warlord era, a new associational life proliferated vigorously around China. Numerous new types of Chinese communities sprang up. Some, like the Young Men's Christian Association (YMCA), Girls' Life Brigade, and sports leagues, utilized models that had been developed in the West. Others, like the World-Wide Ethical Society, blended a Protestant-style congregational structure with Confucian ideology and decorum.[16]

All around the world during the heyday of the global missionary societies, these newly introduced cultural technologies produced the very kinds of outcomes the missionaries sought. For instance, missionaries in twentieth-century Korea proudly reported that the meetings of the Woman's Aid Society (founded in 1900 and modeled on an American Methodist women's organization) always followed the orderly procedures of a roll call, inquiries after absent members, the reading of previous minutes, and verbal committee reports. It was music to missionaries' ears to hear Korean women declare that, after living for decades without a name, on the day of their baptism within the mission church they had received a personal name that gave them an independent identity as a follower of Christ.[17]

At other times, however, these cultural technologies facilitated ventures that the missionaries found undesirable. For example, early Korean charismatic movements that grew out of mission churches beginning in the early 1900s relied heavily on the revival meeting format introduced by Methodist missionaries. These revival meetings had a distinctive timetable and slate of activities, including Bible study, congregational prayer, public confession of sins, and healing, coordinated to foster an atmosphere of emotional intensity and spiritual receptivity.[18] Missionaries initially encouraged these revivals, but revival movements later grew into full-fledged, independent Pentecostal and charismatic movements that became competitors of missionary churches. In China, LMS congregants such as Wei Enbo, a Beijing silk merchant, cut their teeth as leaders within missionary churches and then harnessed the evangelistic and experiential power of revivals to build their own followings.

The Western missionary societies' cultural technologies did not enrich rival native Christian movements alone but also had significant uptake in secular spheres such as Chinese political movements. Many of the zealous young intellectuals striving to "save China" learned significant lessons from Christianity's organizational structures. For instance, Yun Daiying, who became a Communist organizer, gained some key ideas in organization from a YMCA camp, with its mix of recreation, socializing, and self-improvement lectures, all framed within a sweeping moral ideological vision. Yun's later organizational work in the anarchist Mutual Aid Society and, by early 1922, the Chinese Communist Party would build on inspiration Yun gleaned from this encounter with Christian organizational models.[19] Mao Zedong also gained organizational experience with the YMCA. In 1922 Mao participated in a "mass education campaign" sponsored by the YMCA in Changsha, provincial capital of Hunan. Mao and his Communist associates adapted some of the vocabulary in the YMCA's 1,000-character primer for the campaign so that students learned about peasants and workers and the history of the Russian Revolution.[20] But the structure of the primer, as well as the organizational framework within which the campaign occurred, came from the YMCA.[21]

Beyond organizational structures, a second cultural technology LMS missionaries pioneered in China was a system for making Bible readers out of people who were illiterate. As Protestants emphasizing the authority of the word of God, LMS missionaries worked to make it available to as many people as possible by printing Bibles and encouraging group Bible study.[22] By contrast, in their first century or so in China, Catholic missionaries and native Christian leaders tended to concentrate on liturgical and pastoral texts. Subsequent Catholic translations of the Bible were only partial, up until the 1960s. During Mass, literate congregants could read from a prayer book, but the less literate could simply chant the rosary.[23] This ideal of universal literacy within the religious community was also novel within a Chinese context. Ordinary people did not need to know how to read in order to worship a deity at a Buddhist or Daoist temple, consult a divination or feng shui expert, or quote ancient maxims that circulated within everyday speech.

In North China, the LMS missionaries invented new phonetic scripts, a cultural technology that arose from their desire to bring the Bible to speakers of local dialects, including women who could not read Chinese characters. They also introduced new forms of gatherings and communities founded on shared reading and study of the Bible (for instance, Sunday worship and Bible studies ran on a seven-day weekly schedule, which was entirely different from a traditional Chinese calendar). In the 1920s and 1930s, LMS missions in North China actively promoted the use of Wang-Peill phonetic script within church congregations and also in public medical and educational institutions.[24] Ultimately the majority of transmitters of the script were not foreign missionaries but native Chinese people, and a significant proportion of these were not Christians. For example, bedridden patients in LMS hospitals could learn the script while recovering from illness or surgery. Proficient patients then instructed others. Phonetic script was a stepping stone to learning Chinese characters.[25] Mission texts were often printed in double columns, with phonetic on one side and characters on the other, allowing people to teach themselves at their own pace. This opened up the formerly elite world of character literacy to members of the working classes, facilitating upward mobility.

Many who had learned phonetic script through contact with LMS missionary institutions could reapply their learning in another setting. Some found jobs teaching phonetic script within hospitals.[26] In some villages in the North China countryside, villagers purchased books and organized classes on their own, with those who could already read teaching those who wanted to learn.[27]

The significance of the LMS development of phonetic script was not merely an increase in literacy but the establishment of a new kind of community held together by the authority of a sacred text to which all had direct access. This Bible-centered community culture reduced Chinese Christians' dependence on foreign leadership and added weight to moralistic and intellectual discourse within the community.[28] Textual communities enabled some women to gain employment as "Bible women," which also gave them religious authority. Bible women received a salary from the local church to meet with other women, explain Bible stories, and teach other women to read the Bible themselves (usually in phonetic script).[29]

The True Jesus Church and Other Native Chinese Christian Churches

Ironically, LMS success in introducing Bible-centered religious communities eventually allowed native Chinese Christians to establish their own churches and reject missionary control. In many instances native church movements including the True Jesus Church, Jesus Family, and Little Flock, which flourished in the 1920s and 1930s, beat the foreign missionaries at their own game by drawing on their native fluency with Chinese language and culture to argue that foreign missionaries had misinterpreted biblical passages and thus Christian truth. By successfully establishing congregational literacy culture, LMS missionaries provided congregants with tools to challenge their theological interpretations and authority.[30]

Like the tools for literacy, the LMS's structure for local congregational self-governance was also a double-edged sword. The LMS had a strong Congregational ethos that idealized independent, self-governing churches.[31] Self-governing congregations were also logistically desirable, given the expenses of maintaining foreign missionaries overseas, the instability of fluctuating exchange rates, and, above all, the superiority of native Christians over foreign missionaries when it came to evangelizing. Not as immediately as biblical translation efforts, but as soon as local congregations matured to the point of having a critical mass of members, LMS missionaries urged native converts to organize local governing structures.

For example, in 1877, just sixteen years after the advent of LMS activities in the city of Beijing, directed by missionaries, the fledgling congregation held an election for their first native Chinese pastor and selected Ying Shaoku, a former high-ranking official.[32] This ideal notwithstanding, as shown by LMS history not only in China but also in other missions such as South Africa, missionaries were often hesitant to relinquish control, especially when cultural differences exacerbated differences in interpretations of religious orthodoxy.[33]

Starting in the 1910s, native local governance began to take root in LMS congregations in North China, although fully independent churches were not commonplace, especially during a time of natural disasters and civil war.[34] However, Chinese leaders in LMS churches in North China oversaw a wide variety of activities within the church community. In 1917 the Kang Wah Shih Church in the western section of Beijing had 134 names on its membership roll, of whom 80 attended the Sunday service. The chapel hosted numerous meetings on Sunday, multiple weekday afternoon meetings, and an evening meeting every night except for Saturday. In addition to the main service on Sunday, there were special afternoon meetings for women and children, Bible classes, Sunday school, and group prayer sessions.[35]

Chinese-led congregations developed creative new approaches to congregational life. In 1930, the local Christians in a village outside Cangzhou decided to celebrate Christmas Day with a feast, but, instead of consuming pork and other expensive delicacies, they cut these items from the menu and put the money toward a combined offering of over six dollars (worth approximately one hundred dollars in 2023) for the benefit of the poor in the village, including fifty "old men, widows, and poor children."[36] However, sometimes local Christians' independent initiatives alarmed missionaries. In one Cangzhou church, two of the local Chinese deacons established a primary school, for which they used the church building even though there was no Christian instruction as part of the curriculum. The foreign missionaries felt uneasy but did not interfere. After several months, the school was forced to close due to financial difficulties, to the missionaries' relief.

Mature native congregations began to act independently in their theology and practices, sometimes to missionaries' dismay. In one church to the south of Cangzhou in 1927, an entire LMS congregation converted to the native, Pentecostal, restorationist True Jesus Church founded by Wei Enbo, the Beijing silk merchant and LMS convert.[37] Missionary Evan E. Bryant described the congregation's newly adopted method of corporate prayer, which involved "repeating ad lib the phrases 'Hallelujah, Praise be to Jesus,' each person saying it faster and faster, until the rapid united 'praying' becomes a wild ecstatic babble, accompanied in the case of some with physical tremours, and shakings, and other manifestations akin to Boxer, India, and Sudanese religious raptures. Those who excel in these are said to have got 'the Holy Spirit' and the gift of tongues."[38] Another missionary, Edith Murray, reported with frustration that LMS congregants who joined the True Jesus Church departed from the staid LMS worship style and became more charismatic. "Everyone talked about dreams and visions," she wrote wryly. "We did not experience any, because we 'had not received the Spirit'"; "Oh how hard we strove to teach them about the holy Spirit as revealed in Scripture, and as proved in our own experience, but they would not believe us. Every meeting became a pandemonium, as soon as any attempt at prayer was made. All kneeling, bodies swaying about and trembling all over, they would start repeating, 'Hallelujah, praise Jesus,' but almost immediately lose themselves in inarticulate sounds. One night after an address on Isaiah LIII [53], they went on like that for forty minutes, until I really thought they were mad."[39]

The case of the Cangzhou congregations shows how native Christians could redeploy physical resources like the church building, ecclesiastical resources such as leadership experience, and even charismatic resources such as the heightened emotion and divine expectation of a revival meeting. Indeed, most converts to the new independent churches came not from the ranks of the "heathen" but from the pews of mission organizations, giving rise to accusations of "sheep-stealing." Organizational models and processes originally instituted by missionaries could now be repurposed in independent Chinese churches led by native Christians.[40] With self-conscious awareness of political trends in republican China, the leaders of the True Jesus Church eventually formulated a church constitution and a system of representative assemblies that melded ecclesiastical forms with the procedures, languages, and structural checks and balances of Western liberal democracy.[41] In this sense their application of cultural technologies was strikingly modern and also hybrid.

In fact, the gift of tongues, or glossolalia, popularized by Pentecostals in Wales, Korea, the United States, and other places in the early twentieth century was itself a cultural technology strikingly adapted to the doubt and skepticism of the modern age. American Pentecostals and the Chinese Pentecostals who absorbed their views believed that speaking in tongues was a sign of the presence of the Holy Spirit—a veritable "indicator light" for the presence of the divine. Within the True Jesus Church in China, tongues-speaking created an entirely new form of language that was neither the common language of vernacular Chinese nor the foreign language of the European missionaries but rather a primordial language of repeated syllables. In subsequent years, church leaders developed teachings to detect the physical manifestations of authentic tongues-speaking under the influence of the Holy Spirit, such as a tireless repetition that could be maintained for hours or certain movements of the body. So fine-tuned did they become in this technology of tongues that in 2010, when I visited a church meeting, leaders walked among a group of new initiates speaking in tongues, examining them carefully and placing a sticker on the clothing of those who exhibited the signs of those who had truly received the Holy Spirit.[42]

Thus the British missionaries who came to China and the native Chinese people who entered into mission spaces engaged in a complex set of negotiations. For the purpose of converting Chinese people to Christianity and establishing sustainable Christian communities, LMS missionaries introduced new tools, including phonetic scripts to foster literacy and organizational structures to foster self-governance. Both of these cultural technologies were effective and successful to the point that they overran the missionaries' original intentions and took on a life of their own, spreading beyond the mission environment.

The Global Church of Jesus Christ of Latter-day Saints in the Nineteenth, Twentieth, and Twenty-First Centuries

Like the LMS, during the nineteenth century the Church of Jesus Christ of Latter-day Saints created mission and congregational networks throughout the world and propagated a suite of cultural technologies that could be appropriated and redeployed at the grassroots. The centralized chains of command, reporting back to Nauvoo and Salt Lake City instead of London, served as hubs for gathering and redistributing spiritual, textual, and material resources. As in the case of the LMS, however, the "peripheral" endeavor expanded far beyond the scale of the "central" administration, creating a new demographic center of gravity that ultimately transformed the theology of the center.

For example, at the outset in 1837, England was not the center of ecclesiastical administration. Far from being a small, insignificant node in a mission network, however, for a period of time it was the church's demographic center. In 1840 there were over 3,500 Latter-day Saints in England, more than were yet resident in the church's appointed American gathering place, the city of Nauvoo.[43] By 1851, there were 33,000 Latter-day Saints in England, almost triple the number of church members in Utah.[44] In 1851 a British Mission publication, the *Pearl of Great Price*, began circulating. This compilation of scriptural translation texts produced by Joseph Smith, along with some historical material, contained many of the doctrines that now make Mormonism distinctive. In 1880 this mission publication was made part of the faith's standard works.[45]

A twentieth-century example of the periphery transforming the center is the case of how the building of a temple in Brazil, a racially diverse country, was directly linked to the rescinding of the racial ban on priesthood ordination and temple rites that had existed within the church since 1852. This ban grew out of racial animus and racialist hierarchies pertaining to America's history of enslaving Black people, and over the course of over a century had been buttressed by numerous authoritative statements from church leaders in support of the ban. However, seeing the sacrifices Latter-day Saints of African descent in Brazil were making to build the temple, even though they were banned from setting foot inside, and working closely with dedicated Brazilian leaders moved Latter-day Saint Church President Spencer W. Kimball to seriously seek a revelation changing the status quo. This change came in 1978, just prior to the opening of the São Paulo temple.[46]

Like the True Jesus Church, the nineteenth-century Church of Jesus Christ of Latter-day Saints was a restorationist church, an offshoot of establishment

Christianity that was discursively rooted in biblical precedents while decisively oriented toward contemporary problems. Under the leadership of Joseph Smith, the formation of the Church of Jesus Christ of Latter-day Saints drew on existing forms in antebellum American religion (the Methodist general conference, the Baptist immersion baptism, the culture of the Bible in nineteenth-century America, charismatic revivalism, the language of rights and citizenship, the communitarian and sexual experimentation of alternative Christianities such as the Oneida community and the Shakers, and so on).[47] Like the True Jesus Church, the Church of Jesus Christ of Latter-day Saints produced something its missionaries could display as tangible proof of miracles: the Book of Mormon, translated from a set of gold plates delivered by an angel.[48] The increasingly accessible technology of print and the cultural technology of an evidence of divine revelation (both testimonials from contemporary witnesses and the actual physical Book of Mormon that could be held in the hands) melded into one.

Like the LMS and the True Jesus Church, the Church of Jesus Christ of Latter-day Saints developed distinctive organizational structures. These organizational structures will be the final example of cultural technologies I will discuss in this chapter. Both Joseph Smith and Brigham Young, the first two leaders of the Church of Jesus Christ of Latter-day Saints, had strong organizational sensibilities, though these manifested themselves in different ways.

John Durham Peters points out that Joseph Smith "was intensely interested in experimenting with and inventing new modes of familial, ecclesiastical, governmental, and social organization."[49] Jonathan Stapley's work on Mormon liturgy argues that Joseph Smith fundamentally reimagined heaven as a durable network of eternally linked individuals that could be experienced right now, on earth.[50] These eternal sealings, as Samuel Brown's work has shown, promised power over death that would have been extremely relevant in the mid-nineteenth century, a time when death was an open door.[51] This power over death and ability to bind relationships for eternity was also part and parcel of plural marriage, since, in a time when many people were widows and widowers, many people already had more than one spouse (though not living at the same time). By reinventing marriage and kinship structures through temple sealings and adoptions, Joseph Smith offered Latter-day Saints new opportunities for connection, belonging, and perpetuation of cherished relationships.[52] In Kirtland and Nauvoo, Smith drew on elements of the Old Testament to construct temples within which the Saints could perform rites and processes they believed connected them to primordial Christian worship and gave them access to divine power and protection. He introduced clothes (temple garments) with properties of protection from harm and evil.[53]

In terms of organization, Joseph Smith created innumerable groupings within the church, including the Relief Society (for women), the Council of Fifty (a political governing body of fifty men), the First Presidency (with Smith as president, along with two counselors), the Quorum of the Seventy (men tasked with preaching and establishing new church congregations), and the Quorum of the Twelve Apostles (Smith's most trusted associates). These often-overlapping organizational structures within the church created a charismatic redundancy that allowed the church to survive after the defection of prominent leaders, the assassination of the Prophet, attrition, and relocation. In a mission setting, this cellular structure of groups within groups allowed a small number of Latter-day Saints to hold together throughout an initial establishment period and then eventually expand in organizational complexity as numbers increased. For instance, in Germany in the early 1920s, most Latter-day Saint branches were anchored by the Relief Society, the women's organization. In Cologne, Relief Society activities were effectively all-congregation activities, with men attending.[54] In the late twentieth century in Mongolia, an initial surge of female university student converts led to the Relief Society being organized and staffed with local leadership before a congregational unit was formally established.[55] In both cases, redundancy in congregational organizations allowed Latter-day Saint communities to start small and gradually scale up.

Brigham Young, for his part, experimented with dynamic forms of church governance and culture. He created a city in which most addresses oriented themselves in relation to the temple block: 700 East, for instance, was a street running north and south, seven blocks east of the temple; 3300 South was a street running east and west, thirty-three blocks south of the temple. This cultural technology of the grid system meant that every single address in Salt Lake City would proclaim the relevance of the Latter-day Saints' sacred spatial center. He commissioned the building of the Tabernacle, a building carefully shaped and proportioned to magnify the voice of a speaker at the Saints' large conference gatherings. He introduced what must have been the only legal no-fault divorce in nineteenth-century America in order to manage some of the relationship difficulties introduced by the practice of plural marriage.[56]

Just as in the case of the LMS's use of phonetic script to connect illiterate speakers of local Chinese dialects to a shared culture of Bible reading and study, in the winter of 1853–54, Young created a phonetic script to connect non-English speakers of European dialects to the Anglophone linguistic currency of the Saints' Great Basin kingdom. This script was called the Deseret Alphabet, with an orthography that completely replaced Roman letters and erased idiosyncrasies of the English language.[57] According to Kenneth R. Beesley and Dirk Elzinga, "Because it was a phonemic alphabet, providing one letter to represent each phoneme (each distinctive sound) of English, words were always 'spelled by sound.'"[58] The Deseret Alphabet did not enjoy the same popularity in Utah as Wang-Peill phonetic script in North China. However, the existence of an 1860 English–Hopi vocabulary written in the Deseret Alphabet by Marion Jackson Shelton, who lived in the Hopi village of Orayvi from 1859 to 1860, suggests that by this point the alphabet had spread far enough to be picked up and applied to linguistic tasks at hand. Perhaps its phonemic simplicity lent itself to efficient transcription of Hopi words and phrases.

Both Joseph Smith and Brigham Young created new organizational structures in order to support their charismatic claims and visions. Yet on numerous occasions, these organizational structures developed an independent strength that threatened their authority. In the case of Joseph Smith, the Relief Society, run by Joseph's wife Emma, which Joseph had directed to be "a kingdom of priests," in 1844 released a 1,200-word document denouncing plural marriage, which Joseph had been clandestinely but busily implementing in certain Latter-day Saint circles in Nauvoo.[59] When opposition to Brigham's leadership arose, as in the case of the Godbeites in 1869, dissenters drew on Latter-day Saint publishing habits to amplify their resistance.[60]

Helmuth Hübener's anti-Nazi resistance, discussed earlier, had a foil in the way his pro-Nazi branch president made use of his church leadership position to promote Nazi ideas. Both of these German Latter-day Saints exemplify the use of cultural technologies within global Mormonism in the twentieth century. In the twenty-first century, numerous other examples come to mind. Contemporary Latter-day Saints may not speak in tongues like nineteenth-century members including Brigham Young, who spoke, sang, and interpreted tongues, but, like the members of the True Jesus Church, American Latter-day Saints have also developed a cultural technology for publicly displaying divine presence: tears. In American Latter-day Saint testimony meetings and general conferences, when grown men and women weep copiously, a reverent silence falls across the assembly. Tears are seen as a sign of the verity of their testimony, the overpowering presence of the Spirit. This technology is usually not mastered by children, but teenagers learn to cultivate it, often through expressing love for their family members, which begins to build a sort of connecting bridge to feeling "moved by the Spirit."

Like the True Jesus Church members for whom tongues-speaking was a way to refute the secularism of the age, in addition to tears, Latter-day Saints around the world have access to international networks that supply them with sacred distance. In unfamiliar settings, speaking unfamiliar languages, those symbols, forms, and processes that remain consistent with their native experience take on new power. Young eighteen- and nineteen-year-old missionaries in a foreign country or different part of their own country have unusually intense emotional and spiritual experiences that form a set of bedrock religious references and confirmations. Those who wonder why the church sees value in sending out missionary teenagers for short periods of time that only afford them rudimentary mastery of local languages have mistaken a technology of conversion for a technology of retention, and indeed, young Latter-day Saints retain their parents' religious beliefs at higher rates than most other Protestants in America (though these numbers are declining for all religions). Older members visiting a temple in a foreign country, or attending a meeting while traveling, also find in this overlay of unfamiliar and familiar a similar intensification and amplification of their religious beliefs and experiences.

In general conference broadcasts streamed over the internet, Latter-day Saints see fellow church members in Korea, New Zealand, South Africa, Samoa, and many other countries singing the same hymns, showing the same physical posture for prayer, reading the same sacred texts, and so on. In this sense (like the Book of Mormon, relying both on media technology and the cultural technology of a mediatized divine occurrence) such multilingual, multisite hymn broadcasts are a cultural technology that both authenticates and artificially creates global presence and unity. Latter-day Saints in Utah enjoy the legitimating sound of people in Honduras singing "We Thank Thee, O God, for a Prophet" in Spanish but do not have to confront the specter of their hatred for "illegal immigrants." Latter-day Saints in poorer countries imagine universal kinship as children of God, without having to confront other members' immense wealth and ignorance of their lives. Ironically, the smallness of Mormonism allows for a distinctive, robust global presence, and having such direct access to global networks dramatically expands the opportunities of Latter-day Saints throughout their life cycles, even into retirement, with the system of "senior missionaries" who often serve in foreign locations.

In every religious tradition, from Hinduism to Catholicism, and in every place, religions supply cultural technologies, and religious people adapt, appropriate, and innovate. But one place where cultural technologies are especially dynamic is in the borderlands of mission. Even when the missionaries of the London Missionary Society or the True Jesus Church or the Latter-day Saints fail to convert, or to retain for the long term, they may succeed in introducing an idea, a process, or a format that sticks. From improving the recruitment and camaraderie of the Chinese Communist Party in the 1920s to placing a young millennial American in a position to work in Poland for eighteen months and eventually pursue a career in international diplomacy that lasts long after her church participation, the cultural technologies that overflow the formal boundaries of global Christian mission often find eager uptake. More universal than doctrines or creeds, longer-lasting than material objects, and more resilient than formal organization, cultural technologies may well be the most lasting legacy of Christian missions.

CHAPTER 10

Missing Missiology
Latter-day Saint Missionary Pragmatism and the Search for Scholarship

David Golding

In 2013, Latter-day Saint historian and missiologist Ronald E. Bartholomew organized a roundtable discussion between fellow scholars about prevailing categories used by missiologists to classify Christian communities. At issue was the prior grouping of Latter-day Saints as "marginal" and "heterodox" Christians within certain publications and membership requirements of certain scholarly societies.[1] Seeking to participate professionally in mission studies, the group of roundtable discussants argued for basic recognition of Latter-day Saints as missional by tradition, Christian by religiosity, and independent relative to Orthodox, Catholic, and Protestant confessions. Editors and association leaders soon adjusted their taxonomies, identifying Mormon communities as "independent." The door for missiological participation had opened; Bartholomew and others joined missiological guilds and delivered the first presentations by Latter-day Saint members at the International Association for Mission Studies and American Society of Missiology conferences. Latter-day Saint scholars had now started the first professional collaborations in the field of missiology despite sustained missionary activity dating back more than 180 years.[2]

The Church of Jesus Christ of Latter-day Saints continued to administer its missionary organizations without noticeable regard to individual scholarly activity, just as it had since the early twentieth century—via a central Missionary Department headed by the Missionary Executive Committee and a worldwide network of missions led by mission presidents.[3] Church members engaged in volunteer service that averaged annually over 34,000 full-time proselytizing missionaries between 1975 and 2020, each year in that period equivalent to between two and three times the number of Protestant missionaries from North America, Great Britain, and Western Europe in 1890, or 8 percent of the total number of Christian foreign missionaries in mid-2021.[4] Deep inquiries into systematic missiology preceded the nineteenth-century boom in Protestant missions, and yet the contemporaneous and geographically similar phenomenon in the Latter-day Saint context grew from a pragmatic concern for preaching and gathering converts. Not until the late twentieth century did hints of theological interest in Latter-day Saint missionary work appear in a scattering of published articles. This enterprise recruited and sustained a highly active missionary staff on a distinct impulse from Protestant and Catholic counterparts, without agents, voluntary societies, religious orders, or missiological training.

Despite the Latter-day Saint community's absence of missiology, the historical study of its missionaries has not lacked volume or enthusiasm. The *Studies in Mormon History* bibliography registered over 1,700 publications on the subject of mission history before 2021, and the Church History Library in Salt Lake City houses thousands of manuscript histories compiled by hundreds of Latter-day Saint mission organizations since the early 1800s.[5] Few of these products venture beyond insular interests, however. Syntheses of this body of research remain inchoate. For mission historians to consider Latter-day Saints' effects on the missionary encounter, transnational networks, and globalization, they must attend to such fundamental questions as *What is Latter-day Saint mission?* and *What constitutes the Latter-day Saint missionary encounter?*, as well as accounting for Latter-day Saint mission history at large. The scholarly agenda will run differently than the historiographical development seen in Protestant mission studies—precisely for the Latter-day Saints' missing missiology.

With "missing missiology," I imitate David J. Bosch, who in his noteworthy work *Transforming Mission* intended the book's title to present an ambiguity. "Transforming" functioned as both adjective and present participle, describing both the transformative type of mission and the activity of transforming (of which "mission" is the object).[6] I intend both syntaxes of "missing" to describe (1) how the Latter-day Saint missionary enterprise has historically lacked a coherent missiology and (2) how Latter-day Saint missiologists, when facing academic barriers to participation, envied the deep trove of theological scholarship enjoyed within a broader missiological guild. My set of questions are historical and only elliptically missiological. They stem from what seems a fundamental inquiry into the Latter-day Saint experience: How does one best square the intensity among Latter-day Saints toward missionary work along all stages of their history with their relative absence of theological and theoretical concern for mission?

The chasm between developed missiology and such would-be missiologists owed itself to a pattern of pragmatism—Latter-day Saints perpetuated a cycle of proselytizing first and measuring effectiveness second. For the bulk of the nineteenth century, terms of success often converged around bringing convert immigrants to a central gathering place, a settlement corridor in the North American Intermountain West. They anticipated a millennial age inaugurated by the second coming of Jesus Christ and sought to fashion a holy society safe from doomsday calamities. This apocalypticism began to wane at the turn of the century, bringing more concerted attention to maintaining permanent congregations abroad. Adapting to increasingly diverse proselytizing zones, where Latter-day Saints would pursue a distributed network of gathering places, the "stakes of Zion" throughout the world, further abstracted indicators of missionary success from earlier pragmatism. Mission scholarship beckoned some with lines of inquiry entertained by Protestant theorists many decades before.

Protestant Missiologies, Latter-day Saint Missionaries

Mission studies more broadly emerged from Protestants' engagement in world evangelism. Where missiologies—meaning systematic rationales, theologies, and schemes developed as answers to the biblical commission to preach Christianity—were articulated, mission studies followed. By comparison, Latter-day Saints undertook a scheme of achieving a gathering of the covenant faithful. They proselytized before the Book of Mormon was published in 1830 and spread in all directions before founding prophet Joseph Smith was killed in 1844. Unlike their Protestant neighbors, the Latter-day Saints proceeded with minimal instruction, and though material to assemble a mission theology existed in the Book of Mormon and revelations of Joseph Smith, missionaries took considerably less pains to explain the missionary mandate before embarking on audacious preaching tours. They concerned themselves with apologetics and Bible proofs and virtually ignored Protestant missiological and antimission debates.[7] The void persisted into even serious treatments of Mormon philosophy and theology published in the twenty-first century.[8]

Whereas Euro-American Protestant missionaries faced the challenge of mounting and maintaining a decentralized enterprise, Latter-day Saints worked under a central administration of priesthood leadership and deferred their own preaching to first receiving a missionary call from such leaders. In justifying the mission endeavor to differing denominational constituencies, Protestants theorized about mission and how to integrate the Great Commission with voluntary and interdenominational action.[9] Latter-day Saints, however, responded to an open invitation to preach and ignored the long list of professional qualifications circulating among Protestant agents, favoring instead Peter's series of Christian virtues in the New Testament. A desire to preach and basic Christian conduct were enough for a Latter-day Saint candidate to be recommended for formal missionary service.[10]

Varieties of Protestant Missiology and Mission Historiography

Academic approaches to mission history gained momentum in the eighteenth century as seminaries and denominational boards assessed missions to Native Americans and Jewish people and developed plans for "foreign missions." Sponsoring institutions advanced a confessional agenda, intending missiology to identify strategy, justify a biblical mandate, and articulate missionary qualifications.[11] As missionary societies dispatched agents to gather funds and professional missionaries to open stations across the globe, administrators accounted for the enterprise in terms of printed Bibles, sizes of congregations, outpost expenditures, and numbers of "native assistants."[12] The study of missions engaged theology most prominently, with a growing contingent of "theorists" who rationalized new modes of church planting and new methods of proselytism. Reports from the field persuaded society administrators that the conversion of the world remained attainable, notwithstanding the relatively wide domain of the unevangelized, those yet unvisited by the missionaries. Missionary discourse, particularly mission theory, centered on an expansionist outcome, leaving no nation untouched and no auditor unpreached until the entire "heathen" could be given to Christ as "an inheritance."[13]

At the World Missionary Conference in 1910, the Protestant mission establishment convened in Edinburgh to address factors complicated by a century of proselytism and encounters between missionaries and diverse religions.[14] Lectures, reports, atlases, surveys, and anecdotes together urged academic attendees to professionalize mission studies by lending social science disciplines and cooperating in scholarship, as opposed to furthering ecumenical projects. Kenneth Scott Latourette, a former missionary to China, incorporated Chinese studies into Yale Divinity School and ambitiously endeavored to track Christianity in all its branches across history with his seven-volume *History of the Expansion of Christianity*.[15] Between the 1920s and 1950s, the American missionary academy renegotiated the expansionist narrative of Latourette's cohort, leading toward a stronger critique against superiority complexes and triumphalism inherent in the era's missiological methods.[16]

A more robust historiography of missions, previously centered on and often written by missionaries, followed Latourette, with social anthropology influencing research methods. Bengt Sundkler and John B. Taylor consulted Africanists in applying the tools of social science to Christian history in Uganda and South Africa. Their studies inspired others to minimize or even ignore the institutional aims of the sending agencies and instead to draw from field research to note relations between colonial officials and missionaries. Historians at elite universities took notice and challenged prior imperial histories by incorporating the perspectives of religion and the outgrowths of the missionary encounter.[17] John K. Fairbank complained before the American Historical Association in 1968 that the foreign missionary had become "the invisible man of American history."[18] Others led by William R. Hutchison and Daniel Bays responded to the concern, arguing that enterprises of American Protestant missions and cultural projects to "civilize" indigenous and non-Christian peoples were entangled in each other. While Fairbank championed the pursuit of a secular historiography on missions, missiologists like Stephen Neill held firm to the triumphalist outlook. "The age of missions is at an end," Neill declared in his *History of Christian Missions*; "the age of mission has begun."[19] Neill's colleagues who had treated the missions as a revolutionary force in the spread of modernity maintained an ecumenical and confessional orientation despite a growing school of academic historians sounding their postmodern, postcolonial, and Marxist critiques.[20] The accusation that missionaries were complicit in spreading Western hegemony distanced missiologists and confessional historians from the secular academy. The possibility of such serious offenses demanded serious investigation; with religious pluralism flourishing in various mission environments and new Christianities emerging in the Global South, missiologists commenced a crucial revision of missiology at large.[21]

In and after the linguistic turn in broader historiography, a branch of study began to develop that engaged neither in missionary apologetics nor in critical theory. Historians of this school brought questions of power dynamics to the missionary encounter, finding in the realms of public discourse and ideology evidence of complicated interactions. Fairbank's "invisible" missionary came to resemble one who did not conform to the dominant, white, masculine, mainline Protestant type. Catholics, Moravians, Pentecostals, nondenominational evangelicals, and most especially women and Indigenous missionaries all appeared to have participated in and even sustained immense world-networks of evangelizers and receiving peoples. Institutions and political powers did not capture the whole story. Pivoting the focus away from governments and organizations toward the people in the trenches of the intercultural encounters made missionary history (as opposed to mission history) a palatable and informative line of study for historians suspicious of imperialistic modes of spreading religion.[22]

The new focus on Indigenous agency accommodated gender analysis and extended research beyond the native-evangelizer encounter. From 1997, the year Amanda Porterfield published her study of Mary Lyon and the Mount Holyoke missionaries and Dana L. Robert published her history of American women missionaries, gender analysis commanded a wide range of missionary studies on topics from women's organizational activities in promoting missions to maternalism within missionary households.[23] This body of research overturned previous assumptions that men directed the missions and women merely joined in as married companions. Women appear in history who both subverted and exercised authority, fortified and undermined colonial regimes, exported religion to foreign environments, and imported foreign religion to home environments. The scene of the mission stations, native churches, schoolhouses, and hospitals resembles a feminine space where women creatively adapted their religion and deliberately enforced their morality on others.[24]

The trend in scholarship for both confessional and secular domains moved toward a complexity model recognizing the prevalence of intense frictions in the missionary encounter. Missionaries and receiving peoples exhibited traits far outside the simple binary of colonizer-colonized. As such, the traits explain the mechanics of identity formation, religious and cultural hybridity, globalization and localization, and conversion and affiliation. By the twenty-first century, four themes emerged that drove missionary history: race, conversion, imperialism, and hitherto overlooked sites of encounter. Race, conversion, and imperialism command attention as *processes*, a novel perspective when compared to prior histories that treated these as norms.[25]

When viewed as effects in motion constructed by people over time, such processes invite wholly different questions about missionaries and proselytes: Who adheres to a concept of race? Who participates in fashioning an empire? Who is objectified by social constructs? What motivates people to hold their various orientations? While American missionary history kept a tight radius around British, French, and Spanish colonies in North America, other sites of encounter have increasingly attracted interest. Oceania and the Middle East offer encounters in which missionaries, by colonialist and proselytizing measures, appear to have failed in their objectives. Historians working in these areas have observed changes to local nationalism and education brought about by inter-religious exchanges. Political forces stimulating nineteenth-century Zionism arose from American missionaries attempting to fulfill an expectation borne of biblical millennialism.[26] Still other scholars found missionaries and proselytes in the Middle East locked in a perpetual impasse, failing to convert or be converted by each other.[27]

While broader trends in American missionary historiography refined critiques of the Euro-American missionary, missiological historians regrouped. Following widespread backlash against missions during periods of decolonization in the mid-twentieth century, the seminary-based contingent of American missiologists formed the American Society of Missiology (ASM) in 1973. The journal *Practical Anthropology* was transferred to the ASM and renamed *Missiology: An International Review*. Roman Catholic evangelicals and Protestant missiologists contributed to its pages, often directly confronting the postcolonial critique and engaging a world-orientation in gathering case studies to bear on missiology.[28] The missiological community produced sweeping revisions to prevailing missiologies, offering enough non-Western and decolonized perspectives for Mark Noll to extol missiologists as best poised to answer the crises of historical analysis occasioned by the linguistic turn and well protected against "the silence of deconstructive solipsism."[29]

In 1989, the Pew Charitable Trust awarded the Overseas Ministry Studies Center research funds to study Christianity worldwide just as prominent African scholar Lamin Sanneh argued that the colonialist paradigm, even when under scrutiny, kept Western guilt at the center of mission studies. Pew funds reached 110 different scholars and were channeled by a committee eager to answer Sanneh's vision of an interdisciplinary and international agenda. By 1992, the term "world Christianity" came into use as a more expansive orientation to what were formerly termed "mission studies." By 2000, other centers and groups founded on a world Christianity project arose with continued support. The Yale-Edinburgh Group, begun in 1992 between the two divinity schools to study missions with rigorous academic and missiological methods, eventually favored world Christianity as an approach to mission history that draws from postcolonial and global theories and perspectives.[30] Two extensive book series from William B. Eerdmans and Brill presses published more than eighty titles on Christian missions between 1990 and 2019, each the product of revitalized schools of missiological approaches to history.[31]

Practicalities of Latter-day Saint Mission

Latter-day Saints, by contrast, never ran a defense or recruitment campaign based on systematic missiology. The first preaching circuits formed from impromptu responses to revelations dictated by Joseph Smith beginning in 1829.[32] Dozens of revelations that followed articulated many evangelistic routines, such as sounding apocalyptic warnings to households and congregations; welcoming visitors and their spiritual diversity to church meetings; reasoning out of the Bible in discussions with clergy of other churches; initiating converts through baptism and confirmation rites; ordaining priests and elders; establishing small branches; holding regular conferences; assisting converts in relocating to a Zion-like city in the United States; dusting their feet when rejected; performing healings by the laying on of hands; exhorting repentance; publishing and delivering copies of the revelations; and alerting Native American audiences to the Book of Mormon.[33] Earliest preachers sometimes paused their labors to copy new revelations into their diaries, and an occasional elders' school assembled for preservice studies in scripture, theology, and civics.[34] Nearly all materials available to preachers and elders were produced and compiled extemporaneously; only a short series of theological lectures offered a catechism resembling a systematic theology.[35]

Preaching and ministry preceded the "missionary" category by some years. Church elders assumed the role of evangelizing, frequently employing the term "mission" to describe departing home for preaching tours before they adopted the title "missionary" or referred to each other as "missionaries." The rhetorical nuances resembled prevailing Protestant vernacular of the early 1800s that generally associated "minister" with reviving lapsed Christians, "missionary" with proselytizing among the unevangelized, and "apostle" with a first-contact missionary or preparer of new mission fields.[36] Joseph Smith's dictated revelations referenced "preaching" and "ministry" as a primary task of church elders without mentioning "missionaries." The first ordinations of "missionaries" occurred in 1835 in a meeting dispatching four men on a mission to the "Lamanites," a Book of Mormon name Latter-day Saints identified with Native Americans and a community they treated as residing in "foreign lands."[37] The first elders sent to Great Britain in 1837 regarded their mission as inaugurating a broader gathering effort that a new church periodical reported as a foreign mission, with the church now needing to maintain correspondence with "our missionaries." Elders continued to preach among "every State of the Union" whereas "messengers" labored in lands faraway enough to precipitate chronicling their correspondence.[38] Joseph Smith spoke of "missionaries" in terms of distant preaching, enlisting Apostle Orson Hyde to visit Jerusalem in the 1840s and instructing a general audience that the missionaries traversed nations abroad.[39] Throughout the rest of the century, Brigham Young and his successors assigned scores of church members on various nonproselytizing missions to industrialize and colonize regions of the North American West, even issuing "mission calls" but infrequently calling recipients of such assignments "missionaries."[40] The thriving traffic of evangelizers, proselytizers, and ministers mounted without a specific missionary identity or class.

The missionary concept, therefore, grew in tandem with international engagement. But unlike Euro-American Protestant societies, Latter-day Saints recruited missionaries on a universal gathering model—all nations deserved proselytism, and due to a "new and everlasting covenant" occasioned by the revelations of Joseph Smith, even previously baptized Christians needed baptism and confirmation into the Latter-day Saint fold.[41] Concentrated articulations of missionary identity surfaced more often within the missions abroad in contexts of immediate confrontations within the missionary encounter and practical concerns for expanding the church.

The closest to a Rufus Anderson, Robert Speer, John Mott, or Pearl Buck among the Latter-day Saints was Alvin R. Dyer, who as a mission president in the 1950s penned a number of treatises on the doctrines of missionary work intended for his corps of missionaries, or John A. Widtsoe, who prepared a course of study in 1939 on the principles of church government that explained mission organization as a function of priesthood.[42] But despite their relative verbosity about missionary work, neither Dyer nor Widtsoe displayed a philosophical interrogation of mission beyond a basic outline. Reid L. Neilson proposed the Latter-day Saints followed a missionary model based on a Euro-American pattern, perhaps the most conscious work to date of situating the Latter-day Saints' missionary activities within the larger missiological context.[43] But scholars are still left with essay-length treatments and nothing resembling a wide synthesis of mission theory or history.

Within the Church of Jesus Christ of Latter-day Saints, administrators solicited reports from the beginning and consulted with missionaries about keeping a steady flow of immigrants from disparate branches toward a centralized Zion community. An early freelance period grew into an active emigration scheme, with mission offices in Great Britain serving as a hub of relocation services and proselytizing dispatches until the 1890s. The highest leaders in the First Presidency and Quorum of the Twelve Apostles supervised the handful of missions, the collections of transient branches roughly bounded to a region and presided over by mission presidents and sometimes apostles. With the decline of Latter-day Saint polygamy at the turn of the twentieth century, church leaders phased out the mass emigration effort and implemented a permanent congregation-building system. Between 1898 and 1951, this system era experienced a sustained bureaucratization by which officers and activities came under the purview of more expressly delineated hierarchies and roles. With the ordination of the new staunchly missionary-minded church president David O. McKay in the 1950s came a modernization of mission work. McKay and other mission presidents standardized mission government, processes, activities, policies, and curricula into a centrally defined and replicable program. Missionary preaching became plainer until rote delivery of short lessons predominated. Instruction manuals encouraged missionaries to accept a modest purpose and trust a simple message to achieve adequate results. Rates of baptism and door-to-door proselytizing prevailed over alternative measures of the missionary program's success. A surge after 2012 occasioned by a policy adjustment to minimum age requirements invited reconsiderations of saturation effects, as the increase in personnel did not correlate with an increase in new church members. The central Missionary Department orchestrated multifaceted approaches through social media and other formats, launching several initiatives that engage regular members, local congregations, and certified missionaries in missionary work.[44]

This cursory summary of the Latter-day Saint missionary enterprise highlights the administrative orientation that remained constant. Regular members initially sensed a more existential preoccupation than their more established Protestant neighbors—their small numbers called for all hands on deck and gathering converts to a central community before an imminent apocalypse. The urgency edged out philosophizing on missiological themes. Freelancers and mission administrators alike devoted energies to testing methods against rising or falling rates of baptism. While influential Protestant theorists worked at a reasoned system for launching and sustaining missions, Latter-day Saints engaged in outreach heedless of theory, and later scholars treated mission theology elliptically as pragmatic concerns of finding hospitable mission fields commanded greater attention.[45] The missing missiology predisposed later observers to search for a scholarly discourse to investigate Latter-day Saint missionary work.

Protestant and Latter-day Saint Mission-Historical Interests

The complexity model that has reified the transnational and transreligious channels of the missionary encounter might expose Latter-day Saint historical effects. Already women's history and gender analysis have produced fresh comparisons and new knowledge about Latter-day Saint missions.[46] In calling for a decolonization of the broader Mormon community, some scholars have noticed the potential for a postcolonial approach, particularly in the long history of Latter-day Saint migrations, resettlement, and missionary interactions among Indigenous peoples.[47] Studies keen on the dimension of race within the Latter-day Saint encounter have identified reinforcing effects and suggest missionary influences on church restrictions toward people of color.[48] Work on globalization, imperialism, indigeneity, and twentieth-century Mormonism has multiplied, yet opportunities to integrate such methods with missionary history remains. A survey history of

Latter-day Saint missions and the missionary encounter that could employ complexity and transnational models in decentering the missionary experience from an administrative paradigm would present new parameters for microhistories. How Latter-day Saints throughout history and the world have conceptualized their evangelism—in a word, their missiology—could afford a new lens for identifying larger processes of adaptation, retrenchment, and development.

CHAPTER 11

American Missionaries and the Struggle for Control of Christianity's Symbolic Capital

David A. Hollinger

When the São Paulo businessman Ulisses Soares was added to the Quorum of Twelve Apostles in 2018, the Church of Jesus Christ of Latter-day Saints brought the Global South into its own governance structure in a highly visible fashion. Yet the Latter-day Saint governance structure, like that of the Roman Catholic Church, enables populations in the North Atlantic West to maintain their traditional control. Not so with many of the major Protestant groups, whose governance arrangements give much more power to rank and file members throughout the denomination, including those residing beyond the United States. American Methodists eager to recognize same-sex marriage are outvoted by Methodist delegates from Africa and Latin America. The Anglican Communion has witnessed an African bishop perform a rite of exorcism on a British gay priest in the shadows of Westminster Abbey. A majority of the Seventh-day Adventists in the United States have been trying for decades to ordain women, but since only about 10 percent of that eighteen-million-member denomination live in the United States, the American Adventists are outvoted every time by the biblical literalists of the Global South, who repeatedly invoke the Apostle Paul's first letter to the Corinthians, which declares unequivocally that women are to remain silent in churches, that it is disgraceful for a woman to speak at all in church, and that if she has a question she should ask her husband.[1]

A consequence of these differences in ecclesiastical rules is that some confessions, like the Methodists, the Episcopalians, and the Adventists, confront more directly than the Mormons, the Catholics, and quite a few of the mainstream Protestant groups the challenge presented to Christianity by the dramatic increase in the numbers of professing Christians in the Global South. But even when constitutional arrangements do not enable affiliates abroad to determine policies for American churches, the growth of Global South Christianity plays importantly into the long-term rivalry in the United States between ecumenical, liberal constructions of the faith and evangelical, conservative constructions of it. This rivalry is most visible between large families of institutions: on the one hand, the ecumenical, so-called mainline churches associated with the National Council of Churches and the *Christian Century* and, on the other hand, the more conservative churches associated with the National Association of Evangelicals and *Christianity Today*. But the ecumenical-evangelical divide is also present within a number of the mainline, ecumenical confessions, and the case of the Adventists reminds us that this rivalry is found within the fundamentalist-evangelical churches, too.

A Presbyterian minister in Minneapolis who said she had just returned from a walk in the park with the Apostle Paul would be referred to counseling. The same might happen even to a small-town Alabama pastor of a Foursquare Gospel congregation, but not necessarily to a Pentecostal minister in Uganda. Dreams like Daniel's are no longer confined to a distant Mediterranean antiquity. Testimony of that order is offered in churches of the present day. Many African bishops espouse doctrines long since regarded as anachronistic and obscurantist by most educated European and American divines, yet still defended by some American evangelicals who welcome new allies. The authority to speak for Christianity is slipping away from the Enlightenment-influenced Protestants and Catholics who have fought hard to get it. The more that Christianity comes to be defined by the American evangelicals who have found a champion in Donald Trump, the more marginal becomes the standard-issue liberal Protestantism for which Barack Obama and Hillary Clinton are poster children, and the more on the defensive become the small group of beleaguered evangelical leaders who struggle against Trump's enduring influence. Control of the symbolic capital of Christianity is at stake.

The increase of Christian numbers in the Global South and their decline in the North Atlantic West is a world-historical event the significance of which is only beginning to be seriously debated. A missionary project involving the sending churches of the historically Christian North Atlantic West and the receiving populations of the rest of the world has been largely replaced by an ostensibly undifferentiated global Christianity. This decentering of the historical heartland of Christianity was driven by the increased agency of the Indigenous populations of the receiving countries, who eventually and loudly declared that they were no less Christian than their missionary teachers. This decentering was also advanced by the diminution of imperialist and colonialist attitudes on the part of the sending churches, many of whom worked hard to de-westernize Christianity. This decentering was further effected by the relative secularization of much of the Global North. As the numbers of church goers and the cultural authority of religion declined in Britain, the Netherlands, the Scandinavian countries, Canada, and the United States, the upsurge of Christianity in what used to be called the Third World became all the more striking. Observers began to speak of a "seismic shift," according to which the old faith migrated southward without changing its identity.[2]

Here, I want to address some of the apparent dynamics in that world-historical event, calling attention to a vast and multifaceted process to which the Church of Jesus Christ of Latter-day Saints may well play a creative role in the global Christian future. Latter-day Saints are relative latecomers but increasingly important participants, given the church's size and huge international range, Many of the contributions to this volume address the challenges that missionaries—including Mormon missionaries, but many others too—have faced in trying to clarify just what converts were being invited to join. What kind of community (often called "the Body of Christ") did the missionaries have in mind and try to exemplify? The history of missions reveals more sharply than any other aspect of religious history the priorities of believers. When you try to bring "foreign" peoples (and just what does that mean?) into your spiritual orbit, what exactly do you have in mind, and how do you explain it? Missionaries and their supporters often speak of "bringing people to Christ," but what that actually means has varied considerably. This book helps us understand how missionaries and their supporters have confronted the challenge of self-definition for themselves and the constituencies in their own natal communities.

I will begin my contribution to this inquiry with the career of the American Methodist, E. Stanley Jones, hailed by *Time* magazine in the 1930s as the world's greatest missionary. Year after year following his arrival in India in 1907, Jones found that the experience of living with Hindus was changing him. He decided that the culture of his American upbringing was hopelessly provincial. Spending a lot of time with Hindus led Jones to conclude that American Protestants were more of an obstacle to a genuinely Christian world than Hinduism was. He celebrated Gandhi as Christlike. He operated an ecumenical ashram. Jones condemned the ancient caste system of India, but "our white-caste idea" in America is worse, he said, because it is "opposed to our faith." Jesus, declared

Jones with great passion, was color-blind, but American Christians are not. Jones's years in India made him take seriously the radical universalism of Galatians 3:28 to the effect that in Christ there was no Jew or Gentile, not slave nor free, and so on. Imploring his American coreligionists to give ground to the East, Jones sketched a vision of India as a bride of Christ. We of the West must "trust India with the Christ and trust Christ with India," he argued.[3]

Jones developed this pluralistic view of the world and of the Christian faith itself in dozens of books, the most famous of which was *The Christ of the Indian Road*, first published in 1925. This book reads remarkably like the multiculturalist manifestos of the 1990s. I was an active participant in the multiculturalist debates of that decade and after, and in that setting I was struck with how the curricular reforms of schools and the pronouncements of college diversity officers and the manifestos of the progressive pundits followed the precise logic and structure of the liberal Protestant missionary theorists of a half-century before. Jones endorsed the world's cultural diversity and insisted that Christ traveled many "roads" quite different from those on which Americans had made their own spiritual journeys. Jones was a flaming cultural pluralist, eager to recognize and appreciate the vast variety of human societies and their customs and beliefs. "We want the East to keep its own soul," he said. The Indians and the Chinese and the Africans everywhere should be actively discouraged from copying the ways of life that Americans often assumed were Christian.[4]

Many of Jones's contemporaries resisted this outlook as too liberal and as insufficiently affirmative about the superiority of the Christ of the American road. Those of "us" who have been Christians for centuries have a deeper understanding of the faith than those who have just recently heard the gospel for the first time, it was said. The gospel has complexities that the new converts in Brazil and the Congo and China cannot be expected to grasp right way. We Americans and Europeans need to retain leadership. But even defenders of this traditional view, reluctant to embrace distant tribes into the Body of Christ unsupervised, understood that Jones had hit on crucially important issues. *The Christ of the Indian Road* sold 400,000 copies in its first four years and in that brief time was translated into fourteen languages.

Jones was but one of many missionaries of the 1920s and 1930s who reported that their experience in the field had changed them, changed their view of the Christian faith, changed their view of the missionary project, changed their view of other religions, and changed their view of the United States. Frank Laubach, a Congregational missionary to the Philippines, preached that the future of Christianity was Asian and that the peoples of Asia as they became Christian would transform the faith into something truly able to speak to the entire human race. Books, journal articles, lectures while on furlough, and reports to missionary boards and denominational officials conveyed a steady stream of demands for reassessment, coming especially from the mission fields in India, China, Japan, and what was then called the Near East.[5]

Several of us who are contributors to this book have written about the liberalization of many of the missionaries, but the historical profession as a whole has not yet registered the extent to which some of the missionaries of the 1920s and 1930s were just as sensitive to the character and interests of Indigenous peoples as were the celebrated anthropologists, Margaret Mead and Ruth Benedict—and, no doubt, just as blind in some ways. The notion that missionaries are always racists and imperialists, while anthropologists are not, dies hard. This popular notion is simply false. Anyone who has read Daniel Fleming and Frank Rawlinson realizes that the liberal missionaries were right there with the legendary anthropologists in attacking racism, ethnocentrism, and imperialism.[6]

By the 1920s the American Protestant foreign missionary endeavor was more than a century old. Missionaries had long reported being enlarged by their experience in the field. But never before the 1920s had there been such an outpouring of this testimony, and never before had a critical edge been remotely as prominent in accessible magazines and other public forums. The missionaries who were sent abroad after about 1900 by the major Protestant groups—the Presbyterians, the Congregationalists, the Methodists, the Episcopalians, the Dutch Reformed, the Disciples of Christ, and the Northern Baptists—had been differently educated than those who had served in the 1830s or 1870s or even the 1890s. The seminaries and colleges that prepared the new generation of missionaries taught them about the history of what were just then being called the world's "Great Religions." The superiority of Christianity was not called into question, but a basic familiarity with the beliefs and practices of Buddhists and Hindus and Muslims had come to be expected of new recruits. This prior knowledge, which was based extensively on the experience of the earlier missionaries, many of whom wrote impressively learned works, equipped the new generation of missionaries to more quickly view with sympathy and understanding the beliefs and practices of Indigenous peoples. What made for change, then, was not simply the impact of alterity; that impact differed depending on the frame of mind and feeling the Western missionaries brought to their experience abroad.[7]

A second kind of knowledge contributed to this liberalized frame of mind. It derived not from the mission field but from philologists and archaeologists based largely in the universities of Europe and the United States. The seminaries and colleges of the turn of the twentieth century provided a more deeply historical understanding of the scriptures than had been the norm in earlier generations. Many early twentieth-century missionaries had learned that the book of Isaiah was written by at least three different authors living centuries apart and that Paul's letters had been written under specific historical circumstances. They had also learned that several of those letters were not even written by Paul himself. These modern missionaries and the leaders of their supporting groups at home were also dealing with the insistence of the biblical scholars that many of the prescriptions of the New Testament were designed for a world that was expected to end very soon, perhaps within Paul's own lifetime. The letters were not designed for a situation like the one modern Christians faced, in which they were building institutions and communities for the long haul. Elizabeth Clark's most recent book, *The Fathers Refounded*, reminds us of what a difficult challenge this scholarship was for Christians who were accustomed to thinking the Bible was designed to speak directly to them in their own time and place.[8] There are, after all, 31,102 verses in the Bible, every one of which, the scholars explained, was deeply embedded in a particular history. When an individual or group invoked scriptural warrant, they were making a choice responsive to their own circumstances and interests.[9]

Even the truest of faiths, then, had been created by real people in real time, and even the choice of what ancient documents should be included in the canon was made by other real people in real time under specific historical conditions and amid honest and deep conflicts within the early Christian community. This recognition of the historicity of Christianity made the educated missionaries sensitive to the historical circumstances of the Indigenous peoples they dealt with on a daily basis. Instead of the stark pagan-Christian dichotomy, the more liberal missionaries came to see the religions of the world as stages of spiritual growth. God had shared some of his power with other faiths. Christians had more divinity, but it was a mistake to deny the spiritual substance and integrity of the world's other faiths.

Both of these elements of historical knowledge—the higher criticism and an appreciation for world religions—played into the fundamentalist-modernist dispute for which the 1920s and 1930s are now remembered. Fundamentalists wanted no part of the higher criticism and disparaged as a distraction the empathic study of non-Christian religions. While the fundamentalist-modernist dispute is usually depicted in our textbooks as focused on evolution, this is something of a misunderstanding. The Presbyterians, the Baptists, and other denominations of the period found arguments about missions to be more important and more deeply vexing.

There were plenty of fundamentalist missionaries, too, schooled most often in a variety of Bible institutes, not at Princeton, Yale, Harvard, or Union

Theological Seminaries. As Joel Carpenter has pointed out, the gap in education was great. The two groups of Protestants fought each other in the various mission fields, especially in China. Some of the leading modernists, like John Leighton Stuart, the president of the missionary-connected Yenching University and later US ambassador to China, were tried for heresy during the ferocious conflicts of the 1920s and 1930s. Quite a few of the missionaries who began to speak in ecumenical voices were driven out of conservative churches, gravitating mostly to the Congregationalists and the Episcopalians.[10]

As these quarrels proceeded, a persistent point of tension between the two groups was how much respect should be offered to Indigenous populations, whether they had converted to Christianity or not. If the locals had converted, the question usually took form as to how much authority should be yielded to the new Christians. The fundamentalists repeatedly accused their modernist rivals of turning over too much responsibility and ecclesiastic power to the Chinese, or Japanese, or Bengali, or Tamil, or Turkish, or Arab converts. If the locals had not converted to Christianity, the question usually took form as to how much deference should be shown to the people who remained committed to pagan religions. The fundamentalists were adamant that preaching and conversion should remain the center of the missionary project, while their opponents moved toward social service and what they called teaching by example, exemplifying the Christian life rather than preaching that without it a soul was bound for hell. The schools, hospitals, and public health projects of the ecumenical liberals were generally designed to help entire Indigenous communities, including nonbelievers.[11]

These mission-focused conflicts of the 1920s and 1930s did much to institutionalize the ecumenical-evangelical divide that has largely defined American Protestantism from the World War II era all the way to the present. On the ecumenical side, often still called "mainline," there is the well-educated leadership of those classic denominations and the prestigious old seminaries like Union, Chicago, Yale, and the Pacific School of Religion. On the evangelical side of this great divide there is Fuller Seminary in Pasadena and Liberty University and Biola University and Wheaton College and the Southern Baptists and the Assemblies of God and the Nazarenes and the Adventists.

This divide has many sources in economy, class, and culture, and it would not do to ascribe the depth and durability of this divide exclusively to the ways in which the experience of foreign peoples affected American Protestants.[12] But that experience did play a large role in the history of that divide. Time after time, when the ecumenicals took another step to renounce what they thought were paternalistic, imperialist, colonialist, and racist features of the missionary project, the evangelical leadership rose up in horror and affirmed the traditional ideology of missions, accusing the liberals of substituting politics for religion. During the 1940s, for example, ecumenical missionary Edwin D. Soper published *The Philosophy of the Christian World Mission*, a comprehensive theoretical treatise advocating greater empathic identification with Indigenous peoples and an appreciation for the styles of Christianity being developed by converts all over the world. Evangelical theorist Harold Lindsell replied with a volume of his own, *A Christian Philosophy of Missions*, declaring that only an inerrant Bible could be the basis for salvation and that missionaries were abandoning the faith if they pulled away from that emphasis. Lindsell described his work as "a final theology of missions," insisting that his ideas were true for all time and were simply a modern articulation of the Gospels and the letters of Paul. Nothing had changed, and nothing ever would, so long as Christians were true to their faith. Christianity was not a historical entity but a divine, transcendent one, with an eternal structure.[13]

The ecumenists of the 1950s and 1960s were at great pains to respond to the self-declared interests of Indigenous peoples and to treat every church in Nigeria or Mexico or China or India as the full equal of the churches in Boston or Boise or Buffalo or Bloomington. Manifesto after manifesto of those decades proclaimed that every community in the North Atlantic West was no less a target for missionary work than were the most "primitive" or remote sections of Angola or Thailand. The very idea of sending and receiving was, in this liberal view, a mistake. The historically mainline churches cut back on their foreign missionary projects so that a greater and greater percentage of the American Protestant missionaries abroad were evangelicals who continued to prioritize preaching. Evangelical missionaries in the field sometimes described the ecumenical World Council of Churches as a greater obstacle to Christian progress than the pagan religions of Africa. In 1966 nearly a thousand evangelical leaders gathered at Wheaton College to fight the insidious ecumenical menace and declared resoundingly that the gospel of salvation through Christ should be unashamedly preached to every living human being and not put aside in favor of social service endeavors. During these late 1960s years, while the ecumenical churches were increasingly opposed to the Vietnam War, evangelical institutions by and large supported that war, which, as David Swartz has shown, the missionary leadership of Fuller Theological Seminary characterized as a welcome opportunity to spread the Protestant gospel to historically Catholic and Buddhist Indochina.[14]

The two largest and most important conclaves of the late 1960s and early 1970s perpetuated this dialectic. The World Council of Churches meeting at Uppsala in 1968 was one; the Billy Graham–organized evangelical conclave at Lausanne, Switzerland, in 1974 was the other.

The *Christian Century* celebrated the Uppsala meeting as the historic moment when "the service impulse" was finally liberated from the project of making the world Christian and when Protestants were finally and fully authorized to use whatever means they could to serve "the poor, the defenseless, and abused, and the forgotten." Uppsala recognized that the problem to be addressed, the *Century*'s correspondent asserted, was no longer pagans in remote areas but corporate managers in the West "who erode human dignity" and deny power to anyone they can control. The traditional role of missions, insisted one prominent commentator, was now advanced by a host of secular agencies—including progressive business enterprises—with no reference whatsoever to God and the Bible.[15]

The evangelicals castigated all this but gradually and grudgingly gave ground on the issue of service. In 1974 at Lausanne, the largest evangelical missionary meeting ever held, the official line changed to accept and indeed to affirm service projects as relevant to the spread of the gospel. Although the Lausanne conferees did not admit it, their speeches followed closely the speeches liberals made fifty years earlier about the connection of service to the gospel. The Lausanne meeting held the line against heretical theological ideas and against any kind of partnership with non-Christian religions. Harold Lindsell was again one of the main evangelical voices, railing against his favorite enemy, the World Council of Churches. The ecumenists of the World Council forget, complained Lindsell, several crucial truths: "Some men are lost . . . there is a hell, and . . . those who die without having personally made a profession of faith in Jesus Christ are [forever] lost."[16]

By the 1970s more of the evangelical missionaries were better educated than previously and in the field often behaved more like the ecumenical missionaries. As the most recent scholarship shows, some of the evangelical missionaries experienced the same kind of deprovincialization experienced by the ecumenical missionaries in previous decades. But the overwhelming majority of the evangelical intelligentsia supporting and training the missionaries, as Grant Wacker has pointed out, still resisted the sympathetic study of world religions enacted with great sophistication in the liberal seminaries.[17] This evangelical intelligentsia, as Molly Worthen has shown, was highly intellectual about issues they cared about, such as scriptural inerrancy, but they were slow to condemn the blatant anti-intellectualism of Billy Graham's mantra that the Bible says what it means and means what it says.[18]

By the 1980s there became visible a gradually developing but major irony in the American foreign missionary project: the ecumenicals who were originally the most eager to recognize the self-declared interests and feelings and priorities of Indigenous peoples found that the Indigenous peoples who converted to

AMERICAN MISSIONARIES AND THE STRUGGLE FOR CONTROL 161

Christianity gravitated toward the style of Christianity advanced by their evangelical rivals. The simple salvation narrative pushed by the evangelical missionaries turned out to win many more souls than the Christian-life-exemplified mode of religious witness favored by the ecumenicals. Aspects of scripture downplayed by the ecumenicals had real resonance. Speaking in tongues and other apparently direct experiences of the Holy Spirit proved very appealing in many African, Asian, and Latin American communities. This owed much to local circumstances and cultural traditions, as Philip Jenkins, Brian Stanley, Richard Elphick, Robert Frykenberg, and others have established. Jenkins correctly observes that in the eyes of some poor and persecuted peoples, "the book of Revelation looks like not a weird book, but a true prophecy on an epic scale." The notion of one's dictatorial government in Africa being the Antichrist, Jenkins continues, "is not a bizarre religious fantasy but a convincing piece of political analysis." The American evangelical missionaries found that their emphasis on the evils of homosexuality played quite well in many Indigenous communities, given local traditions. Parts of the gospel that the ecumenists had found relatively unimportant caught on even among many of the converts the ecumenicals did make.[19]

The legacy of the ecumenical Protestant missionary project in the developing world was enormous, especially in education and medicine and public health. But much of that legacy appeared in secular institutions in Thailand and India and Nigeria and China, and so on, while the ecumenicals were losing control of the churches in those countries. This paralleled what happened to the ecumenicals in the United States: their chief legacies took form outside the churches. As N. J. Demerath III, Christian Smith, and a number of other scholars like to say, the ecumenicals won the United States but lost the church. The United States is not so much a secular society as it is a post-Protestant one.[20] But this had massive consequences for the control of the symbolic capital of Christianity. The American evangelicals soon figured out that Global South Christians could be used as weapons. See, most of the Christians in the world are closer to us, the evangelicals, than to you, the liberals!

Lots of the liberals wondered just how they should react when they watched a video of a Kenyan bishop blessing Sarah Palin in her own Assembly of God church in 2008, praying that the vice presidential candidate would be kept safe from witches.[21] Millions of American and European Christians wondered just how inclusive their own religion had become. Some wondered if their own discomfort might be racist.

Now, not all Christians in the Global South have presented these challenges. Throughout the transition to which I refer, and right down to the present day, various American liberal Protestants, as well as evangelicals, have experienced and do experience fulfilling visits to affiliated congregations in South Africa and Ecuador and Sri Lanka. But there is no question, as Melani McAlister has established, that evangelicals are more comfortable with more of Global South Christianity than are their liberal counterparts.[22] World Christianity as a whole looks more conservative, more ostensibly orthodox, when the Christians of the Global South are counted as part of the faith for which the American evangelicals claim to be the most legitimate voices.

But how big a deal is world Christianity? Isn't Christianity in decline? Are we not experiencing massive secularization? Not at all, say critics of the secularization narrative. The religiosity of the Global South has come to the rescue of those who resist the secularization narrative of modern history. Many popular and scholarly voices insist that we now live in a postsecular age. There is a good bit of confident laughter at the secularization theorists of a half-century ago.

Attractive as the new talk of a postsecular age may be to persons anxious about the fate of Christianity, there are empirical and conceptual problems with the use of the Global South to refute classical secularization theory. The social location for the appeal of supernaturalist ideas and practices has actually continued to be exactly where predicted. According those theorists of half a century ago, building on Max Weber, traditional belief in supernatural authority and deference to institutions claiming to speak for that authority are most likely to diminish when four historic conditions have come into existence: (1) literacy and scientific knowledge are widespread, (2) physical insecurity has been sharply reduced by technology and military peace, (3) democratic political institutions have empowered a larger segment of the citizenry, and (4) populations have moved from homogeneous rural communities to diverse urban environments. Only the last of these conditions is common in the flourishing Christian communities of the Global South today. Moreover, within the United States, Pentecostalism most flourishes where some of these conditions—notably a high level of education—do not exist, either. And the percentage of nonbelievers is the highest among the populations most highly educated in science and the liberal arts. The use of the Global South to refute classic secularization theory simply fails the most elementary tests of history and social science.[23]

But if questions about secularization are easily answered, questions about how the remaining Christians of the Global North are connected, or not connected, to those of the Global South are more complicated.

Are all individuals and groups who profess to be Christian really part of the same faith? And who decides? And for what purposes? Brian Stanley, a leading voice among those who insist that Christianity is still the same entity but has simply experienced the "seismic shift" to the south, raises haltingly and tentatively the question of "whether Christianity has conquered Indigenous religionists or whether Indigenous religions and cultural perspectives have succeeded in converting Christianity." Stanley's uncertainty about the direction of causation—Where is Christianity its own agent, and where might it have been subverted by foreign agents?—is inspired largely by what he sees in the Global South. Stanley here echoes a long-standing concern in missionary discourse about syncretism, the mixing of religious traditions. When does the mixing get to the point that what matters about Christianity is buried in the mix? Now, internal diversity and disputes over authenticity are not new to Christianity, well beyond disputes about syncretism. Catholics and many kinds of Protestants have challenged each other's claim to be true Christians. Are Mormons really Christians? And so on. Persons claiming the banner of orthodoxy have often alleged that their liberal enemies have been taken over by secularism, that Enlightenment influences have pushed aside what makes Christianity truly Christian. This was the standard complaint of fundamentalists against modernists. Stanley, who describes himself as a "British evangelical," speaks in that tradition, positing a true Christianity that is at risk of being corrupted by other influences.[24] True Christianity. What's that?

It is exactly at this point in the discourse that the concept of the Third Church has come to play a vital role. This concept keeps the potentially dangerous appearances of the Holy Spirit at a certain distance while retaining them to enlarge the size of contemporary Christianity. There is Catholicism and there is Protestantism, say Philip Jenkins and a number of other scholars; these are the first two churches, both variations on the Christian project. And then there is a third church, the Christians of the Global South. The concept of the Third Church allows one to have it both ways: the discomforting aspects of Global South Christianity are counted as fully Christian for statistical purposes but not fully part of either the Protestant or the Catholic churches, even if formally affiliated. The concept of the Third Church functions somewhat like the three-fifths clause of the original federal constitution, which enabled white southerners to claim the slave population for governance purposes while not freeing the Black people and not welcoming them fully in their own society. Some groups today do bring the Nigerians and the Indonesians into full juridical authority, as we have seen, but the great strategic value of the concept of the Third Church for American Christians who do not subject themselves to rules voted on by Global South Christians is that these American Christians are still able to claim the numbers of the Global South Christians when measuring the size of Christianity and when ostensibly refuting secularization theory and when declaring that Christianity's center of theological gravity is conservative rather than liberal. As with the two-thirds clause, one can get credit for their numbers but can keep them at a certain distance.

But scholars do not need to be bound by the constructions of Christianity offered by Christians, conservative or liberal. Scholars report above all to an epistemic rather than a religious community. We can address the varieties and dynamics of the Christian project the same way we address racism, socialism, Puritanism, fascism, Romanticism, imperialism, Islamic fundamentalism, liberalism, and a variety of other movements and persuasions. Scholars are free to develop their own sense of what defines a project and what its borders are; we don't have to be bound by the self-definitions of individuals and groups. Donald Trump may deny he is a racist, but scholars are not obliged to take his word for it.

Scholars understand that insofar as Christianity is a single project at all, it is a prodigious one with many particular varieties, all of which necessarily overlap with other projects and draw upon prior historical matrixes. When does Christianity define something and when is Christianity simply a rider on the back of something else? The separation of the Christian movement from Judaism was not a quick and easy thing for the people who brought it about. Every episode in what we call Christian history is a result as well as a cause, a vehicle as well as an engine, a consequence of prior influences no less than a force in its own right. In that respect, the witchcraft-engaging Christianities of the Global South are rather like the Jewish foundations of Jesus's ministry, part of the matrix out of which some particular new thing emerges. Consider the Masowe Apostolic Church of Zimbabwe as an example. This church declares that there is no reason to study the Bible other than to learn from it how people can access the Holy Spirit by themselves.[25] What analytic purchase do we get on the members of this church by saying of them that they are Christians? Some, perhaps, but surely not much. When scholars assess the size and reach of the Christian project, might they decide to assign relatively little weight to the Masowe Church? What might such decisions do to the statistical counts of Christians in the world?

The challenge of deciding what shall count as Christian has been strikingly compounded by the recent religious politics of the United States in the age of Donald Trump. Amid endless references to the fact that 81 percent of white evangelicals supported Trump in the 2016 election and have continued to do so post-2020 according to opinion polls, a remarkable debate has emerged as to who is a real evangelical. Are many of those claiming to be evangelicals not even rightly called Christians? A 2019 collection of essays by the nation's leading historians of evangelicalism illustrates this debate.

Evangelicals: Who They Have Been, Are Now, and Could Be contains many variations on the suggestion that "real" evangelicals are actually not so enthusiastic about the deeply anti-intellectual, frankly authoritarian, sexually promiscuous media personality and billionaire who won the White House. Socially and culturally retrograde elements of the population have latched onto evangelical slogans while having no understanding of the theology that is actually the core of evangelicalism. The label has been indiscriminately applied by unsophisticated pollsters and the press. Jonathan Edwards and George Whitfield would not recognize the pro-Trump population as evangelical. Most African Americans are evangelicals, too, and the press ignores this diversity of the movement. The panorama of evangelical thought and action today includes many examples of sensible, humane, and intellectually creative work. True evangelical Christianity is being confused with impostors at worst and just a diluted fragment of it at best.[26]

The issue is engaged with by other scholars who insist that evangelicalism has become exactly what it shows itself to be in the support of Trump and is accurately represented as such by the press. The evangelical intellectuals who try to distance evangelicalism from Trump are kidding themselves, argues Kristin Du Mez in *Jesus and John Wayne: How White Evangelicals Corrupted a Faith and Fractured a Nation*. Whatever theological positions may have defined evangelicalism in the past, Du Mez argues, the white Americans who have come by the early twenty-first century to fill the pews of evangelical churches embrace exactly the crudely authoritarian and patriarchal values that Trump has shown himself to stand for. "By the time Trump arrived proclaiming himself their savior, conservative white evangelicals had already traded a faith that privileges humility and elevates 'the least of these' for one that derides gentleness as the province of wusses." Evangelicals, Du Mez continues, "did not cast their votes despite their beliefs, but because of them."[27]

Just as the ecumenical Protestant missionaries gradually lost control of the character of Christianity in Africa, Asia, and Latin America, and just as they yielded most of the symbolic capital of Christianity in the United States to their evangelical rivals, so the "respectable" evangelicals lost control of American evangelicalism.

Just what is Christianity, and who decides? These questions are very old, but never have their answers been less clear than today. The struggle for control of the symbolic capital of Christianity is worth watching, both for those inside the community of faith and those outside it. The most obvious stakeholders are persons who profess Christianity. But there is more to it. Christianity is such a large part of the United States that all Americans have a stake in what Christianity is and just who controls it.[28]

Acknowledgments

We delight in acknowledging the generosity and contributions many have given to this book and the symposium that preceded it. Two sponsors offered crucial support for both efforts: the Church History Department of the Church of Jesus Christ of Latter-day Saints and the Neal A. Maxwell Institute for Religious Scholarship at Brigham Young University (BYU). We thank their past and present leaders, especially Steven E. Snow, LeGrand R. Curtis Jr., Reid L. Neilson, Matthew J. Grow, and J. Spencer Fluhman, who delivered institutional resources for our project and advocated for our success. Matthew McBride in the Church History Department championed our endeavors, connected us with key resources at critical stages, and in many respects worked as a third organizer. Brent M. Rogers expedited processes that secured vital funds. Spencer McBride collaborated early in the process and shared successes gained from an earlier symposium hosted at the Church History Library to open doors for us and our participants.

Many contributed their spare time and expertise in chairing and participating in symposium sessions, providing event support, offering chapter reviews, and lending research. For these contributions we thank Deborah Gates, Jessica Nelson, David Grua, Lisa Olsen Tait, Blair Hodges, Richard Holzapfel, Ussama Makdisi, and Joe Chelladurai. We also thank colleagues at our respective workplaces: the Church History Department and BYU's Department of History. This book's first editor, Michael McGandy, brought keen reviews and recommendations that enhanced our work beyond typical editorial guidance. Sarah Grossman was instrumental during the COVID-19 pandemic and its many disruptions. We thank her and other staff at Cornell University Press for their excellent assistance and for accommodating unusual transitions and arrangements.

This book straddled a global pandemic, and without many dedicated friends and family—their concern, adaptability, positivity, patience, and humanity—we certainly could not have brought this project to completion. David extends his deepest appreciation to Camille, Kenny, Samantha, Aidan, and Olivia Golding, who offered constant motivation and absorbed his shortcomings with care and encouragement. Christopher thanks Karim, Sofia, Joaquin, Oscar, and Paloma for their love and support.

NOTES

Foreword

1. E. Myers Harrison, *Blazing the Missionary Trail* (Eaton, IL: Van Kampen Press, 1949), 52.

2. Many fine works could be added to this list. Some of the early influential investigations include James Axtell, *The Invasion Within: The Contest of Cultures in Colonial North America* (New York: Oxford University Press, 1985); Francis Paul Prucha, "Two Roads to Conversion: Protestant and Catholic Missionaries in the Pacific Northwest," *The Pacific Northwest Quarterly* 79, no. 4 (October 1988): 130–137; and Albert G. Raboteau, *Slave Religion: The Invisible Institution in the Antebellum South* (New York: Oxford University Press, 1978).

3. Julie Byrne, *The Other Catholics: Remaking America's Largest Religion* (New York: Columbia University Press, 2016), 5, 11.

Introduction

1. Julius O. Beardslee to Amos Augustus Phelps, October 26, 1839, Rare Books Department, Boston Public Library. Available online via *Digital Commonwealth*, https://ark.digitalcommonwealth.org/ark:/50959/5h73zz40x; Aaron F. Farr, Diary, September 15, 1852, January 12, 1853, MS 1800, Church History Library, Salt Lake City, Utah (hereafter CHL); Aaron Farr to Brigham Young, December 16, 1853, Brigham Young General Correspondence, Incoming, 1839–1877, General Letters, 1840–1877, Brigham Young Office Files, CR 1234 1, CHL.

2. Farr, Diary, January 12, 1853.

3. Farr, Diary, January 23, 1853; Farr to Young, December 16, 1853.

4. Reid L. Neilson and R. Mark Melville, eds., *The Saints Abroad: Missionaries Who Answered Brigham Young's 1852 Call to the Nations of the World* (Provo, UT: Religious Studies Center, 2019), xx–xxii.

5. Jeffrey Cox, *The British Missionary Enterprise since 1700* (New York: Routledge, 2008), 93–102; William R. Hutchison, *Errand to the World: American Protestant Thought and Foreign Missions* (Chicago: University of Chicago Press, 1987), 45.

6. Emily Conroy-Krutz, *Christian Imperialism: Converting the World in the Early American Republic* (Ithaca: Cornell University Press, 2015), 54–59.

7. "A Special Conference of the Elders of the Church of Jesus Christ of Latter-Day-Saints, Assembled in the Tabernacle, Great Salt Lake City, August 28th, 1852, 10 o'clock, a.m., Pursuant to Public Notice," *Deseret News* 2, no. 23 (September 18, 1852): 1, 4;

Neilson and Melville, *Saints Abroad*, xxiii–xxvi; Laurie F. Maffly-Kipp, "Assembling Bodies and Souls: Missionary Practices on the Pacific Frontier," in *Practicing Protestants: Histories of Christian Life in America, 1630–1965*, ed. Laurie F. Maffly-Kipp, Leigh E. Schmidt, and Mark Valeri (Baltimore: Johns Hopkins University Press, 2006), 51–76.

8. David A. Hollinger, *Protestants Abroad: How Missionaries Tried to Change the World but Changed America* (Princeton: Princeton University Press, 2017), 10–12; Brian Stanley, *Christianity in the Twentieth Century: A World History* (Princeton: Princeton University Press, 2018), 193–201; Melani McAlister, *The Kingdom of God Has No Borders: A Global History of American Evangelicals* (New York: Oxford University Press, 2018), 197–203.

9. See Arthur F. Glasser, "The Evolution of Evangelical Mission Theology since World War II," *International Bulletin of Missionary Research* 9, no. 1 (January 1985): 9–13.

10. David Golding, "Gender and Missionary Work," in *The Routledge Handbook on Mormonism and Gender*, ed. Amy Hoyt and Taylor G. Petrey (London: Routledge, 2020), 171–173; Richard O. Cowan, "The Seventies' Role in Worldwide Church Administration," in *A Firm Foundation: Church Organization and Administration*, ed. David J. Whittaker and Arnold K. Garr (Provo, UT: Religious Studies Center, 2011), 578–580; Matthew Bowman, *The Mormon People: The Making of an American Faith* (New York: Random House, 2012), 191–192.

11. Brian Russell Franklin, "America's Missions: The Home Missions Movement and the Story of the Early Republic" (PhD diss., Texas A&M University, 2012), 246–249. Home mission campaigns among Mormon communities continued into the late 1800s in Utah and the North American West; see Jana Kathryn Riess, "'Heathen in Our Fair Land': Presbyterian Women Missionaries in Utah, 1870–90," *Journal of Mormon History* 26, no. 1 (Spring 2000): 165–195; Peggy Pascoe, *Relations of Rescue: The Search for Female Moral Authority in the American West, 1874–1939* (New York: Oxford University Press, 1990).

12. Reid L. Neilson, "The Nineteenth-Century Euro-American Mormon Missionary Model," in *Go Ye into All the World: The Growth and Development of Mormon Missionary Work*, ed. Reid L. Neilson and Fred E. Woods (Provo, UT: Religious Studies Center, 2012), 65–90; R. Lanier Britsch, *Moramona: The Mormons in Hawai'i*, 2nd ed. (L'āie, HI: Jonathan Napela Center for Hawaiian and Pacific Islands Studies, 2018), 1–22.

13. Farr to Young, December 16, 1853.

14. Case studies of competition and conflict between Protestant and Mormon missionaries in the nineteenth century include Maffly-Kipp, "Assembling Bodies and Souls," 72–75, and Karen M. Kern, "'They Are Not Known among Us': The Ottomans, the Mormons, and the Protestants in the Late Ottoman Empire," in *American Missionaries and the Middle East: Foundational Encounters*, ed. Mehmet Ali Doğan and Heather J. Sharkey (Salt Lake City: University of Utah Press, 2011), 138–144.

15. Neil J. Young, *We Gather Together: The Religious Right and the Problem of Interfaith Politics* (New York: Oxford University Press, 2016), 31–32, 89–93, 189–203.

1. Heathen Landscapes

1. Thomas Smith Grimké, *Address on the Power and Value of the Sunday School System in Evangelizing Heathen and Reconstructing Christian Communitys, and on the Southern Enterprize of the American Sunday School Union* (Philadelphia, 1834), 6.

2. Grimké, *Address*, 7.

3. Grimké, *Address*, 8.

4. John Newton Brown, ed., *Fessenden & Co.'s Encyclopedia of Religious Knowledge: Or, Dictionary of the Bible, Theology, Religious Biography, All Religions, Ecclesiastical History, and Missions* (Brattleboro: Fessenden and Co., 1836), s.v. "HEATHEN, (from heath, barren, uncultivated)."

5. Isaiah 35:1, 7. (King James Version).

6. Isaiah 34:9, 13. (KJV).

7. Amy DeRogatis shows how home missionaries (those within the United States) made similar assumptions about how orderly landscapes, preferably mapped onto a grid, reflected the state of white inhabitants on the frontier, in *Moral Geography: Maps, Missionaries, and the American Frontier* (New York: Columbia University Press, 2003).

8. Willie James Jennings, *The Christian Imagination: Theology and the Origins of Race* (New Haven: Yale University Press, 2011), 24.

9. See, for instance, Barbara Mann, *Spirits of Blood, Spirits of Breath: The Twinned Cosmos of Indigenous America* (New York: Oxford University Press, 2016); Sue Fawn Chung and Priscilla Wegars, *Chinese American Death Rituals: Respecting the Ancestors* (Walnut Creek: AltaMira Press, 2005).

10. Jennings, *Christian Imagination*, 39.

11. Jennings, *Christian Imagination*, 43.

12. Alexander VI, *Inter Caetera*, papal bull, May 4, 1493.

13. Henry Whitfield, *Strength out of Weakness: Or a Glorious Manifestation of the Further Progresse of the Gospel amongst the Indians in New-England Held Forth in Sundry Letters from Divers Ministers and Others to the Corporation Established by Parliament for Promoting the Gospel among the Heathen in New England, and to Particular Members Thereof since the Late Treatise to that Effect, Formerly Set Forth by Mr Henry Whitfield Late Pastor of Gilford in New-England* (London: Corporation for Promoting the Gospel among the Heathen in New England, 1652).

14. See William Cronon, *Changes in the Land: Indians, Colonists, and the Ecology of New England* (New York: Hill and Wang, 1983).

15. Cotton Mather, *India Christiana: A Discourse, Delivered unto the Commissioners, for the Propagation of the Gospel among the American Indians which Is Accompanied with Several Instruments Relating to the Glorious Design of Propagating Our Holy Religion, in the Eastern as Well as the Western, Indies* (Boston: B. Green, 1721), 28–29, italics in the original.

16. Johnson v. M'Intosh, U.S. 576 and 577, 21.

17. Johnson v. M'Intosh, 21.

18. Steven T. Newcomb, *Pagans in the Promised Land: Decoding the Doctrine of Christian Discovery* (Golden, CO: Fulcrum Publishing, 2008).

19. On the American turn toward the globe, see Emily Conroy-Krutz, *Christian Imperialism: Converting the World in the Early American Republic* (Ithaca: Cornell University Press, 2015).

20. See Martin Brückner, *The Geographic Revolution in Early America: Maps, Literacy, and National Identity* (Chapel Hill: University of North Carolina Press, 2006).

21. Morse also had a stake in key evangelical movements of the antebellum era; he helped found the missionary magazine *Panoplist*, Andover Theological Seminary, the New England Tract Society, and the American Bible Society. *American National Biography Online*, s.v. "Jedidiah Morse," by Elizabeth Noble Shor, published online February 2000, http://www.anb.org/articles/13/13-01182.html.

172   NOTES TO PAGES 13–19

22. Jedidiah Morse, *The American Universal Geography: or A View of the Present State of All the Empires, Kingdoms, States and Republicks in the Known World, and of the United States of America in Particular* (Boston: Thomas and Andrews, 1805), 14.

23. Morse, *American Universal Geography*, 10.

24. Morse, *American Universal Geography*, 13.

25. Morse, *American Universal Geography*, 14–15.

26. Morse, *American Universal Geography*, 432. Chapter 9 in this volume by Melissa Wei-Tsing Inouye details how Chinese "heathenism" was turned into a reason for their lack of attention to more than basic subsistence.

27. Morse, *American Universal Geography*, 497.

28. See Roxann Wheeler, *The Complexion of Race: Categories of Difference in Eighteenth-Century British Culture* (Philadelphia: University of Pennsylvania Press, 2000), esp. 35.

29. Bruce Harvey, *American Geographics: U.S. National Narratives and the Representation of the Non-European World, 1830–1865* (Stanford, CA: Stanford University Press, 2001), 39. Italics in original.

30. See for instance, Wheeler, *Complexion of Race*; George Fredrickson, *Racism: A Short History* (Princeton, NJ: Princeton University Press, 2002); Rebecca Goetz, *The Baptism of Early Virginia: How Christianity Created Race* (Baltimore: Johns Hopkins University Press, 2012).

31. Sylvester Johnson, *African American Religions, 1500–2000: Colonialism, Democracy, and Freedom* (Cambridge: Cambridge University Press, 2015), 392. Italics in original.

32. Conroy-Krutz, *Christian Imperialism*.

33. Jedidiah Morse, *A Sermon, Delivered before the American Board of Commissioners for Foreign Missions, at Their Annual Meeting in Springfield, Massachusetts, September 19, 1821, Published by Order of the Board* (Boston: American Board of Commissioners for Foreign Missions, 1821), 6.

34. Morse, *Sermon*, 6.

35. Morse, *Sermon*, 3.

36. Morse, *Sermon*, 5.

37. Morse, *Sermon*, 6.

38. Morse, *Sermon*, 24.

39. See Fredrickson, *Racism*; Wheeler, *Complexion of Race*; and especially Goetz, *Baptism of Early Virginia*.

40. Morse, *Sermon*, 25.

41. Morse, *Sermon*, 26.

2. Before "Woman's Work for Woman"

1. Ermina Nash to Jeremiah Evarts, March 12, 1825, Papers of the American Board of Foreign Missions, Houghton Library, Harvard University (ABC), ABC 6, vol. 5. She would serve in the household of the Potters at the Choctaw mission.

2. Foreign Missionary Society of Boston and Vicinity Records, June 18, 1823, ABC 28.2.

3. Dana Robert, *American Women in Mission: A Social History of Their Thought and Practice* (Macon, GA: Mercer University Press, 1997); Mary Kupiec Cayton, "Canon-

izing Harriet Newell: Women, the Evangelical Press, and the Foreign Mission Movement in New England, 1800–1840," in *Competing Kingdoms: Women, Mission, Nation, and the American Protestant Empire, 1812–1960*, ed. Barbara Reeves-Ellington, Kathryn Kish Sklar, and Connie Shemo (Durham, NC: Duke University Press, 2010), 69–93; Amanda Porterfield, *Mary Lyon and the Mount Holyoke Missionaries* (New York: Oxford University Press, 1997); Ashley Moreshead, "'Beyond All Ambitious Motives': Missionary Memoirs and the Cultivation of Early American Evangelical Heroines," *Journal of the Early Republic* 38, no. 1 (Spring 2018): 37–60; Barbara Reeves-Ellington, "Women, Protestant Missions, and American Cultural Expansion, 1800–1938: A Historiographical Sketch," *Social Sciences and Missions* 24 (2011): 190–206.

4. Cayton, "Canonizing Harriet Newell."

5. William Potter to Samuel Worcester, June 19, 1819, ABC 6, vol. 1.

6. William Potter to Samuel Worcester, March 25, 1820 ABC 6, vol. 1; William Potter to Samuel Worcester, September 24, 1819, ABC 6, vol. 1.

7. Louise Battelle to ABCFM, January 5, 1822, ABC 10, vol. 3.

8. Hannah Thatcher to Samuel Worcester, February 16, 1820, ABC 6, vol. 2.

9. Ellen Stetson to Jeremiah Evarts, November 13, 1819, ABC 6, vol. 2.

10. American Board of Commissioners for Foreign Missions, "Address of the Prudential Committee," *Missionary Herald*, January 1828, 27–31.

11. William Swan, *Letters on Missions* (Boston: Perkins and Marvin, 1831).

12. As she explained in her letter, "He turned an eye upon me that I shall never forget, and which seemed to search my inmost soul, while he recounted some of the necessary qualifications of a missionary. I was mute from a sense of what I had said and a consciousness of my unworthiness and unfitness for so arduous and responsible an undertaking, I resolved at once to say or think no more about it." Emily Root to ABCFM, [Lenox], n.d. [1826], ABC 6, vol. 6.

13. Flora Post to Jeremiah Evarts, August 11, 1829, ABC 6, vol. 5.

14. Sadler's letter also noted that she was "willing to go out single or married as the Lord shall direct." Letter on behalf of Miss Adeline Sadler to ABCFM, May 25, 1837, ABC 6, vol. 12.

15. See, for example, Stetson to Evarts, November 13, 1819. Stetson would be appointed to the Cherokee missions.

16. Emphasis in original. Abigail Kimball to Benjamin Wisner, April 18, 1835 [actually 1834], ABC 6, vol. 10.

17. Robert, *American Women in Mission*; Porterfield, *Mary Lyon and the Mount Holyoke Missionaries*.

18. Emphasis in original. Rev. John A. Douglass to Rufus Anderson, April 22, 1834, ABC 6, v. 10.

19. James W. Robbins to ABCFM, September 21, 1821; Anna Bunham to ABCFM, December 26, 1821, ABC 6, vol. 4.

20. Rev. Shubael Bartlett to Jeremiah Evarts, 22 October, 1822, ABC 10, vol. 3.

21. Emphasis in original. Cynthia Thrall to Jeremiah Evarts, October 14, 1823, ABC 6, vol. 4.

22. The candidate files can be found in ABC 6, with some twenty-four volumes prior to 1860. Domestic correspondence can be found in ABC 1.1 and ABC 10. ABC 10 contains fifty volumes before 1860.

23. On the constructed nature of archives, see Marisa J. Fuentes, *Dispossessed Lives: Enslaved Women, Violence, and the Archive* (Philadelphia: University of Pennsylvania Press, 2016); Antoinette Burton, *Dwelling in the Archive: Women Writing House, Home, and History in Late Colonial India* (New York: Oxford University Press, 2003).

24. William Gregory to Rev. Thomas Haweis, October 15, 1798, LMS Candidates' Papers, Box 6, Folder 33; Report of Examiners for J. Guard and W. Hawkins, 1798, LMS Candidates' Papers, Box 6, Folder 42.

25. William Benyon to LMS, January 6, 1825, Papers of the London Missionary Society, School of Oriental and African Studies, LMS Candidates' Papers, Box 1, Folder 47.

26. David Griffiths to Rev. George Burder, December 6, 1819, LMS Candidates' Papers, Box 6, Folder 38.

27. John Dryden to LMS, August 1, 1837, LMS Candidates' Papers, Box 1, Folder 1.

28. Emmeline Geller to Dr. Mulleus, June 30, 1875, LMS Candidates' Papers, Box 6, Folder 5.

29. Louise Battelle to ABCFM, January 5, 1822, ABC 10, vol. 3.

30. On the earlier history of the Bombay missionaries' discomfort with female missionaries, see Emily Conroy-Krutz, "The Forgotten Wife: Roxanna Nott and Missionary Conceptions of Marriage," *Journal of Early American Studies* 16, no. 1 (Winter 2018): 64–90.

31. ABCFM to "Dear Madam," April 19, 1825, ABC 1.01, vol. 5; Rufus Anderson to Mrs. S. Hastings, March 27, 1826, ABC 1.01, vol. 7.

32. Abigail Kimball to Benjamin Wisner, April 18, 1835 [actually 1834], ABC 6, vol. 10.

33. November 27, 1816 [1817?]: "Answered a letter from Rev. Chester Wright, Montpelier, VT, on the question of employing unmarried females" (176), ABC 1.01, vol. 1.

34. Matthew McBride, "'Female Brethren': Gender Dynamics in a Newly Integrated Missionary Force, 1898–1915," *Journal of Mormon History* 44, no. 4 (October 2018): 40–67; David Golding, "Gender and Missionary Work," in *The Routledge Handbook on Mormonism and Gender*, ed. Amy Hoyt and Taylor G. Petrey (London: Routledge, 2020), 169–186.

3. Humanitarian Encounter in Late Ottoman Turkey

1. In this chapter, Ottoman and Turkish names are used in conformity with their presentation in Ottoman official documents instead of the pre-Ottoman naming preferred in American diplomatic, state, and missionary documents. Therefore, instead of "Smyrna" or "Aintab" I opt for "Izmir" or "Antep." Further, the transliteration of Ottoman Turkish names follows the pattern adopted by the *International Journal of Middle Eastern Studies*. Words that are common in English are given in their common usage. For example, instead of "Halep," as used in Ottoman documents, I prefer to use "Aleppo."

2. In its early connotation, the word "heathen" primarily signified "pagans," such as Native American tribes of the United States and peoples of India and China. Later on, it included all unevangelized communities regardless of geography, such as Jews, "more benighted parts of the Roman Catholic world," "nominal Christians of West-

ern Asia"—i.e., Armenians, Assyrians, Yezidis, Chaldeans, Nestorians, and Maronites—and Muslims and "nominal" Muslims of the Near East, such as the Druzes of Mount Lebanon and the Nusayris of Southeastern Anatolia. Rufus Anderson, *Memorial Volume of the First Fifty Years of the American Board of Commissioners for Foreign Missions*, 4th ed. (Boston: American Board of Commissioners for Foreign Missions, 1861), 80.

3. Daniel O. Morton, *Memoir of Rev. Levi Parsons, First Missionary to Palestine from the United States: Containing Sketches of His Early Life and Education, His Missionary Labors in This Country, in Asia Minor and Judea, with an Account of His Last Sickness and Death*, 2nd ed. (Burlington: Chauncey Goodrich, 1830).

4. "Asiatic Turkey" comprises just about all the territories of modern-day Turkey, with the exception of the Eastern Thrace, which is within the boundaries of today's Turkey.

5. It will be useful to briefly provide background information on the administrative division of the Ottoman Empire. In the post-Tanzimat period, the administrative division of Ottoman lands was largely organized along the line of the French Napoleonic Code in that the Regulation for the Provinces (*Vilâyet Nizamnamesi*) of 1864 replaced the earlier division of the provinces by state (*eyalet*) with a new division by province (*vilâyet*). The Regulation for the Provinces was soon followed by the General Provincial Regulation (*Vilâyet-i Umumiye Nizamnamesi*) of 1867 and the General Regulation for Provincial Administration (*İdare-i Umumiye-i Vilâyet Nizamnamesi*) of 1871. The empire was divided into provinces (*vilâyet*), which were further divided into sub-provinces (*sancak* or *liva*), districts (*kaza*), subdistricts (*nahiye*), and towns (*karye*). The province was governed by a governor (*vali*), who presided over a provincial administrative council (*vilâyet idare meclisi*) with an advisory function that was composed of leading officials and representatives of the Muslim and non-Muslim populations. The highest civil authority of a subprovince was a subgovernor (*mutasarrıf*), who headed an administrative council (*liva idare meclisi*) with a similar composition and function to that of the provincial council. District and subdistrict were governed by *kaimmakam* and director (*müdür*) respectively, the first of whom presided over a similar advisory council. In accordance with the increasing centralization, the highest civil authority in town went from an *imam* to a headman (*muhtar*), who was appointed by the center. For the time period in question, 1876–1909, given the tight control of Abdülhamid II, the administrative divisions of the Ottoman Empire remained pretty consistent. For an alphabetized list of the names of Ottoman administrative divisions by province, see *Osmanlı Asırlarında Türk Devleti'nin Mülki İdare Taksimatı ve Yer İsimlerinin Mukayeseli Tahlili: I. Bölüm Vilayet, Sancak, Kaza, Nahiye Itibariyledir, 1324–1325/1906–1907* [Administrative divisions of the Turkish state and comparative analysis of location names during the Ottoman centuries: 1st volume in terms of province, subprovince, district, subdistrict, 1324–1325/1906–1907] (Istanbul: T.C. Başbakanlık Devlet Arşivleri Genel Müdürlüğü, Osmanlı Arşivi Daire Başkanlığı, Tasnif Şubesi Müdürlüğü Araştırma Grubu, 1989).

6. Selim Deringil, "Legitimacy Structures in the Ottoman State: The Reign of Abdülhamid II (1876–1909)," *International Journal of Middle East Studies* 23, no. 3 (August 1991): 345–359; Selim Deringil, *The Well Protected Domains: Ideology and Legitimation of Power in the Ottoman Empire, 1876–1909* (London: I. B. Tauris, 1998); İlber Ortaylı, *Tanzimattan Sonra Mahalli İdareler, 1840–1878* [Local administrations in the post-Tanzimat period,

1840–1878] (Ankara: Sevinç Matbaası, 1974); Carter Findley, *Bureaucratic Reform in the Ottoman Empire: The Sublime Porte, 1789–1922* (Princeton: Princeton University Press, 1980).

7. "Six New Relief Stations Opened," *The Christian Herald and Signs of Our Times* 19, no. 3 (January 15, 1896): 45.

8. Erzincan was a subprovince of Erzurum province; Harput was a subprovince of Ma'mûretü'l Azîz (Elazığ) province; Mardin was a subprovince of Diyarbekir province; and Gemerek was a subdistrict of Ankara province.

9. "Six New Relief Stations Opened," 45.

10. Margaret E. Sangster, "Mrs. Sangster on Armenia," *The Christian Herald and Signs of Our Times* 19, no. 3 (January 15, 1896): 45.

11. BOA (*Başbakanlık Osmanlı Arşivleri*, Prime Ministry Ottoman Archives, now Presidency of Republic of Türkiye, Directorate of State Archives, Ottoman Archives with the continuing former abbreviation of BOA), Sadaret, Mektubi Mühimme Kalemi Evrakı (BOA. A. MKT.MHM.), 688/6, 4 Mart 1896 (H-19-09-1313).

12. "Six New Relief Stations Opened," 45. Named after Abdülhamid II, Hamidieh cavalry, officially called Hamidiye Light Cavalry Regiments (*Hamidiye Hafîf Süvari Alayları*) and largely composed of Kurdish tribes, was established in 1891 to suppress the Armenian uprisings in the eastern provinces of the Ottoman Empire that peaked in the last decade of the nineteenth century.

13. "Six New Relief Stations Opened," 45.

14. "Ten Relief Stations Now Open," *The Christian Herald and Signs of Our Times* 19, no. 4 (January 22, 1896): 67.

15. BOA. A. MKT.MHM., 688/6, H-19-09-1313. During the Ottoman centuries, because Ottomans did not have official surnames, foreign individuals were referred to in Ottoman documents by either their first or last names. Therefore, "Mr. Howard" (*Mösyö Howard*) was mentioned as such in the related document. There is a "Mr. Howard" listed as a correspondent of the *Christian Herald* in its January 22 issue. "Mr. Howard" is identified as W. W. Howard, the Armenian representative of the *Christian Herald*, in BOA (Directorate of Presidential State Archives, Ottoman Archives) Hariciye Nezareti, Siyasi (BOA. A. HR.SYS.), 2741/32, 21 Mart 1896 (M-21-03-1896).

16. "Memalik-i ecnebiyede iane komiteleri tarafından toplanan akçaların bu komitelerin adamları vasıtasıyla tevzigine, hükümet-i senniye tarafından müsaeede olunamayub, caneb-i seniul cevahib hazreti taccariden ihsan buyurulan ianeti, muhtacine lieclul tevziğ, İslam ve Hristiyan mütebananından mahallerinde teşkil eden komisyonlar marifetiyle taksime muvafakat olunmuş olduğu beyanıyla, Amerika'da toplanan ianetin dahi zikr olunan komisyonlar marifetiyle tevzine birşey denilemez." (Since the distribution of monies in the Ottoman territories, collected by aid committees in foreign countries, through their own agents is not allowed by the Ottoman government, similar to how the aid for the needy, granted by the Sultan His Exalted Highness, is distributed through local commissions composed of Muslim and Christian dignitaries, the aid collected in the United States will be distributed on the same pattern [in Ottoman lands].) BOA. A. MKT.MHM., 688/6, H-19-09-1313.

17. BOA. A. MKT.MHM., 688/6, H-19-09-1313.

18. BOA (Directorate of Presidential State Archives, Ottoman Archives) Hariciye Nezareti, Siyasi (BOA. HR.SYS.), 2741/50, 12 Haziran 1896 (M-12-06-1896).

19. BOA. HR.SYS., 2741/50, M-12-06-1896.

20. BOA. HR.SYS., 2741/50, M-12-06-1896.

21. BOA. HR.SYS., 2741/50, M-12-06-1896.

22. BOA (Directorate of Presidential State Archives, Ottoman Archives) Hariciye Nezareti, Siyasi (BOA. HR.SYS.), 54/4, 13 Ağustos 1896 (M-13-08-1896).

23. "Christian Herald gazetesinin vilayet-i şahanede mütemekkin Ermeniler için şimdiye kadar cem etmiş olduğu ianenin Amerika misyonları vasıtasıyla tevzi edildiği ve bu sebeble Nasraniyeti nesre firsat buldukları ve misyonerlerin ahali-i Hristiyaniyeyi, Protestan ve Katolik mezheblerine imaliyeye sağ ettikleri ve vesai-i lazime ile keyfiyetin mümkün olduğu derece tahkikiyle ilâveten mutalaa ile arz ve isari." Referred to in BOA. HR.SYS., 54/4, M-13-08-1896. This was followed by another communiqué of the Grand Vizierate on June 8, 1896, to the Aleppo province reiterating the content and urgency of the imperial decree. Italics added. BOA. HR.SYS., 54/4, M-13-08-1896.

24. BOA. HR.SYS., 54/4, M-13-08-1896.

25. BOA. HR.SYS., 54/4, M-13-08-1896.

26. BOA. HR.SYS., 54/4, M-13-08-1896.

27. BOA. HR.SYS., 54/4, M-13-08-1896.

28. BOA. HR.SYS., 54/4, M-13-08-1896.

29. BOA (Directorate of Presidential State Archives, Ottoman Archives) Sadaret, Mektubi Mühimme Kalemi Evrakı (BOA. A. MKT.MHM.), 752/15, 27 Haziran 1895 (H-04-01-1313).

30. BOA. A. MKT.MHM., 752/15, H-04-01-1313.

31. The imperial decree was not specified in the Cabinet minutes.

4. Dueling Orientalisms

1. Findlay married Isabella Ratray in c. 1844. Mission in the Scottish Highlands was considered the Church of Scotland's first foreign mission because of the Gaelic language barrier and the "pagan" beliefs that were prevalent there.

2. Ross Findlay and Linnie Findlay, eds., *Missionary Journals of Hugh Findlay: India-Scotland* (Ephraim, UT: Ross Findlay and Linnie Findlay, 1973), 1.

3. Findlay and Findlay, *Missionary Journals of Hugh Findlay*, 1.

4. Michael Fry, "'The Key to Their Hearts': Scottish Orientalism," in *Scotland and the 19th-Century World*, ed. Gerard Carruthers, David Goldie, and Alastair Renfrew (Amsterdam: Rodopi, 2012), 138.

5. Fry, "Key to Their Hearts," 147–149.

6. Fry, "Key to Their Hearts," 149.

7. Jane Rendall, "Scottish Orientalism: From Robertson to James Mill," *The Historical Journal* 25, no. 1 (March 1982): 69.

8. Matthew 24:14 (King James Version); Richard Ballantyne to Nathaniel Jones, April 14, 1854, in Journal, November 1853–May 1854, 114–118, Richard Ballantyne Papers, MS 467, Church History Library, Salt Lake City, Utah; Ballantyne, Journal, April 16–24, 1854, 118–122.

9. Findlay and Findlay, *Missionary Journals of Hugh Findlay*, 40.

10. John Murray Mitchell, *In Western India: Recollections of My Early Missionary Life* (Edinburgh: David Douglas, 1899), 23.

11. Mitchell, *In Western India*, 23; emphasis in original.

12. See Mitch Numark, "Translating Dharma: Scottish Missionary-Orientalists and the Politics of Religious Understanding in Nineteenth-Century Bombay," *Journal of Asian Studies* 70, no. 2 (May 2011): 471–500. Numark argues that for these missionaries religions were "systems" based upon scripturally derived doctrines and behaviors, not popular practices and ideas. Reliance on custom, tradition, and the authority of priests for knowledge of one's religion, rather than knowing one's religious scriptures for oneself, was one explanation the Scots gave for why Indians did not know their own religions.

13. Numark, "Translating Dharma," 473–474; emphasis in original.

14. Numark, "Translating Dharma," 474; emphasis in original. Numark also links their efforts to make their work scientific with their Scottish education.

15. See R. Lanier Britsch, *Nothing More Heroic: The Compelling Story of the First Latter-day Saint Missionaries in India* (Salt Lake City: Deseret Book, 1999).

16. Findlay and Findlay, *Missionary Journals of Hugh Findlay*, 27.

17. Findlay and Findlay, *Missionary Journals of Hugh Findlay*, 29.

18. Subhashis Pan, "Negotiating Scottish 'Distinctiveness'(?): Unmasking the British Conquest and the Construction of Empire in the 19th Century Indian Subcontinent," *Rupkatha Journal on Interdisciplinary Studies in Humanities* 12, no. 5 (2020): 6.

19. Emily Conroy-Krutz, *Christian Imperialism: Converting the World in the Early American Republic* (Ithaca, NY: Cornell University Press, 2015), 24.

20. Conroy-Krutz, *Christian Imperialism*, 64.

21. See chapter 10 by David Golding in this book.

22. Conroy-Krutz, *Christian Imperialism*, 68.

23. Conroy-Krutz, *Christian Imperialism*, 68.

24. An extract from *Daily News* quoted in Findlay and Findlay, *Missionary Journals of Hugh Findlay*, 8–9.

25. Findlay and Findlay, *Missionary Journals of Hugh Findlay*, 9.

26. Findlay and Findlay, *Missionary Journals of Hugh Findlay*, 13; emphasis in original.

27. Findlay and Findlay, *Missionary Journals of Hugh Findlay*, 41.

28. Conroy-Krutz, *Christian Imperialism*, 14.

29. John Santosh Murala, oral history, interview by R. Lanier Britsch, May 6, 2014, in author's possession.

30. Pan, "Negotiating Scottish 'Distinctiveness,'" 1–2.

5. Shoshone Worlds, Bannock Zions

1. "The Logan Temple," *The Deseret News*, June 4, 1884, 14.

2. Christopher Kimball Bigelow, *Temples of the Church of Jesus Christ of Latter-day Saints* (San Diego: Thunder Bay Press, 2018), n.p.; Carroll Van West, "Architecture," in *The Rocky Mountain Region*, ed. Rick Newby (Westport, CT: Greenwood Press, 2004), 11.

3. Charles Dibble, "Interview with George M. Ward," August 1, 1945, typescript, Utah Humanities Research Foundation Records, 1944–1945, J. Willard Marriott Library, University of Utah, Salt Lake City, Utah, 13.

4. Kristen Moulton, "At Bear River Massacre Site, the Names of the Dead Ring Out," *The Salt Lake Tribune*, January 30, 2013.

5. Brigham Madden, *The Northern Shoshone* (Caldwell, ID: Caxton Press, 1980), 197.

6. Amelia J. Frost, "Indian Work in Idaho: Address of Amelia J. Frost, Blackfoot, Idaho," *Home Mission Monthly* 20, no. 9 (July 1906): 232–233.

7. Ed Edmo is related to Edward Edmo Jr. but is not the same person.

8. Ed Edmo, "Shoshone-Bannock Creation Legend," Lewis and Clark Tribal Legacy Project, video, 4:30, https://lc-triballegacy.org/wp/wp-content/uploads/2021/04/EEdSho1A-creationlegend.mp4, accessed December 1, 2020.

9. Annie Pike Greenwood, *We Sagebrush Folks* (Moscow, ID: University of Idaho Press, 1988), 253.

10. Richard Francaviglia, *Believing in Place: A Spiritual Geography of the Great Basin* (Reno, NV: University of Nevada Press, 2003), 47.

11. Stephen J. Crum, *The Road on Which We Came* (Salt Lake City: University of Utah Press, 1994), 2.

12. Crum, *The Road on Which We Came*, 3.

13. I first encountered this quote in Donna Healy, "Smallpox Fears Stir Memories of Heavy Toll Indians Suffered," *Billings Gazette*, January 24, 2003, https://billingsgazette.com/news/local/smallpox-fears-stir-memories-of-heavy-toll-indians-suffered/article_93eaa022-c43f-5d79-98a2-7f68f1f17f8a.html. See also Richard Glover, ed., *David Thompson's Narrative 1784–1812* (Toronto: The Champlain Society, 1962), excerpted in *Our Hearts Fell to the Ground: Plains Indian Views of How the West Was Lost*, ed. Colin G. Calloway (Boston: Bedford of St. Martin's Press, 1996), 43.

14. Cited in Healy, "Smallpox Fears."

15. Pekka Hämäläinen, *The Comanche Empire* (New Haven: Yale University Press, 2008), 75.

16. Recently, the Oceti Sakowin Oyate historian Nick Estes has argued that the portrayal of fur trade relationships as creating a "middle ground" misses the sexual exploitation of Native women. Although scholars like Richard White and Sylvia Van Kirk did not completely dismiss the violence that existed within fur trade families, Estes has called for a greater emphasis on sexual coercion and physical violence. See Sylvia Van Kirk, *Many Tender Ties: Women in Fur Trade Society, 1670–1870* (Norman: University of Oklahoma Press, 1983); Richard White, *The Middle Ground: Indians, Empires, and Republics in the Great Lakes Region, 1659–1815* (New York: Cambridge University Press, 1991); and "Our History is Our Future with Nick Estes," *The Dig*, June 29, 2019, https://thedigradio.com/podcast/our-history-is-the-future-with-nick-estes-2/.

17. Peter Silver, *Our Savage Neighbors: How Indian War Transformed Early America* (New York: W. W. Norton, 2008). See also Jill Lenore, *The Name of War: King Philip's War and the Origins of American Identity* (New York: Vintage Books, 1998).

18. 2 Nephi 30:6, *The Book of Mormon* (Salt Lake City, UT: Church of Jesus Christ of Latter-day Saints, 1981).

19. "Indianola Ward Relief Society, Minutes, September 16, 1880," in *The First Fifty Years of Relief Society: Key Documents in Latter-day Saint Women's History*, ed. Jill Mulvay Derr, Carol Cornwall Madden, Kate Holbrook, and Matthew J. Grow (Salt Lake City: Church Historians Press, 2016), 483–486.

20. "Indianola Ward Relief Society, Minutes."

21. Thomas D. Brown, *Journal of the Southern Indian Mission*, ed. Juanita Brooks (Logan: Utah State University Press, 1972), 63.

22. Brown, *Journal of the Southern Indian Mission*, 35.

23. Darren Parry, "Indian Way of Life," *The Herald Journal*, August 3, 2017, https://hjnews.com/full-text-of-Darren-parrys-talk-at-the-osa-heritage-day/article_1d8b59df-8f9a-546f-ae78-20f4f9a8db60.html.

24. Scott Christensen, *Sagwitch: Shoshone Chieftain, Mormon Elder, 1822–1887* (Logan: Utah State University Press, 1999), 84.

25. "Shoshone Latter-day Saint Photographs, 1909," PH 9714, Church History Library, Salt Lake City, Utah.

26. "Shoshone Latter-day Saint Photographs, 1909."

27. Cited in Kass Fleisher, *The Bear River Massacre and the Making of History* (Albany: State University of New York Press, 2004), 64.

28. Ing, "Buzz of the Burg," *Idaho State Journal* 49, no. 304 (February 21, 1951): 4, https://newspapers.com/image/20818842.

29. Amelia J. Frost, "The Bannocks and Shoshones," *Home Mission Monthly* 2, no. 4 (February 1907): 82–83.

30. Frost, "Bannocks and Shoshones," 83.

31. "Indian Babe Possesses Royal Blood: Infant Takes Spotlight at Fort Hall," *Salt Lake Tribune*, October 4, 1939, 10, https://newspapers.com/image/598549736.

32. Bonnie Sue Lewis, *Creating Christian Indians: Native Clergy in the Presbyterian Church* (Norman: University of Oklahoma Press, 2003), 145.

33. "Indian Babe Possesses Royal Blood," 10.

34. Marie Crawford, "The Old and the New Indian Marriage," *Home Mission Monthly* 24, no. 4 (February 1910): 83–84.

35. Crawford, "Old and the New Indian Marriage," 83–84.

36. Brenda Child, Masterclass, Montana State University, October 29, 2018.

37. Amelia J. Frost, "The Bannocks and Shoshones," *The Idaho Republican*, February 22, 1907, 1, https://newspapers.com/image/60112381/7.

38. "Fort Hall Indian Reservation Makes Ideal Home for Three Indian Tribes," *The Idaho Republican*, May 6, 1919, 1, 8, https://www.newspapers.com/image/601146091.

39. "Visits Mission," *The Idaho Republican*, November 14, 1921, 1, https://newspapers.com/image/601215212.

40. "Local and Personal," *Twice-A-Week Twin Falls Times*, October 15, 1915, 5, https://newspapers.com/image/566009742.

41. "Local Happenings," *Bingham County News*, May 26, 1922, 1, https://newspapers.com/image/375408387.

42. "Blackfoot Represented at Salt Lake School," *The Idaho Republican*, April 2, 1920, 5, https://newspapers.com/image/601176641.

43. "Picturesque Exhibits at the Blackfoot Fair," *The Idaho Republican*, September 8, 1916, 8, https://newspapers.com/image/601152566.

44. "Origin of the Word 'Blackfoot,'" *The Idaho Republican*, February 7, 1921, 4, https://newspapers.com/image/601210952.

45. "Origin of the Word 'Blackfoot,'" 4.

46. "Origin of the Word 'Blackfoot,'" 4.

47. *Bingham County History* (Blackfoot, ID: Bingham County Centennial Book Committee, 1985), 109.

48. This information on Lillian comes from my aunt Deloris, who also shared that Lillian went by "Teba." This is partially corroborated by her obituary. "Lillian Tendore," *Idaho State Journal*, November 29, 1963, 2, https://newspapers.com/image/15837018.

49. Undated photograph in author's possession.

50. "Understanding Indian Religion," *Idaho State Journal*, November 16, 1973, 26, https://newspapers.com/image/24767235.

51. "June Eloise Miera Obituary," Legacy.com, March 9, 2020, https://www.legacy.com/us/obituaries/idahostatejournal/name/june-miera-obituary?id=8788285.

52. Postcard c. 1935 in author's possession.

53. Postcard c. 1935 in author's possession.

54. Michele Welch, "Interview with Mae Timbimboo Parry," May 2, 2006, transcript, Utah Women's Walk Oral Histories, Utah Valley University, Orem, Utah, 7–8, https://uvu.contentdm.oclc.org/digital/api/collection/womenswalk/id/9/download.

55. Welch, "Interview with Mae Timbimboo Parry," 8–9.

56. Welch, "Interview with Mae Timbimboo Parry," 9.

6. Traveling Elders

1. David Livingstone, *Missionary Travels and Researches in South Africa: Including a Sketch of Sixteen Years' Residence in the Interior of Africa, and a Journey from the Cape of Good Hope to Loanda on the West Coast; Thence across the Continent, Down the River Zambesi, to the Eastern Ocean* (London: John Murray, 1857; New York: Harper & Brothers, 1858).

2. Christraud M. Geary, "Missionary Photography: Private and Public Readings," *African Arts* 24, no. 4 (1991): 48.

3. Brigham Young, Speeches before the Utah Territorial Legislature, January 23 and February 5, 1852, George D. Watt Papers (MS 4534), Church History Library, Salt Lake City, Utah.

4. Francis M. Lyman to Warren H. Lyon, October 2, 1903, cited in Evan P. Wright, *A History of the South African Mission*, vol. 2 (n.p., n.d.), 8, spelling corrected by Wright.

5. Francis M. Lyman, "Editorial: Are Negroes Children of Adam?" *The Latter-day Saints' Millennial Star*, December 3, 1903, 777.

6. David A. Hollinger, *Protestants Abroad: How Missionaries Tried to Change the World but Changed America* (Princeton: Princeton University Press, 2017), 304n24.

7. T. Jack Thompson, "Capturing the Image: African Missionary Photography as Enslavement and Liberation," Day Associates Lecture, June 29, 2007, Yale Divinity School, New Haven, Connecticut, 3.

8. Hollinger, *Protestants Abroad*, 304n24.

9. Jay M. Todd, "Improvement Era," in *Encyclopedia of Mormonism: The History, Scripture, Doctrine, and Procedure of the Church of Jesus Christ of Latter-day Saints*, vol. 2, ed. Daniel H. Ludlow (New York: Macmillan, 1992), 678.

10. For a history of the *Improvement Era*, see Todd, "Improvement Era," and Doyle L. Green, "The Improvement Era—The Voice of the Church (1897–1970)," *Improvement Era*, November 1970, 12–14, 19–20.

11. "New President for the African Mission," *Improvement Era*, August 1911, 900.

12. Frank J. Hewlett, "In Sunny Africa," *Improvement Era*, August 1912, 880.

13. Sarah Robbins and Ann Ellis Pullen, *Nellie Arnott's Writings on Angola, 1905–1913: Missionary Narratives Linking Africa and America* (Anderson, SC: Parlor, 2011), 75. For a discussion of mission and travel narratives in early twentieth-century America, see pp. 73–79.

14. Syed Manzurul Islam, *The Ethics of Travel: From Marco Polo to Kafka* (Manchester: Manchester University Press, 1996), vii.

15. Islam, *The Ethics of Travel*, vii–viii.

16. Casey Blanton, *Travel Writing: The Self and the World* (New York: Routledge, 2002), 2.

17. Steve Clark, introduction to *Travel Writing and Empire: Postcolonial Theory in Transit*, ed. Steve Clark (London: Zed Books, 1999), 3.

18. Sara Mills, *Discourses of Difference: An Analysis of Women's Travel Writing and Colonialism* (London: Routledge, 1991), 86.

19. "Messages from the Missions," *Improvement Era*, September 1908, 889.

20. Orville W. Cutler, "The Cape to Cairo Railroad," *Improvement Era*, April 1916, 490.

21. Ali A. Mazrui, "The Re-Invention of Africa: Edward Said, V.Y. Mudimbe, and Beyond," *Research in African Literatures* 36, no. 3 (2005): 70–71.

22. Anne Maxwell, *Colonial Photography and Exhibitions: Representations of the "Native" People and the Making of European Identities* (London: Leicester University Press, 1999).

23. V. Y. Mudimbe, *The Invention of Africa: Gnosis, Philosophy, and the Order of Knowledge* (Bloomington: Indiana University Press, 1988) and *The Idea of Africa* (Bloomington: Indiana University Press, 1994).

24. Edward W. Said, *Orientalism* (New York: Pantheon, 1978).

25. Patrick Brantlinger, "Victorians and Africans: The Genealogy of the Myth of the Dark Continent," *Critical Inquiry* 12, no. 1 (1985): 166.

26. Paul S. Landau, "An Amazing Distance: Pictures and People in Africa," in *Images and Empires: Visuality in Colonial and Postcolonial Africa*, ed. Paul S. Landau and Deborah D. Kaspin (Berkeley: University of California Press, 2002), 2.

27. For example, David Livingstone, "Discoveries in Africa," *Deseret News*, February 22, 1860, 2; "Dr. Livingstone Alive and Well," *Deseret Evening News*, November 23, 1867, 2.

28. David Livingstone to John Murray, May 22, 1857, MS 42420, National Library of Scotland, Edinburgh, Scotland.

29. David Livingstone to John Murray, November 27, 1864, and March 3, 1865, MS 42421, National Library of Scotland, Edinburgh, Scotland.

30. Livingstone, *Missionary Travels*, 519.

31. "Monument to David Livingstone, the Missionary and Explorer," *Deseret Evening News*, March 31, 1903, 11. The *Willmar Tribune* of Willmar, Minnesota, printed the same image two months later, making no reference to Livingstone's work as a missionary ("Monument to David Livingstone, Explorer," *Willmar Tribune*, May 30, 1903, 4). On the competing elements of Livingstone's legacy, see John M. MacKenzie, "David Livingstone—Prophet or Patron Saint of Imperialism in Africa: Myths and Misconceptions," *Scottish Geographical Journal* 129 (2013): 277–291, and Justin D. Livingstone, *Livingstone's "Lives": A Metabiography of a Victorian Icon* (Manchester: Manchester University Press, 2014).

32. Orson M. Rogers, "Native Races of South Africa," *Improvement Era*, June 1909, 625–635. Rogers, of Salt Lake City, Utah, was set apart for his mission on October 9, 1906, by Rulon S. Wells (Missionary Department Missionary Registers, 1860–1959, Book C, 1894 April 27–1906 October 16, 246 [CR 301 22], Church History Library, Salt Lake City, Utah).

33. Rogers, "Native Races of South Africa," 625.

34. See, for example, Robert Moffat, *Missionary Labours and Scenes in Southern Africa* (London: John Snow, 1846), and W. P. Livingstone, *Mary Slessor of Calabar: Pioneer Missionary* (London: Hodder and Stoughton, 1915). The frontispiece for Livingstone's *Missionary Travels* is of the Mosi-oa-Tunya, or Victoria Falls; however, the first image after the frontmatter and just before the narrative commences is of Livingstone (Livingstone, *Missionary Travels*, frontispiece and between xi and 1).

35. In this chapter, "k——" denotes *kaffir*, a derogatory term.

36. Jochen S. Arndt, "What's in a Word? Historicising the Term 'Caffre' in European Discourses about Southern Africa between 1500 and 1800," *Journal of Southern African Studies* 44, no. 1 (2018): 59–75.

37. Arndt, "What's in a Word?"

38. Rogers, "Native Races of South Africa," 632.

39. W. Paul Reeve, *Religion of a Different Color: Race and the Mormon Struggle for Whiteness* (Oxford: Oxford University Press, 2015), 191–192, 207.

40. Rogers, "Native Races of South Africa," 626–627.

41. Max Perry Mueller, *Race and the Making of the Mormon People* (Chapel Hill: University of North Carolina Press, 2017), 13, 62.

42. "Messages from the Missions," *Improvement Era*, February 1909, 316. Jones, of Cedar City, Utah, was set apart for his mission on June 25, 1907, by Francis M. Lyman (Missionary Department Missionary Registers, 1860–1959, Book D, 1906 October 23–1919 July 4, 13 [CR 301 22], Church History Library, Salt Lake City, Utah).

43. "Lesson III: Genealogy and Literature: Third Week in February: Racial History: Ham: His Descendants and Tribes," *Relief Society Magazine*, January 1918, 51–57.

44. "Ham: His Descendants and Tribes," 52–53.

45. Sheffield, of Kaysville, Utah, was set apart for his mission on March 7, 1905, by George Albert Smith (Missionary Department Missionary Registers, 1860–1959, Book C, 211).

46. Paul Jenkins and Christraud Geary, "Photographs from Africa in the Basel Mission Archive," *African Arts* 18, no. 4 (1985): 56, and T. Jack Thompson, "Capturing the Image: African Missionary Photography as Enslavement and Liberation," Day Associates Lecture, June 29, 2007, Yale Divinity School, New Haven, Connecticut, 15.

47. June B. Sharp, Journal, July 21, 1914, MS 14361, Church History Library, Salt Lake City, Utah.

48. Rogers, "Native Races of South Africa," 627.

49. Rogers, "Native Races of South Africa," 628, 630.

50. Where European clothing is mentioned, it is usually in comparison to African clothing (see, for example, Hewlett, "In Sunny Africa," 884–885).

51. T. J. Tallie, "Sartorial Settlement: The Mission Field and Transformation in Colonial Natal, 1850–1897," in "Preaching the Civilizing Mission and Modern Cultural Encounters," edited by Diego Olstein and Stefan Hübner, special issue, *Journal of World History* 27, no. 3 (September 2016): 389–410.

52. See, for example, June B. Sharp, Photograph Album (PH 8123), and Willis E. Spafford, Mission Photographs (PH 10341), Church History Library, Salt Lake City, Utah.

53. Geary, "Missionary Photography," 53.

54. John M. MacKenzie with Nigel R. Dalziel, *The Scots in South Africa: Ethnicity, Identity, Gender and Race, 1772–1914* (Manchester: Manchester University Press, 2007), 102.

55. Jeffrey Grant Cannon, "Church of Scotland Periodicals and the Shaping of Scottish Opinion Regarding South African Apartheid and the Central African Federation, c. 1912–c. 1965" (PhD diss., University of Edinburgh, 2021), 29–30, 239–240.

56. Reeve, *Religion of a Different Color*, 56–57.

57. Hollinger, *Protestants Abroad*, 297.

58. Sharp, Journal, May 2, 1913, August 1, 1913, and August 6, 1914.

59. Sharp, Journal, July 21, 1914.

60. Mohamed Adhikari, "Hope, Fear, Shame, Frustration: Continuity and Change in the Expression of Coloured Identity in White Supremacist South Africa, 1910–1994," *Journal of Southern African Studies* 32, no. 3 (2006): 467–487.

61. Church of Jesus Christ of Latter-day Saints, Record of Members, Johannesburg Branch (CR 375 8, Reel 6498), Church History Library, Salt Lake City, Utah.

62. Sharp, Journal, January 5, 1913, and Alexander Lester Stoddard, Journal, July 2, 1917, MS 7365, Church History Library, Salt Lake City, Utah.

63. Stoddard, Journal, July 2, 1917.

64. Lavina F. Anderson, "Nicholas Groesbeck Smith: A Documentary History, 1881–1945" (unpublished manuscript), 165, cited in Russell Stevenson, "The Branch of Love: A Black History Month Tribute to Valentine's Day," *Times and Seasons* (blog), February 14, 2015, http://timesandseasons.org/index.php/2015/02/the-branch-of-love-a-black-history-month-tribute-to-valentines-day.

65. Mowbray Branch Cottage Meeting Minutes, 1921–1925 (LR 4578 21), Church History Library, Salt Lake City, Utah; "Mission News: Cape District," *Cumorah's Southern Cross*, March 1932, 46.

66. Gordon W. Allport, *The Nature of Prejudice* (Cambridge, MA: Addison-Wesley, 1954), 261–281.

67. "Messages from the Missions," *Improvement Era*, March 1908, 389. Simons, of Salt Lake City, Utah, was set apart for his mission on October 9, 1906, by Rudger Clawson (Missionary Department Missionary Registers, 1860–1959, Book C, 246).

68. Wendy J. Deichmann Edwards, "Forging an Ideology for American Missions: Josiah Strong and Manifest Destiny," in *North American Foreign Missions, 1810–1914: Theology, Theory, and Policy*, ed. Wilbert R. Shenk (Grand Rapids, MI: Eerdmans, 2004), 175–176.

69. Josiah Strong, *Our Country: Its Possible Future and Its Present Crisis* (New York: Baker and Taylor for the American Home Missionary Society, 1885), 159–180. Strong dedicated a chapter of this book to the "peril" of "Mormonism" (59–68).

70. For an example of this history, see Alexander Wilmot and John Centlivres Chase, *History of the Colony of the Cape of Good Hope: From Its Discovery to the Year 1819* (Cape Town: J. C. Juta, 1869). Wilmot and Chase were largely responsible for the English-language historiography of South Africa for decades. The first edition of George McCall Theal's influential, pro-(British) settler *Compendium of South African History and Geography* was published in 1874. As prime minister, Cecil John Rhodes appointed him colonial historian and his work became a major influence on the history taught in South Africa into the 1990s (William H. Worger, "Southern and Central Africa," in *The Oxford History of the British Empire: Volume V: Historiography*, ed. Robin W. Winks [Ox-

ford: Oxford University Press, 1999], 513–515). In 1893, the assistant secretary of the Royal Geographic Society, John Scott Keltie, published his book *The Partition of Africa*, in which he supported expansion, arguing that missionaries and explorers before 1875 did valuable work in preparing the ground for later colonialism. For twenty years the general outlines of discussion followed Keltie's approach (John E. Flint, "Britain and the Scramble for Africa," in Winks, *The Oxford History of the British Empire: Volume V: Historiography*, 452). In addition to appointing Theal colonial historian, Rhodes appointed Wilmot to investigate the origins of Great Zimbabwe—an endeavor that later served to prop up Rhodes's expansion into Central Africa. In support of those aims, Rhodes's sometime employee Harry Johnston, who at other times served as a colonial representative of the government in Whitehall, wrote pro-imperial books like *British Central Africa* (1897) and *The Colonisation of Africa by Alien Races* (1899). Rhodes's attempts to control the narrative of British imperialism resulted in calls for Britain to assert itself as the only power in the region (Worger, "Southern and Central Africa," 515).

71. H. L. Steed, "Cape Town of Today," *Improvement Era*, August 1909, 768–775. Steed, of Corrine, Utah, was set apart for his mission on June 30, 1908, by Joseph F. Smith (Missionary Department Missionary Registers, 1860–1959, Book D, 30).

72. Steed, "Cape Town of Today," 775.

73. Steed, "Cape Town of Today," 768.

74. John M. MacKenzie, *The British Empire through Buildings: Structure, Function and Meaning* (Manchester: Manchester University Press, 2020), 4.

75. Steed, "Cape Town of Today," 771.

76. "City Hall Cape Town," postcard, June B. Sharp photograph album, 1912–1915, Church History Library, Salt Lake City, Utah.

77. "Railroad Expansion in South Africa," *Scientific American* 87, no. 16 (October 18, 1902): 252–253.

78. "The Coal Fields of Natal," *Scientific American* 88, no. 3 (January 17, 1903): 36; "The Cape to Cairo Railroad," *Scientific American* 88, no. 22 (May 30, 1903): 414.

79. Cutler, "The Cape to Cairo Railroad," 490–492. Cutler, of Salt Lake City, Utah, was set apart for his mission on December 2, 1913, by J. Golden Kimball (Missionary Department Missionary Registers, 1860–1959, Book D, 163).

80. Cutler, "The Cape to Cairo Railroad," 490–491.

81. Cutler, "The Cape to Cairo Railroad," 491–492.

82. The Hewletts were born in England and living in Salt Lake City when they were set apart for their mission on July 26, 1911, Emily by Charles W. Penrose and Franklin by Anthon H. Lund (Missionary Department Missionary Registers, 1860–1959, Book D, 110).

83. "New President for the African Mission," 900; Frank J. Hewlett, "In Sunny Africa: III—The Transvaal," *Improvement Era*, April 1913, 550–551.

84. Hewlett, "In Sunny Africa: III," 552.

85. Hewlett, "In Sunny Africa: III," 551.

86. Franklin J. Hewlett, "In Sunny Africa: II—The New U. S. A.," *Improvement Era*, November 1912, 45, 46, 51.

87. Hewlett, "In Sunny Africa: II," 51.

88. Hewlett, "In Sunny Africa: III," 549.

89. Ralph A. Badger, "Groote Schuur—A Sketch," *Improvement Era*, February 1908, 257–266.

90. Badger, "Groote Schuur," 260.

91. Brian Stanley, "Gardening for the Gospel: Horticulture and Mission in the Life of Robert Moffat of Kuruman," in *Pathways and Patterns in History: Essays on Baptists, Evangelicals, and the Modern World in Honour of David Bebbington*, ed. Anthony R. Cross, Peter J. Morden, and Ian M. Randall (London: Spurgeon's College and the Baptist Historical Society, 2015), 354–368.

92. Badger, "Groote Schuur," 264.

93. Nicholas G. Smith, "Cecil John Rhodes: A Thrilling Story of Achievement," *Improvement Era*, July 1916, 808.

94. Smith, "Cecil John Rhodes," 810.

95. B. H. Jacobson, "Oxford and the Rhodes Scholarships," *Improvement Era*, August 1908, 802.

96. Brigham H. Roberts, "Sphere of Y. M. M. I. A. Activities: An Appeal to the Parents and Priesthood of the Church," *Improvement Era*, January 1913, 199–202.

97. Farrell Ray Monson, "History of the South African Mission of The Church of Jesus Christ of Latter-Day [sic] Saints, 1853–1970" (master's thesis, Brigham Young University, 1971), 31.

98. F. W. Reitz, *Een Eeuw van Onrecht*, 2nd ed. (Dordrecht: Morks and Geuze, 1900), 26; quotation from the English edition, F. W. Reitz, *A Century of Wrong* (London: "Review of Reviews" Office, 1900), 43. The Dutch original reads, "De heer Rhodes, met die verraderlijke dubbelzinnigheid, die het blijvend kenmerk der Britsche politiek in Zuid-Afrika is, werkte openlijk in het nauwste verband met de Koloniale Afrikaners, terwijl in het geheim hij met het jingoïsme een complot tegen de Afrikaners en de Afrikaansche Republikeinen smeedde."

99. Frank J. Hewlett, "A Jaunt in South Africa," *Improvement Era*, April 1914, 508.

100. Sharp's album contains fifteen photographs, but it is unclear whether he took them all or if they are the extent of his collection.

101. Alfred J. Gowers Jr., "Kimberley and the Diamond Fields," *Improvement Era*, February 1912, 316–321. Gowers, of Nephi, Utah, was set apart for his mission on October 4, 1910, by Anthony W. Ivins (Missionary Department Missionary Registers, 1860–1959, Book D, 92).

102. "Messages from the Missions," *Improvement Era*, April 1912, 561–562; Hewlett, "In Sunny Africa," 880. Shurtliff, of Baker, Oregon, was set apart for his mission on March 21, 1911, by George F. Richards (Missionary Department Missionary Registers, 1860–1959, Book D, 103).

103. Laura Moench Jenkins, "The Widow's Mite," *Relief Society Magazine*, September 1917, 501–502.

104. Hewlett, "In Sunny Africa," 885.

105. Hewlett, "In Sunny Africa," 885–886.

106. Malcolm L. Robinson, "Most Distant Branch on Earth," *Improvement Era*, October 1919, 1097. Robinson, of Kanab, Utah, was set apart for his mission on May 17, 1916, by Francis M. Lyman (Missionary Department Missionary Registers, 1860–1959, Book D, 204).

107. Levi Edgar Young, "'Mormonism' and the Modern Man," *Improvement Era*, October 1914, 1103. Young was called to the First Council of Seventy in 1909 and from

1913 to 1929 was a member of the General Board of the Young Men's Mutual Improvement Association, which published the *Improvement Era*.

108. Joseph M. Tanner, "Problems of the Age: Dealing with Religious, Social and Economic Questions and their Solution: A Study for the Quorums and Classes of the Melchizedek Priesthood," *Improvement Era*, July 1918, 804–805.

109. Brian Stanley, "From 'the Poor Heathen' to 'the Glory and Honour of All Nations': Vocabularies of Race and Custom in Protestant Missions, 1844–1928," *International Bulletin of Missionary Research* (January 2010): 3.

7. Earthquakes, Mudslides, and Hurricanes

1. Global Volcanism Program, "Report on Nevado del Ruiz (Colombia)," in *Scientific Event Alert Network Bulletin* 10, no. 5 (May 1985), ed. L. McClelland, Smithsonian Institution, https://doi.org/10.5479/si.GVP.SEAN198507-351020; Global Volcanism Program, "Report on Nevado del Ruiz (Colombia)," in *Scientific Event Alert Network Bulletin* 10, no. 7 (July 1985), ed. L. McClelland, Smithsonian Institution, https://doi.org/10.5479/si.GVP.SEAN198507-351020; Barry Voight, "The 1985 Nevado del Ruiz Volcano Catastrophe: Anatomy and Retrospection," *Journal of Volcanology and Geothermal Research* 44 (1990): 361–363.

2. Voight, "Report," 365–367.

3. Robert W. Decker and Barbara Decker, *Mountains of Fire: The Nature of Volcanoes* (New York: Cambridge University Press, 1991), 4.

4. Walter Sullivan, "Studies Find Warnings of Volcano Were in Vain," *New York Times*, June 29, 1986.

5. Decker and Decker, *Mountains of Fire*, 4–5.

6. Sullivan, "Studies."

7. Sullivan, "Studies."

8. Bradley Graham, "Red Cross Sees Toll up to 20,000," *Washington Post*, November 15, 1985.

9. Bradley Graham, "Survivors Recall Night of Horror," *Washington Post*, November 15, 1985.

10. Graham, "Red Cross"; Randy Frame, "A Year of Major Tests for Evangelical Relief Agencies," *Christianity Today*, January 17, 1986.

11. Art Toalston, "Baptists Join Relief Efforts after Colombian Volcano Erupts," *Baptist Press*, November 14, 1985, 4.

12. Art Toalston, "Baptists Give Volcano Victims Medicine, Supplies, Compassion," *Baptist Press*, November 25, 1985, 1–2; Art Toalston, "'Center of Hope' Opens Doors to Help Armero's Survivors," *Baptist Press*, January 7, 1986, 1–2.

13. Frame, "A Year." The Association of Evangelical Relief and Development Organizations formed in 1978 with twelve initial member agencies. "Who We Are," Accord Network, accessed August 20, 2019, https://www.accordnetwork.org/who-we-are.

14. Matthew 25:31–46 (New Revised Standard Version); Luke 10:25–37 (NRSV).

15. This literature on humanitarian and development aid, particularly from faith-based organizations, is too vast to cite comprehensively here, but recent works that address these themes include David King, *God's Internationalists: World Vision and the Age of Evangelical Humanitarianism* (Philadelphia: University of Pennsylvania Press,

2019); Heather Curtis, *Holy Humanitarians: American Evangelicals and Global Aid* (Cambridge, MA: Harvard University Press, 2018); Michael Barnett, *Empire of Humanity: A History of Humanitarianism* (Ithaca, NY: Cornell University Press, 2013); Ann Marie Wilson, "Taking Liberties Abroad: Americans and International Humanitarian Advocacy, 1821–1914" (PhD diss., Harvard University, 2010); David Ekbladh, *The Great American Mission: Modernization and the Construction of an American World Order* (Princeton: Princeton University Press, 2010); Ian R. Tyrrell, *Reforming the World: The Creation of America's Moral Empire* (Princeton: Princeton University Press, 2010); Rachel McCleary, *Global Compassion: Private Voluntary Organizations and U.S. Foreign Policy since 1939* (New York: Oxford University Press, 2009); Gerard Clarke and Michael Jennings, *Development, Civil Society and Faith-Based Organizations: Bridging Sacred and the Secular* (Basingstoke: Palgrave Macmillan, 2008); Wendy Tyndale, *Visions of Development: Faith-Based Initiatives* (Aldershot: Ashgate, 2006); and Katherine Marshall and Lucy Keough, *Finding Global Balance: Common Ground between the Worlds of Development and Faith* (Washington, DC: World Bank, 2005).

16. King, *God's Internationalists*; Curtis, *Holy Humanitarians*. See also Brian Steensland and Phil Goff, *The New Evangelical Social Engagement* (New York: Oxford University Press, 2014); Melani McAlister, *The Kingdom of God Has No Borders: A Global History of American Evangelicals* (New York: Oxford University Press, 2018). David Stoll has also written about Latin American frustration with US evangelicals for engaging in "disaster evangelism," in particular the assumption US evangelicals held about the potential for "material benefits [to] open a heart to the gospel." See David Stoll, *Is Latin American Turning Protestant? The Politics of Evangelical Growth* (Berkeley: University of California Press, 1990), 12.

17. Briefly, in this period some church leaders who hailed from countries in the Global South began to call on their Western counterparts to abandon their overseas mission fields (as they saw Western missionary work as propagating cultural imperialism and colonialism), grant indigenous leaders control over their local churches, and focus more on achieving social justice than on tallying up ever greater numbers of souls "won" to Christ. Many evangelicals from the United States found this perspective challenging, as they felt that evangelism should be their primary aim, with social action coming as a secondary responsibility. This debate over the orientation of evangelicalism pervaded journals and international conferences throughout the 1960s and 1970s. See Al Tizon, *Transformation after Lausanne: Radical Evangelical Mission in Global–Local Perspective* (Eugene: Wipf & Stock, 2008); Dana Robert, "The Great Commission in an Age of Globalization," in *The Antioch Agenda: The Restorative Church at the Margins*, ed. D. Jeyaraj, R. Pazmino, and R. Petersen, (New Delhi: Indian Society for the Promotion of Christian Knowledge, 2007), 5–22; Lauren F. Turek, *To Bring the Good News to All Nations: Evangelical Influence on Human Rights and U.S. Foreign Relations* (New York: Cornell University Press, 2020).

18. Art Toalston, "Baptists Enlarge Witness as Colombians Ask 'Why?'" *Baptist Press*, December 5, 1985, 2.

19. Mary E. Speidel, "Five Years after Armero, Survivors Find New Life," *Baptist Press*, January 16, 1991, 6.

20. For literature on the spread of evangelicalism in the Global South in the late twentieth century, see Harvey Cox, *Fire from Heaven: The Rise of Pentecostal Spirituality*

and the Reshaping of Religion in the Twenty-First Century (Cambridge, MA: Da Capo Press, 1995); Mark Hutchinson and John Wolffe, *A Short History of Global Evangelicalism* (Cambridge: Cambridge University Press, 2012); Philip Jenkins, *The Next Christendom: The Coming of Global Christianity* (New York: Oxford University Press, 2007); Stephen Offutt, *New Centers of Global Evangelicalism in Latin America and Africa* (Cambridge: Cambridge University Press, 2017); Simon Coleman, Rosalind I. J. Hackett, and Joel Robbins, *The Anthropology of Global Pentecostalism and Evangelicalism* (New York: New York University Press, 2015); Brian Stanley, *The Global Diffusion of Evangelicalism: The Age of Billy Graham and John Stott* (Downers Grove: InterVarsity Press, 2018).

21. Southern Baptist Convention (SBC) Foreign Mission Board, "Foreign Missions Looks Toward 2000 A.D.," January 13, 1976, John David Hughey Papers, AR 711, Box 6, Folder 1, Southern Baptist Library and Historical Archives, Nashville, Tennessee (hereafter SBLHA); Ben Armstrong, *The Electric Church* (Nashville: T. Nelson, 1979), 177. Matthew 28:16–20 details the "Commissioning of the Disciples," specifically the edict to "go therefore and make disciples of all nations, baptizing them in the name of the Father and of the Son and of the Holy Spirit, and teaching them to obey everything that I have commanded you." Matthew 28:19–20 (NRSV).

22. Dana L. Robert, "Shifting Southward: Global Christianity since 1945," *International Bulletin of Missionary Research* 24, no. 2 (April 2000): 52–53.

23. Robert, "Shifting Southward," 52–53; Robert, "The Great Commission," 6–7; Tizon, *Transformation*, 54–58. For an example of the evangelical response to changes in how mainline Protestants approached their global mission, see Donald McGavran's critique of the official statements on mission that the World Council of Churches developed during its Fourth Assembly in Uppsala, Sweden, in 1968: Donald McGavran, "A. Criticism of the WCC Working Draft on Mission 1. Will Uppsala Betray the Two Billion?" reprinted in *The Conciliar-Evangelical Debate: The Crucial Documents, 1964–1976*, ed. Donald McGavran (South Pasadena: William Carey Library, 1977), 233–241.

24. See J. D. Douglas, ed., *Let the Earth Hear His Voice: International Congress on World Evangelization, Lausanne, Switzerland Official Reference Volume* (Minneapolis: World Wide Publications, 1975).

25. C. René Padilla, "Evangelism and the World," in Douglas, *Let the Earth Hear His Voice*, 116–146; Samuel Escobar, "Evangelism and Man's Search for Freedom, Justice and Fulfillment," in Douglas, *Let the Earth Hear His Voice*, 303–318.

26. The Lausanne Covenant, in Douglas, *Let the Earth Hear His Voice*, 5.

27. SBC Foreign Mission Board, "Foreign Missions," 1.

28. The SBC officially adopted the plan in 1977. "Bold Mission Thrust Master Plan Approved," *Baptist Press*, September 21, 1977, 30–31.

29. SBC Foreign Mission Board, "Foreign Missions," 41.

30. SBC Foreign Mission Board, "Foreign Missions," 41.

31. This is not to say that the members of the SBC did not also view social action as an important part of their Christian duty in and of itself, just that, in the context of this specific moment of strategic planning for missions, the SBC and other evangelical organizations emphasized the manner in which humanitarian assistance could benefit their broader evangelistic aims.

32. SBC Foreign Mission Board, "Foreign Missions," 23.

33. SBC Foreign Mission Board, "Foreign Missions," 23.

34. SBC Foreign Mission Board, "Foreign Missions," 27.

35. SBC Foreign Mission Board, "Foreign Missions," 27. Emphasis in original.

36. Matthew 25 (NRSV) includes the Parable of the Judgment, in which Jesus separates the sheep (the saved) from the goats (the damned). The sheep were those who had cared for the sick, poor, and afflicted; addressing them, Jesus stated that "just as you did it to one of the least of these who are members of my family, you did it to me."

37. Dan Martin, "Bold Mission Thrust Gets Major Boost," *Baptist Press*, August 23, 1976, 1. See also John J. Hurt, "Board Said Ready to Meet Disaster Needs Promptly," *Baptist Press*, February 6, 1976, 1–2; Mark Kelly, "Earthquake Makes Japanese Face Spiritual Issues, Missionary Says," *Baptist Press*, January 23, 1995, 1.

38. "Baptist Relief 'a Testimony' in Philippine Disaster Area," *Baptist Press*, August 31, 1976, 1.

39. "Baptist Relief," 1.

40. This language of opportunity became much more common in *Baptist Press* articles about natural disaster relief beginning in the mid-1970s.

41. "Relief Effort Fires Church," *Baptist Press*, September 20, 1979, 4.

42. Charlie Warren, "Baptist Doctors Calm Fears of Guatemala Quake Victims," *Baptist Press*, February 18, 1976, 1.

43. John J. Hurt, "Baptists Rebuild Guatemala, Leave Lasting Impressions," *Baptist Press*, February 1, 1978, 1.

44. "Baptists Mobilize Relief for Ecuador," *Baptist Press*, March 16, 1987, 3; Marty Croll, "Relief Arrives in Ecuador; Baptists Begin Distribution," *Baptist Press*, March 27, 1987, 1.

45. Bill Webb, "Hurricane Blows Open Doors of Opportunity," *Baptist Press*, January 20, 1982, 1.

46. Webb, "Hurricane Blows," 1.

47. Judy Garrett, "Mexico Earthquakes Spawn Church-Starting Project," *Baptist Press*, October 28, 1985, 1.

48. Dan Martin, "'Statistics Have Names': San Antonians in Guatemala," *Baptist Press*, March 12, 1976, 2.

49. "Graham's Global Mission to Reach Japan Quake Survivors, Rwandans," *Baptist Press*, February 9, 1995, 3.

50. "Graham's Global Mission," 3.

51. "Construction Workers Needed to Rebuild Guatemala Churches," *The Pentecostal Evangel*, July 16, 1976, 17.

52. Joye Bowman, "Until the Resurrection," *The Pentecostal Evangel*, April 4, 1976, 5.

53. "Pray for Guatemala Crusades," *The Pentecostal Evangel*, November 13, 1977, 17.

54. "Pray for Guatemala Crusades," 17.

55. Néstor Medina, "The New Jerusalem versus Social Responsibility: The Challenges of Pentecostalism in Guatemala," in *Perspectives in Pentecostal Eschatologies: World without End*, ed. Peter Althouse and Robby Waddell (Eugene: Wipf & Stock Publishers, 2010), 327. I discuss this (and Medina's argument in more detail) in my book *To Bring the Good News to All Nations* and in my 2015 *Diplomatic History* article. See Lauren Frances Turek, *To Bring the Good News to All Nations: Evangelical Influence on Human Rights and U.S. Foreign Relations* (Ithaca, NY: Cornell University Press, 2020); Lauren Frances Turek, "To

Support a 'Brother in Christ': Evangelical Groups and U.S.-Guatemalan Relations during the Ríos Montt Regime," *Diplomatic History* 39, no. 4 (September 2015): 689–719.

56. Medina, "New Jerusalem," 327.

57. Randy Frame, "A Year of Major Tests for Evangelical Relief Agencies," *Christianity Today*, January 17, 1986, https://www.christianitytoday.com/ct/1986/january-17/year-of-major-tests-for-evangelical-relief-agencies.html. As Mark Amstutz, Amy Reynolds, Stephen Offuttt, and other scholars have noted, the number, reach, and size of evangelical humanitarian organizations grew considerably in the decades after World War II. Indeed, the growth was so significant that, by the mid-1970s, the leaders of many of these agencies had begun to seek out greater collaboration and coordination within the evangelical humanitarian NGO community. In 1977, twelve key agencies came together to found the Association of Evangelical Relief and Development Organizations (AERDO), which over time expanded to encompass a wide range of such groups. Interestingly, this move developed concurrently with the broad evangelical effort to coordinate and collaborate on the project of global evangelism that emerged through events such as the International Congress on World Evangelization (ICOWE) and the subsequent Lausanne Movement. For details on post-war NGOs and AERDO, see Mark R. Amstutz, *Evangelicals and American Foreign Policy* (New York: Oxford University Press, 2013), 113; Amy Reynolds and Stephen Offutt, "Global Poverty and Evangelical Action," in *The New Evangelical Social Engagement*, ed. Brian Steensland and Philip Goff (New York: Oxford University Press, 2013), 244. For an example of post-ICOWE efforts at fostering transdenominational evangelistic cooperation and collaboration through the Lausanne Movement, see *Cooperating in World Evangelization: A Handbook on Church/Para-Church Relationships*, Lausanne Occasional Paper 24, 1983, https://www.lausanne.org/content/lop/lop-24.

58. Frame, "A Year of Major Tests."

59. Barrie Doyle, "'Good Samaritan' State: Federal Aid to Religion?," *Christianity Today*, November 10, 1972, https://www.christianitytoday.com/ct/1972/november-10/good-samaritan-state-federal-aid-to-religion.html. USAID required agencies that received funding to avoid proselytism when distributing that aid.

60. W. Stanley Mooneyham, "Ministering to the Hunger Belt," *Christianity Today*, January 3, 1975, https://www.christianitytoday.com/ct/1975/january-3/ministering-to-hunger-belt.html. Emphasis in original.

61. Mooneyham, "Ministering to the Hunger Belt."

62. C. René Padilla, "Evangelism and the World," in Douglas, *Let the Earth Hear His Voice*, 121. See also Carl F. H. Henry, "Strife over Social Concerns," *Christianity Today*, June 4, 1976, https://www.christianitytoday.com/ct/1976/june-4/footnotes.html.

63. Mooneyham, "Ministering to the Hunger Belt."

64. Mooneyham, "Ministering to the Hunger Belt."

65. Mooneyham, "Ministering to the Hunger Belt."

66. Lillian H. Graffam, "What in the World is the World Relief Commission Doing? WRC + Missions + Nationals," *Pulse: Special Report*, Evangelical Missions Information Service, August 1974, 1–2, Collection 309: Records of the National Religious Broadcasters, Box 49, Folder 3: World Relief Commission 1971–1977, Billy Graham Center Archives, Wheaton, Illinois (hereafter BGCA).

67. Graffam, "What in the World," 2.

68. Graffam, "What in the World," 2.

69. Lillian H. Graffam, "A Channel to the Needs of the World," *The Evangelical Beacon* 49, no. 22 (August 3, 1976): 9, http://collections.carli.illinois.edu/cdm/singleitem/collection/tiu_beacon/id/55/rec/11.

70. Ron Lee, "Starvation Takes Its Toll in Famine-Stricken Africa," *Christianity Today*, November 23, 1984, https://www.christianitytoday.com/ct/1984/november-23/starvation-takes-its-toll-in-famine-stricken-africa.html.

71. Lee, "Starvation Takes Its Toll."

72. Lee, "Starvation Takes Its Toll."

73. Graffam, "What in the World," 3.

74. Graffam, "What in the World," 3.

75. Padilla, "Evangelism and the World," 125; Donald McGavran, "The Dimensions of World Evangelization," in Douglas, *Let the Earth Hear His Voice*, 94–100.

76. "Zaire Protestants: A Good First Century," *Christianity Today*, December 15, 1978, https://www.christianitytoday.com/ct/1978/december-15/zaire-protestants-good-first-century.html. Zaire is now known as the Democratic Republic of the Congo.

77. World Relief Commission, News Release #75-8A, July 18, 1975, Collection 309: Records of the National Religious Broadcasters, Box 49, Folder 3: World Relief Commission 1971–1977, BGCA.

78. World Relief Commission, News Release #75-8A; Mission Aviation Fellowship, "Guatemala Report," 1976, Collection 309: Records of the National Religious Broadcasters, Box 49, Folder 3: World Relief Commission 1971–1977, BGCA. Emphasis in original.

79. Lee, "Starvation Takes Its Toll"; Graffam, "A Channel"; Randy Frame, "Africa: Still in Need of Daily Bread," *Christianity Today*, 18 October 18, 1985, https://www.christianitytoday.com/ct/1985/october-18/africa-still-in-need-of-daily-bread.html.

80. James O. Mason, "Humanitarian Aid: The Challenge of Self-Reliance," in *Global Mormonism in the 21st Century*, ed. Reid L. Neilson (Provo: Religious Studies Center, Brigham Young University, 2008), 149–159.

81. Flake does not specifically address evangelism in this chapter, but the language of "demonstrat[ing] the gospel" through relief does echo language used by evangelicals to frame relief work. Garry R. Flake, "Building Bridges of Understanding through Church Humanitarian Assistance," in Nelson, *Global Mormonism in the 21st Century*, 175–180.

8. Inventing Rupture in India and America

1. Limpan Raika, interview with author, Mutaguda, Odisha, India, June 22, 2014. Typescript.

2. The RLDS Church emerged in the American Midwest in the mid-nineteenth century as the second largest Latter Day Saint tradition church. Led by descendants of Joseph Smith Jr., the early and mid-twentieth-century RLDS Church might be best characterized as "neither fully Protestant nor fully Mormon." RLDS members in general hearkened back to an earlier era of Mormonism, the 1830s Kirtland period, as a model for their beliefs and practices. As such, they rejected the Latter-day Saint Church's mid-nineteenth-century practice of polygamy, rejected the doctrines of baptism for the

dead and other Latter-day Saint temple ordinances, embraced the Book of Mormon and Doctrine and Covenants as scripture, maintained that their church had exclusive sacramental and sacerdotal powers, ordained men from all races into a multitiered priesthood, and believed in the doctrine of gathering to the "center place" of Zion (Independence, Missouri). However, they were also influenced by liberal Protestantism, especially currents of the Social Gospel movement that they allowed to flow into their doctrines about Zion. This openness to liberal Protestant theology would be amplified many times over in the 1960s, as will be seen. Roger D. Launius, "'Neither Mormon nor Protestant': The Reorganized Church and the Challenge of Identity," in *Mormon Identities in Transition*, ed. Douglas J. Davies (New York: Cassell, 1996), 52–60; David J. Howlett, "The Death and Resurrection of the RLDS Zion: A Case Study in 'Failed Prophecy,'" *Dialogue: A Journal of Mormon Thought* 40, no. 3 (2007): 115–116.

3. Martin Holbraad, Bruce Kapferer, and Julia F. Sauma, eds., *Ruptures: The Anthropologies of Discontinuity in Times of Turmoil* (London: UCL Press, 2019), 1.

4. Joel Robbins, "On the Paradoxes of Global Pentecostalism and the Perils of Continuity Thinking," *Religion* 33, no. 3 (2003): 221–231; Joel Robbins, Bambi B. Schieffelin, and Aparecida Vilaça, "Evangelical Conversion and the Transformation of the Self in Amazonia and Melanesia: Christianity and the Revival of Anthropological Comparison," *Comparative Studies in Society and History* 56, no. 3 (2014): 559–590; Kimberly Jenkins Marshall, *Upward, Not Sunwise: Resonant Rupture in Navajo Neo-Pentecostalism* (Lincoln, NE: University of Nebraska Press, 2016).

5. Robbins, "On the Paradoxes of Global Pentecostalism," 230.

6. Joel Robbins, "Afterword: Some Reflections on Rupture," in Holbraad, Kapferer, and Sauma, *Ruptures*, 220.

7. Taunalyn F. Rutherford, "The Internationalization of Mormonism: Indications from India," in *Out of Obscurity: Mormonism since 1945*, ed. Patrick Q. Mason and John G. Turner (New York: Oxford University Press, 2016), 37–62; David J. Howlett and John-Charles Duffy, *Mormonism: The Basics* (New York: Routledge, 2016), 156–162.

8. Nandini Sundar, "Introduction: Of the Scheduled Tribes, States, and Sociology," in *The Scheduled Tribes and Their India: Politics, Identities, Policies, and Work*, ed. Nandini Sundar (New York: Oxford University Press, 2016), 1–7.

9. Piers Vitebsky, "Stones, Shamans, and Pastors: Pagan and Baptist Temporalities of Death in Tribal India," in *Taming Time, Timing Death: Social Technologies and Ritual*, ed. Dorthe Refslund Christensen and Rane Willerslev (New York: Routledge, 2013), 120; Piers Vitebsky, *Living without the Dead: Loss and Redemption in a Jungle Cosmos* (Chicago: University of Chicago Press, 2017), 9.

10. Vitebsky, "The Sora 'Tribe'—Animist, Hindu, Christian," online supplement to *Living without the Dead*, 6, http://www.press.uchicago.edu/sites/Vitebsky.

11. Verrier Elwin, *The Religion of an Indian Tribe* (New York: Oxford University Press, 1955); Piers Vitebsky, *Dialogues with the Dead: The Discussion of Mortality among the Sora of Eastern India* (Cambridge: Cambridge University Press, 1993); Vitebsky, *Living without the Dead*.

12. Vitebsky, "The Sora 'Tribe,'" 12.

13. Vitebsky, *Living without the Dead*, 119–123.

14. Vitebsky, *Dialogues with the Dead*, 5; Vitebsky, *Living without the Dead*, 8–9, 21–22, 29–31.

15. Vitebsky, "The Sora 'Tribe,'" 29.

16. Robbins, "The Perils of Continuity Thinking," 224.

17. Vitebsky, *Dialogues with the Dead*, 53. Vitebsky suggests that a better translation of *sonum* would be "Memory," or a form of personhood that is an embodied memory.

18. An article for the RLDS official magazine, the *Saints' Herald*, included a photo with the caption, "Members of a Sora family holding 'sacred Hindu pots' which are to be destroyed prior to the baptismal service." Naomi Russell, "So Much for So Little: A Report on the Growth of the Church in India," *Saints' Herald* 114, no. 1 (January 1, 1967): 9.

19. Vitebsky, *Dialogues with the Dead*, 20; Paul Raito, interview with author, Chudangapur Village, Odisha, India, June 28, 2014, typescript.

20. Baidi Mandal, interview with author, Badakua Village, Odisha, India, June 28, 2014, typescript.

21. Birgit Meyer, "Pentecostalism and Globalization," in *Studying Global Pentecostalism: Theories and Methods*, ed. Allan Anderson, Michael Bergunder, Andre F. Droogers, and Cornelis van der Laan (Berkeley: University of California Press, 2010), 121.

22. David J. Howlett, "Why Denominations Can Climb Hills: RLDS Conversions in Highland Tribal India and Midwestern America, 1964–2001," *Church History* 89, no. 3 (2020): 633–658.

23. James C. Scott, *The Art of Not Being Governed: An Anarchist History of Upland Southeast Asia* (New Haven: Yale University Press, 2009), 325; Vitebsky, "The Sora 'Tribe,'" 20–21.

24. In 2018, American administrators finally imposed their organizational polity onto Sora congregations, and the largest and most rural Sora congregations disaffiliated with the Community of Christ (the name of the RLDS Church since 2001). This included the oldest Sora congregations within the now defunct RLDS East India Mission.

25. Vibha Joshi, *A Matter of Belief: Christian Conversion and Healing in North-East India* (New York: Berghahn Books, 2013), 9; Marshall, *Upward, Not Sunwise*, 15–16.

26. Nathaniel Roberts, *To Be Cared For: The Power of Conversion and Foreignness of Belonging in an Indian Slum* (Berkeley: University of California Press, 2016), 8; Laura Dudley Jenkins, *Religious Freedom and Mass Conversion in India* (Philadelphia: University of Pennsylvania Press, 2019), 136–140.

27. Goldie Osuri, *Religious Freedom in India: Sovereignty and (Anti) Conversion* (New York: Routledge, 2013), 32–33.

28. Goldie Osuri, "The Concern for Sovereignty in the Politics of Anti-Conversion," *Religion Compass* 7, no. 9 (2013): 389.

29. Vitebsky, "The Sora 'Tribe,'" 15–16.

30. Osuri, *Religious Freedom in India*, 32–33.

31. Ronald Neufeldt, "Hindutva and the Rhetoric of Violence: Interpreting the Past, Designing the Future," in *The Twenty-First Century Confronts Its Gods: Globalization, Technology and War*, ed. David J. Hawkins (Albany: State University of New York Press, 2004), 167.

32. As quoted in Sebastian C. H. Kim, *In Search of Identity: Debates on Religious Conversion in India* (New York: Oxford University Press, 2003), 76–77.

33. Osuri, *Religious Freedom in India*, 59.

34. Osuri, *Religious Freedom in India*, 59–60; Jenkins, *Religious Freedom and Mass Conversion in India*, 146–147.

35. Pralay Kanungo, "Hindutva's Entry into a 'Hindu Province': Early Years of RSS in Orissa," *Economic and Political Weekly* 38, no. 1 (2003): 3299–3300; Pralay Kanungo, *RSS's Tryst with Politics: From Hedgewar to Sudarshan* (Delhi: Manohar, 2002), 150–153.

36. Pinky Hota, "Affecting Violence: Development, Religion and Indigeneity in Kandhamal" (PhD diss., University of Chicago, 2012), 167.

37. William T. Higdon, "With the Khonds of Koraput: Saints in India Take the Initiative in Sharing the Gospel," *Saints' Herald* 134, no. 2 (February 1987): 52; Chad Bauman, "Hindu-Christian Conflict in India: Globalization, Conversion, and the Coterminal Castes and Tribes," *Journal of Asian Studies* 72, no. 3 (2013): 633–653.

38. Jenkins, *Religious Freedom and Mass Conversion in India*, 152.

39. Kanungo, *RSS's Tryst with Politics*, 154–156.

40. Jenkins, *Religious Freedom and Mass Conversion in India*, 156.

41. Bauman, "Hindu-Christian Conflict in India," 634.

42. Larry W. Conrad and Paul Shupe, "An RLDS Reformation? Constructing the Task of RLDS Theology," *Dialogue: A Journal of Mormon Thought* 18, no. 2 (1985): 92–103; Mark A. Scherer, *The Journey of a People: The Era of Worldwide Community, 1946 to 2015* (Independence, MO: Community of Christ Seminary Press, 2016), 283; Matthew Bolton, *Apostle of the Poor: The Life and Work of Missionary and Humanitarian Charles D. Neff* (Independence, MO: John Whitmer Books, 2005), 46; David Hollinger, *Protestants Abroad: How Missionaries Tried to Change the World but Changed America* (Princeton: Princeton University Press, 2018).

43. Hiroshi Yamada, *Japan Church History* (Independence, MO: Temple School, Reorganized Church of Jesus Christ of Latter Day Saints, 2000), 59–60; Kisuke Sekine, "Interpreting Our Message to the Japanese," *Saints' Herald* 104, no. 21 (May 27, 1957): 492.

44. Bolton, *Apostle of the Poor*, 35–44.

45. W. Wallace Smith, "Statement on Objectives for the Church," *Saints' Herald* 113, no. 10 (May 15, 1966): 342–344. Neff and two apostles wrote the objectives, but the RLDS Prophet-President W. Wallace Smith published the document under his signature to indicate it was official church policy.

46. William R. Hutchinson, *Errand to the World: American Protestant Thought and Foreign Missions* (Chicago: University of Chicago Press, 1987), 79–80; Dana L. Robert, "The First Globalization? The Internationalization of the Protestant Missionary Movement between the Wars," *International Bulletin of Missionary Research* 26, no. 2 (2002): 54–58.

47. Charles D. Neff, "What Shall We Teach?" *Saints' Herald* 114, no. 21 (November 1, 1967): 726–727.

48. Chrystal Vanel, "Community of Christ: An American Progressive Christianity, with Mormonism as an Option," *Dialogue: A Journal of Mormon Thought* 50, no. 3 (2017): 39–72.

49. Richard P. Howard, "The RLDS Church's Directive on Baptism of Saora Tribal Polygamists: Canonizing Administrative Policy, 1967–1972," in *The Persistence of Polygamy: From Joseph Smith's Martyrdom to the First Manifesto, 1844–1890*, ed. Newell G. Bringhurst and Craig L. Foster (Independence, MO: John Whitmer Books, 2013), 326–357; Bolton, *Apostle of the Poor*, 65–74.

50. *World Conference Bulletin*, April 9, 1972, 168, 170.

51. Doctrine and Covenants (RLDS) 150:10a–b.

52. Richard Price, *The Saints at the Crossroads* (Independence, MO: Price Publishing Company, 1974), 206–207.

53. "World View: Why Are the Dead So Lonely?" *Saints' Herald* 125, no. 1 (January 1978): 15–16, reprinted from Alan R. Beals, George Spindler, and Louise S. Spindler, *Culture in Process*, 2nd ed. (New York: Holt, Rinehart, and Winston, 1973), 107–110.

54. "American Worldview," *Saints' Herald* 125, no. 1 (January 1978): 17, reprinted from E. Adamson Hoebel, *Anthropology: The Study of Man* (New York: McGraw Hill, 1972), 554–557.

55. First Presidency, "The Nature of New Revelation," *Saints' Herald* 131, no. 3 (February 1, 1984): 51.

56. William D. Russell, "The Last Smith Presidents and the Transformation of the RLDS Church," *Journal of Mormon History* 34, no. 3 (2008): 66–68.

57. Jim Cable, "Our International Evangelistic Calling: President McMurray Ponders Sri Lanka and India Journey," *Saints' Herald* 144, no. 6 (June 1997): 226.

58. Eric Hobsbawm and Terence O. Ranger, eds., *The Invention of Tradition* (Cambridge: Cambridge University Press, 1983); Joel Robbins, "Continuity Thinking and the Problem of Christian Culture: Belief, Time, and the Anthropology of Christianity," *Current Anthropology* 48, no. 1 (2007): 5–38. For a critique of thinking about "tradition" as something "invented," see Michael L. Satlow, "Tradition: The Power of Constraint," in *The Cambridge Companion to Religious Studies*, ed. Robert A. Orsi (Cambridge: Cambridge University Press, 2012), 130–150.

9. Technological Christianity

1. Blair R. Holmes and Alan E. Keele, eds. and trans., *When Truth Was Treason: German Youth against Hitler*, 2nd ed. (Provo, UT: Stratford Books, 2020), 148, 159, 191.

2. Holmes and Keele, *When Truth Was Treason*, 156–161.

3. Holmes and Keele, *When Truth Was Treason*, 278.

4. Holmes and Keele, *When Truth Was Treason*, 57.

5. "Helmuth Hübener," Gedenkstätte Deutscher Widerstand, https://web.archive.org/web/20180226043108/https://www.gdw-berlin.de/en/recess/biographies/index_of_persons/biographie/view-bio/helmuth-huebener.

6. John Durham Peters, "Mormonism and Media," in *The Oxford Handbook of Mormonism*, ed. Philip L. Barlow and Terryl Givens (New York: Oxford University Press, 2015), 407.

7. For example, see Geoffrey Winthrop-Young, "Cultural Techniques: Preliminary Remarks," in "Cultural Techniques," ed. Geoffrey Winthrop-Young, Ilinica Iurascu, and Jussi Parikka, special issue, *Theory, Culture, and Society* 30, no. 6 (November 2013): 3–19; Sybille Krämer and Horst Bredekamp, "Culture, Technology, Cultural Techniques—Moving Beyond Text," in Winthrop-Young, Iurascu, and Parikka, "Cultural Techniques," 20–29; Jussi Parikka, "Afterword: Cultural Techniques and Media Studies," in Winthrop-Young, Iurascu, and Parikka, "Cultural Techniques," 147–159.

8. Tom Ullrich, "Working on Barricades and Boulevards: Cultural Techniques of Revolution in Nineteenth-Century Paris," in *Cultural Techniques: Assembling Spaces, Texts*

and Collectives, ed. Jörg Dünne, Kathrin Fehringer, Kristina Kuhn, and Wolfgang Struck (Berlin: Walter de Gruyter, 2020), 23–45.

9. Melissa Wei-Tsing Inouye, "Cultural Technologies: The Long and Unexpected Life of the Christian Mission Encounter, North China, 1900–30," *Modern Asian Studies* 53, no. 6 (November 2019): 2007–2040.

10. Peters, "Mormonism and Media," 411.

11. Inouye, "Cultural Technologies."

12. Shobana Shankar, "Medical Missionaries and Modernizing Emirs in Colonial Hausaland: Leprosy Control and Native Authority in the 1930s," *Journal of African History* 48, no. 1 (March 2007): 45–68; Joachim Kurtz, "Messenger of the Sacred Heart: Li Wenyu (1840–1911) and the Jesuit Periodical Press in Late Qing Shanghai," in *From Woodblocks to the Internet: Chinese Publishing and Print Culture in Transition, circa 1800 to 2008*, ed. Cynthia Brokaw and Christopher A. Reed (Leiden: Brill, 2010), 82–91.

13. David M. Gordon, "Conflicting Conversions and Unexpected Christianities in Central Africa," in *Cultural Conversions: Unexpected Consequences of Christian Missionary Encounters in the Middle East, Africa, and South Asia*, ed. Heather J. Sharkey (Syracuse: Syracuse University Press, 2013), 29–48; Hyaeweol Choi, *Gender and Mission Encounters in Korea: New Women, Old Ways* (Berkeley: University of California Press, 2009), 25; Kwok Pui-lan, "Chinese Women and Protestant Christianity," in *Christianity in China: From the Eighteenth Century to the Present*, ed. Daniel H. Bays (Stanford: Stanford University Press, 1996), 200–201; J. Riley Case, "Interpreting Karen Christianity: The American Baptist Reaction to Asian Christianity in the Nineteenth Century," in *The Changing Face of Christianity: Africa, the West, and the World*, ed. Lamin Sanneh and Joel A. Carpenter (Oxford: Oxford University Press, 2005), 137–139; Ngo Thi Thanh Tam, "The 'Short-Waved' Faith: Christian Broadcasting and Protestant Conversion of the Hmong in Vietnam," in *Mediating Piety: Technology and Religion in Contemporary Asia*, ed. Francis Khek Gee Lim (Leiden: Brill, 2009), 139–158; Young-Hoon Lee, "The Korean Holy Spirit Movement in Relation to Pentecostalism," in *Asian and Pentecostal: The Charismatic Face of Christianity in Asia*, rev. ed., ed. Allan Anderson and Edmond Tang (Eugene: Wipf and Stock, 2011), 413–417.

14. Winthrop-Young, "Cultural Techniques," 7.

15. Inouye, "Cultural Technologies."

16. Melissa Wei-Tsing Inouye, "Miraculous Modernity: Charismatic Traditions and Trajectories within Chinese Protestant Christianity," in *Modern Chinese Religion II: 1850–2015*, 2 vols., ed. Jan Kiely, Vincent Goossaert, and John Lagerwey (Leiden: Brill, 2015), 884–919.

17. Choi, *Gender and Mission Encounters in Korea*, 25, 64, 70.

18. Lee, "Korean Holy Spirit Movement," 413–417.

19. Shakhar Rahav, *The Rise of Political Intellectuals in May Fourth Societies and the Roots of Mass-Party Politics* (New York: Oxford University Press, 2015), 50–58.

20. Stuart Schram, *Mao Tse-Tung* (New York: Penguin Books, 1966), 68–69.

21. Charles A. Keller, "The Christian Student Movement, YMCAs, and Transnationalism," *Journal of American-East Asian Relations* 13 (2004–2006): 62–63.

22. Lori Ferrell, *The Bible and the People* (New Haven: Yale University Press, 2009), 60–62; Lamin Sanneh, *Translating the Message: The Missionary Impact on Culture* (Maryknoll, NY: Orbis Books, 1989).

23. Henrietta Harrison, *The Missionary's Curse and Other Tales from a Chinese Catholic Village* (Berkeley: University of California Press, 2013), 50, 203.

24. Peill's report for 1917 notes reports of early use of Wang-Peill script in Shandong and Fujian as well. Sidney G. Peill, Report for 1917, Cangzhou, London Missionary Society, North China Reports, 1917, Box 8, Council for World Mission Archive, SOAS Library, University of London; numerous LMS missionaries serving in North China during this time mention the benefits of "phonetic" in their reports.

25. Sidney G. Peill, "Paper Written by Request for the 1923 Conference of the China Medical Missionary Association," Council for World Mission Archive, MFC 266.0095. L846CN, fiche 755, Special Collections, Au Shue Hung Memorial Library, Hong Kong Baptist University.

26. Peill, "Paper Written by Request."

27. Ivy Greaves, Report for 1926, Beijing, London Missionary Society, North China Reports, 1926, Box 9, Council for World Mission Archive, SOAS Library, University of London.

28. Joseph Tse-Hei Lee, "Gospel and Gender: Female Christians in Chaozhou, South China," in *Pioneer Chinese Christian Women: Gender, Christianity, and Social Mobility*, ed. Jessie G. Lutz (Bethlehem, PA: Lehigh University Press, 2010), 182–198.

29. Ling Oi Ki, "Bible Women," in Lutz, *Pioneer Chinese Christian Women*, 246–266.

30. Melissa Wei-Tsing Inouye, *China and the True Jesus: Charisma and Organization in a Chinese Christian Church* (New York: Oxford University Press, 2019).

31. Robert Ross, "Congregations, Missionaries and the Grahamstown Schism of 1842–3," in *The London Missionary Society in Southern Africa, 1799–1999: Historical Essays in Celebration of the Bicentenary of the LMS in Southern Africa*, ed. John de Gruchy (Athens, OH: Ohio University Press, 2000), 120.

32. Samuel Evans Meech, Letter, April 25, 1877, Beijing, North China Box no. 1–25, Incoming Letters 1860–1927, Council for World Mission Archive, MFC 266.0095. L846CN, fiche 52-53B, Special Collections, Au Shue Hung Memorial Library, Hong Kong Baptist University.

33. Ross, "Grahamstown Schism," 120–131; Elizabeth Elbourne, "Whose Gospel? Conflict in the LMS in the Early 1840s," in de Gruchy, *The London Missionary Society in Southern Africa*, 132–155.

34. J. D. Liddell, Report for 1917, Beijing countryside, London Missionary Society, North China Reports, 1917, Box 8, Council for World Mission Archive, SOAS Library, University of London.

35. Liddell, Report for 1917.

36. Arnold G. Bryson, Report for 1930, Cangzhou, North China Reports, MFC 266.0095.L846CN, fiche 774, Special Collections, Au Shue Hung Memorial Library, Hong Kong Baptist University.

37. For more on the True Jesus Church, see Xi Lian, *Redeemed by Fire: The Rise of Popular Christianity in Modern China* (New Haven: Yale University Press, 2010); Xi Lian, "A Messianic Deliverance for Post-Dynastic China: The Launch of the True Jesus Church in the Early Twentieth Century," *Modern China* 34, no. 4 (October 2008): 407–441; Chen Yang Kao, "The Cultural Revolution and the Emergence of Pentecostal-Style Protestantism in China," *Journal of Contemporary Religion* 24, no. 2 (May 2009): 171–188; Daniel H. Bays, "Indigenous Protestant Churches in China, 1900–1937: A Pentecostal

Case Study," in *Indigenous Responses to Western Christianity*, ed. Steven Kaplan (New York: New York University Press, 1995), 124–143; and Inouye, *China and the True Jesus*.

38. Evan E. Bryant, Report for 1927, Cangzhou, North China Reports, Council for World Mission Archive, MFC 266.0095 L846CN, fiche 768, Special Collections, Au Shue Hung Memorial Library, Hong Kong Baptist University.

39. Edith S. Murray, Report for 1928, Cangzhou, North China Reports, Council for World Mission Archive, MFC 266.0095 L846CN, fiche 770, Special Collections, Au Shue Hung Memorial Library, Hong Kong Baptist University.

40. Melissa Wei-Tsing Inouye, "Charismatic Crossings: Bernt Berntsen and Wei Enbo, and the Beginnings of Chinese Pentecostal Christianity," in *Global Charismatic and Pentecostal Chinese Christianity*, ed. Fenggang Yang, Joy K. C. Tong, and Allan H. Anderson (Leiden: Brill, 2017), 91–117.

41. Inouye, *China and the True Jesus*, 157–186.

42. Inouye, *China and the True Jesus*, 272.

43. Terryl Givens and Brian Hauglid, *The Pearl of Greatest Price: Mormonism's Most Controversial Scripture* (New York: Oxford University Press, 2019), 11.

44. Givens and Hauglid, *Pearl of Greatest Price*, 12.

45. Givens and Hauglid, *Pearl of Greatest Price*, 1, 11.

46. See Lester E. Bush Jr., "Mormonism's Negro Doctrine: An Historical Overview," *Dialogue: A Journal of Mormon Thought* 8, no. 1 (Spring 1973): 11–68; Armand L. Mauss, *All Abraham's Children: Changing Mormon Conceptions of Race and Lineage* (Urbana: University of Illinois Press, 2003); W. Paul Reeve, *Religion of a Different Color: Race and the Mormon Struggle for Whiteness* (New York: Oxford University Press, 2015); "Brazil: Joy of an Eternal Covenant," Global Histories, The Church of Jesus Christ of Latter-day Saints, https://web.archive.org/web/20200803122550/https://www.churchofjesuschrist.org/study/history/global-histories/brazil/stories-of-faith/br-04-joy-of-an-eternal-covenant?lang=eng.

47. Russell Richey, *The Methodist Conference in America: A History* (Durham, NC: Kingswood Books, 1996); Ferrell, *The Bible and the People*.

48. Terryl L. Givens, *By the Hand of Mormon: The American Scripture That Launched a New World Religion* (New York: Oxford University Press, 2003).

49. Peters, "Mormonism and Media," 412.

50. Jonathan A. Stapley, *The Power of Godliness: Mormon Liturgy and Cosmology* (New York: Oxford University Press, 2018).

51. Samuel Morris Brown, *In Heaven as It Is on Earth: Joseph Smith and the Early Mormon Conquest of Death* (New York: Oxford University Press, 2012).

52. Laurel Thatcher Ulrich, *A House Full of Females: Plural Marriage and Women's Rights in Early Mormonism, 1835–1870* (New York: Alfred A. Knopf, 2017); Brown, *In Heaven as It Is on Earth*; Kathryn M. Daynes, *More Wives than One: Transformation of the Mormon Marriage System, 1840–1910* (Urbana: University of Illinois Press, 2001).

53. Stapley, *The Power of Godliness*.

54. Cologne Branch Relief Society Minutes and Records, 1928–1972, LR 1868 14, Volume 1 (1928–1930), Church History Library, the Church of Jesus Christ of Latter-day Saints, Salt Lake City, Utah.

55. See, for instance, Jill Mulvay Derr, Carol Cornwall Madsen, Kate Holbrook, and Matthew J. Grow, eds., *The First Fifty Years of Relief Society: Key Documents in Latter-day*

Saint Women's History (Salt Lake City: Church Historian's Press, 2016); Matthew J. Grow and R. Eric Smith, eds., *The Council of Fifty: What the Records Reveal about Mormon History* (Provo, UT: Religious Studies Center, 2017); D. Michael Quinn, *The Mormon Hierarchy: Origins of Power* (Salt Lake City: Signature Books, 1994).

56. Daynes, *More Wives than One*.

57. Kenneth Beesley and Dirk Elzinga, eds., *An 1860 English-Hopi Vocabulary Written in the Deseret Alphabet* (Salt Lake City: University of Utah Press, 2015).

58. Beesley and Elzinga, *English-Hopi Vocabulary*, 10.

59. Nauvoo Relief Society, Minutes, July 15, 1843, "A Book of Records, Containing the Proceedings of the Female Relief Society of Nauvoo," Minute Book, March 17, 1842–March 16, 1844, 97, Joseph Smith Papers, https://www.josephsmithpapers.org/paper-summary/nauvoo-relief-society-minute-book/120.

60. Ronald W. Walker, *Wayward Saints: The Godbeites and Brigham Young* (Urbana: University of Illinois Press, 1998).

10. Missing Missiology

1. Such publications included, in particular, the *International Bulletin of Missionary Research* and *World Christian Database*; such scholarly societies included the Yale-Edinburgh Group on World Christianity and the History of Mission, the International Association for Mission Studies, and the American Society of Missiology.

2. Ronald E. Bartholomew, "From the Margins to the Center: Latter-day Saint Integration in the Mission Studies Academy" (presentation, Mormon History Association Annual Meeting, Salt Lake City, Utah, June 9, 2019). Joel Stoker presented at the Yale-Edinburgh Group conference in 2012 on the Mormon missiological enterprise, venturing the first such paper within the predominant mission-historical societies, a preliminary effort compared to the broader body of missiological scholarship.

3. Thomas G. Alexander, "The Church and Its Missions," in *Mormonism in Transition: A History of the Latter-day Saints, 1890–1930*, 3rd ed. (Salt Lake City: Greg Kofford Books, 2012), 223–250; James B. Allen and Glen M. Leonard, *The Story of the Latter-day Saints*, 2nd ed. (Salt Lake City: Deseret Book, 2013), 567–568; Sheri L. Dew, *Go Forward with Faith: The Biography of Gordon B. Hinckley* (Salt Lake City: Deseret Book, 1996), 208, 232; Franklin J. Murdock, Oral History, 1973, OH 89, Church History Library, Salt Lake City, Utah (hereafter CHL); Edwin (Ned) C. Winder, Oral History, 1974, OH 68, CHL.

4. David Golding, "Latter-day Saint Missionaries Called by Year, 1830–2020," May 18, 2021, https://doi.org/10.5281/zenodo.4768754; see Todd M. Johnson and Gina A. Zurlo, eds., *World Christian Database* (Leiden: Brill, 2021). Estimated totals from 1890 calculated from Edwin Munsell Bliss, "Appendix E: Statistical Tables § General Summary," in *The Encyclopaedia of Missions: Descriptive, Historical, Biographical, Statistical*, ed. Edwin Munsell Bliss, 2 vols. (New York: Funk and Wagnalls, 1891), 2:626–634.

5. See *Studies in Mormon History*, Harold B. Lee Library, Brigham Young University, http://smh.lib.byu.edu; Church History Catalog, http://catalog.churchofjesuschrist.org.

6. David J. Bosch, *Transforming Mission: Paradigm Shifts in Theology of Mission* (Maryknoll, NY: Orbis Books, 1991), xv.

7. David Golding, "Mormon Mission in Concept and Practice: From Apocalyptic Gathering to Teaching Salvation," in *World Religions and Their Missions*, 2nd ed., ed. Aaron J. Ghiloni (New York: Peter Lang, 2022), 203–231.

8. Mission theology does not appear in fairly recent reviews of Mormon theology; see Terryl L. Givens, *Wrestling the Angel: The Foundations of Mormon Thought; Cosmos, God, Humanity* (New York: Oxford University Press, 2015); Terryl L. Givens, *Feeding the Flock: The Foundations of Mormon Thought; Church and Praxis* (New York: Oxford University Press, 2017); Charles R. Harrell, *"This Is My Doctrine": The Development of Mormon Theology* (Salt Lake City: Greg Kofford Books, 2011).

9. William R. Hutchison, *Errand to the World: American Protestant Thought and Foreign Missions* (Chicago: University of Chicago Press, 1987).

10. See Wilbert R. Shenk, "The Role of Theory in Mission Studies," *Missiology: An International Review* 24, no. 1 (January 1996): 32. Compare Joseph Smith, "Revelation, February 1829 [D&C 4]," Documents series, Joseph Smith Papers (hereafter JSP), http://josephsmithpapers.org; William Orme, *Memoirs, Including Letters and Select Remains of John Urquhart, Late of the University of St. Andrew's*, 2nd ed. (London: Holdsworth and Ball, 1828); 2 Peter 1.

11. Hutchison, *Errand to the World*.

12. Emily Conroy-Krutz, *Christian Imperialism: Converting the World in the Early American Republic* (Ithaca, NY: Cornell University Press, 2015); Edward E. Andrews, *Native Apostles: Black and Indian Missionaries in the British Atlantic World* (Cambridge, MA: Harvard University Press, 2013); Jay Riley Case, *An Unpredictable Gospel: American Evangelicals and World Christianity, 1812–1920* (New York: Oxford University Press, 2012).

13. Hutchison, *Errand to the World*, chap. 2.

14. Brian Stanley, *The World Missionary Conference: Edinburgh, 1910* (Grand Rapids, MI: William B. Eerdmans, 2009).

15. Dana L. Robert, "Naming 'World Christianity': The Yale-Edinburgh Conference in Historical Perspective" (presentation, Yale-Edinburgh Group Conference, Yale University, New Haven, CT, June 27, 2019); Brian Stanley, "Mission Studies and Historical Research: Past Trends and Future Trajectories," (seminar, Christian Missions in Global History, University of Edinburgh, Edinburgh, UK, October 10, 2012), http://www.history.ac.uk/podcasts/christian-missions-global-history/mission-studies-and-historical-research-past-trends-and; Kenneth Scott Latourette, *History of the Expansion of Christianity*, 7 vols. (New York: Harper and Brothers, 1937–1945).

16. David A. Hollinger, *Protestants Abroad: How Missionaries Tried to Change the World but Changed America* (Princeton: Princeton University Press, 2017), 60–93.

17. Stanley, "Mission Studies and Historical Research."

18. John K. Fairbank, "Assignment for the '70s," *American Historical Review* 74, no. 1 (February 1969): 861–879.

19. Stephen Neill, *A History of Christian Missions* (Baltimore: Penguin Books, 1964), 572.

20. Foremost among this literature is Edward W. Said, *Orientalism* (New York: Random House, 1978), and Jean Comaroff and John Comaroff, *Of Revelation and Revolution*, 2 vols. (Chicago: University of Chicago Press, 1991, 1997); others include Vine Deloria Jr., "Missionaries and the Religious Vacuum," in *Custer Died for Your Sins: An Indian Manifesto* (New York: Simon and Schuster, 1969), 101–124; Vine Deloria Jr., *God*

Is Red: A Native View of Religion (New York: Putnam, 1973); George E. Tinker, *Missionary Conquest: The Gospel and Native American Cultural Genocide* (Minneapolis: Augsburg Fortress, 1993); Arthur Schlesinger Jr., "The Missionary Enterprise and Theories of Imperialism," in *The Missionary Enterprise in China and America*, ed. John K. Fairbank (Cambridge, MA: Harvard University Press, 1974), 336–373; William R. Hutchison and Torben Christensen, eds., *Missionary Ideologies in the Imperialist Era: 1880–1920* (Aarhus: Christensens Bogtrykkeri, 1982).

21. Leaders of this development included David J. Bosch, *Transforming Mission: Paradigm Shifts in Theology of Mission* (Maryknoll, NY: Orbis, 1991); Paul F. Knitter, *One Earth Many Religions: Multifaith Dialogue and Global Responsibility* (Maryknoll, NY: Orbis, 1995); Andrew F. Walls, *The Missionary Movement in Christian History: Studies in the Transmission of Faith* (Edinburgh: T&T Clark; Maryknoll, NY: Orbis, 1996); Adrian Hastings, ed., *A World History of Christianity* (Grand Rapids, MI: William B. Eerdmans, 1999). See also Religious Studies and Mission Studies Section of the Academic Association for Theology and the Administrative Board of the German Association for Mission Studies, "Mission Studies as Intercultural Theology and Its Relationship to Religious Studies," *Mission Studies* 25, no. 1 (April 2008): 103–108. These trends in critical theory followed the larger historiography since the 1970s. The impact of the linguistic turn and Marxism on historical scholarship in addition to foreign missions historiography cannot be overstated; see Elizabeth A. Clark, *History, Theory, Text: Historians and the Linguistic Turn* (Cambridge, MA: Harvard University Press, 2004). In two influential essays, Mark A. Noll argued that missiology was the way through the crises postmodern approaches brought to modern historiography given its central focus on international and global events and processes: Noll, "The Challenges of Contemporary Church History, the Dilemmas of Modern History, and Missiology to the Rescue," *Missiology* 24, no. 1 (January 1996): 47–64; Noll, "The Potential of Missiology for the Crises of History," in *History and the Christian Historian*, ed. Ronald A. Wells (Grand Rapids, MI: William B. Eerdmans, 1998), 106–123.

22. John K. Fairbank thought missionary history particularly insightful for Asian studies and Sinology, a view recent scholarship has confirmed in several noteworthy studies: Alvyn Austin, *China's Millions: The China Inland Mission and Late Qing Society, 1832–1905* (Grand Rapids, MI: William B. Eerdmans, 2007); Liam Matthew Brockey, *Journey to the East: The Jesuit Mission to China, 1579–1724* (Cambridge, MA: Harvard University Press, 2007); Jessie Gregory Lutz, *Opening China: Karl F. A. Gutzlaff and Sino-Western Relations, 1827–1852* (Grand Rapids, MI: William B. Eerdmans, 2008); Xi Lian, *Redeemed by Fire: The Rise of Popular Christianity in Modern China* (New Haven: Yale University Press, 2010); Jonathan Y. Tan, *Christian Mission among the Peoples of Asia* (Maryknoll, NY: Orbis, 2014).

23. Amanda Porterfield, *Mary Lyon and the Mount Holyoke Missionaries* (New York: Oxford University Press, 1997); Dana L. Robert, *American Women in Mission: A Social History of Their Thought and Practice* (Macon, GA: Mercer University Press, 1997).

24. This subfield is deserving of an extended bibliographic essay; the closest to such, though limited mainly to American women missionaries, is Barbara Reeves-Ellington, "Women, Protestant Missions, and American Cultural Expansion, 1800 to 1938: A Historiographical Sketch," *Social Sciences and Missions* 24 (2011): 190–206. Important studies include Margaret Jolly, *Women of the Place: Kastom, Colonialism and Gender in Van-*

uatu (Reading: Harwood Academic Press, 1994); Catherine Brekus, *Strangers and Pilgrims: Female Preaching in America, 1740–1845* (Chapel Hill: University of North Carolina Press, 1998); Mary Taylor Huber and Nancy C. Lutkehaus, eds., *Gendered Missions: Women and Men in Missionary Discourse and Practice* (Ann Arbor: University of Michigan Press, 1999); Lisa Joy Pruitt, *Looking-Glass for Ladies: American Protestant Women and the Orient in the Nineteenth Century* (Macon, GA: Mercer University Press, 2005); Jon F. Sensbach, *Rebecca's Revival: Creating Black Christianity in the Atlantic World* (Cambridge, MA: Harvard University Press, 2006); Susan E. Smith, *Women in Mission: From the New Testament to Today* (Maryknoll, NY: Orbis, 2007); Karen K. Seat, *"Providence Has Freed Our Hands": Women's Missions and the American Encounter with Japan* (Syracuse: Syracuse University Press, 2008); Elizabeth E. Prevost, *Communion of Women: Missions and Gender in Colonial Africa and the British Metropole* (New York: Oxford University Press, 2010); Barbara Reeves-Ellington, Kathryn Kish Sklar, and Connie A. Shemo, eds., *Competing Kingdoms: Women, Mission, Nation, and the American Protestant Empire, 1812–1960* (Durham, NC: Duke University Press, 2010); Jennifer Thigpen, *Island Queens and Mission Wives: How Gender and Empire Remade Hawai'i's Pacific World* (Chapel Hill: University of North Carolina Press, 2014); and Conroy-Krutz, *Christian Imperialism*.

25. The preponderance of diverse topics confirms the interdisciplinary appeal of the new missionary history. The range of topics—in addition to those discussed outside of this note—in missionary history since 2007, even when limited to North American movements, is immense. For instance, indigeneity, imperialism, nationalism, identity, adaptation, democratization, statecraft, education, reverse missions, non-Western missionaries, Pentecostalism, and continental sites of the missionary encounter have all received serious attention in recent scholarly studies. Representative examples include Rachel M. Wheeler, *To Live upon Hope: Mohicans and Missionaries in the Eighteenth-Century Northeast* (Ithaca, NY: Cornell University Press, 2008); Ian R. Tyrrell, *Reforming the World: The Creation of America's Moral Empire* (Princeton: Princeton University Press, 2010); Derek Chang, *Citizens of a Christian Nation: Evangelical Missions and the Problem of Race in the Nineteenth Century* (Philadelphia: University of Pennsylvania Press, 2010); Sarah E. Ruble, *Gospel of Freedom and Power: Protestant Missionaries in American Culture after World War II* (Chapel Hill: University of North Carolina Press, 2012); Hilary E. Wyss, *English Letters and Indian Literacies: Reading, Writing, and New England Missionary Schools, 1750–1830* (Philadelphia: University of Pennsylvania Press, 2012); Rebecca Y. Kim, *Spirit Moves West: Korean Missionaries in America* (New York: Oxford University Press, 2015); and Allan Anderson, *To the Ends of the Earth: Pentecostalism and the Transformation of World Christianity* (New York: Oxford University Press, 2013).

26. Hans-Lukas Kieser, *Nearest East: American Millennialism and Mission to the Middle East* (Philadelphia: Temple University Press, 2010).

27. Ussama Makdisi, *Artillery of Heaven: American Missionaries and the Failed Conversion of the Middle East* (Ithaca, NY: Cornell University Press, 2008).

28. Dana L. Robert, "Forty Years of North American Missiology: A Brief Review," *International Bulletin of Missionary Research* 38, no. 1 (January 2014): 3–8.

29. Noll, "The Potential of Missiology," 106–123.

30. Robert, "Naming World Christianity."

31. Robert Eric Frykenberg and Brian Stanley, eds., *Studies in the History of Christian Missions*, 20 vols. (Grand Rapids, MI: William B. Eerdmans, 2000–2016); Peggy

Brock, James Grayson, and David Maxwell, eds., *Studies in Christian Mission*, 59 vols. (Leiden: Brill, 1990–2023).

32. The earliest extant revelation dates to 1828 but discusses the translation of the Book of Mormon; the first revelation to speak of preaching was dictated in February 1829 (Smith, "Revelation, February 1829 [D&C 4].")

33. On apocalyptic warnings, see Doctrine and Covenants 1, 29, 35, 60, 62 (hereafter "D&C"); on welcoming visitors and spiritual diversity, see D&C 46, 50, 52; on reasoning out of the Bible, see D&C 50, 68; on initiating converts, see D&C 22, 24; on ordaining priests and elders, see D&C 20, 42, 68, 107; on establishing branches, see D&C 20, 72, 107; on holding conferences, see D&C 20, 58; on relocating converts, see D&C 29, 42, 58, 61; on feet dusting, see D&C 24, 60, 99; on healings, see D&C 24; on exhorting repentance, see D&C 5, 18, 73; on publishing the revelations, see D&C 1, 67; on evangelizing with the Book of Mormon among Native American audiences, see D&C 3, 10, 30, 32. For manuscript sources of these sections of the Doctrine and Covenants, see "Sources behind the Doctrine and Covenants," JSP, https://www.josephsmithpapers.org/site/sources-behind-the-doctrine-and-covenants. >

34. Samuel Harrison Smith, Diary, October 15, 1832, MS 4213, CHL; Orson Hyde and Samuel H. Smith, Book of Commandments, Book A, Law and Covenants, c. 1832, MS 4583, CHL; Joseph F. Darowski, "Schools of the Prophets: An Early American Tradition," *Mormon Historical Studies* 9 (Spring 2008): 1–13.

35. Matthew C. Godfrey, Brenden W. Rensink, Alex D. Smith, Max H Parkin, and Alexander L. Baugh, eds., "Appendix 1: First Theological Lecture on Faith, circa January–May 1835; Historical Introduction," in *Documents, Volume 4: April 1834–September 1835*, vol. 4 of the Documents series of *The Joseph Smith Papers*, ed. Ronald K. Esplin and Matthew J. Grow (Salt Lake City: Church Historian's Press, 2016), 457–460.

36. See J. H. T. Kilpatrick, "A Plain Dialogue between Two Brethren, A. & B. of the Baptist Denomination by a Friend to Zion in Georgia" (Philadelphia: Baptist General Tract Society, 1833), reprinted as Tract No. 135 in *The Baptist Manual: A Selection from the Series of Publications of the Baptist General Tract Society, Designed for the Use of Families; And as an Exposition of the Distinguishing Sentiments of the Denomination* (Philadelphia: Tract Depository, 1835), 45–76; Anonymous, *The True Apostleship Not Modern; Or a Refutation of the Claims of the Churches Commonly Called "Irvingite," to an Apostleship and to Spiritual Gifts* (London: James Nisbet, 1838), 37–46.

37. Not to be confused with another mission undertaken by four men in 1830 "to the Lamanites." These four men were John P. Greene, Amos R. Orton, Lorenzo Young, and Phineas H. Young: Oliver Cowdery, clerk, March 7–8, 1835, in Minute Book 1, JSP, https://www.josephsmithpapers.org/paper-summary/minute-book-1/200.

38. Sidney Rigdon, "Prospectus for a New Paper, To Be Published at Kirtland, Geauga Co. Ohio, Called the Elders' Journal of the Church of Latter Day Saints," *The Latter Day Saints' Messenger and Advocate* 3, no. 11 (August 1837): 545–547.

39. Joseph Smith, "Recommendation for Orson Hyde, 6 April 1840," Documents series, JSP; Joseph Smith, "'Church History,' 1 March 1842," Documents series, JSP.

40. Richard H. Jackson, "Geography and Settlement in the Intermountain West: Creating an American Mecca," *Journal of the West* 33, no. 3 (July 1994): 22–34; Leonard J. Arrington, *Great Basin Kingdom: An Economic History of the Latter-day Saints, 1830–1900* (Lincoln, NE: University of Nebraska Press, 1958), 215–223.

41. Golding, "Mormon Mission in Concept and Practice."

42. Alvin R. Dyer, *Messages to the Missionary* (Frankfurt: Alvin R. Dyer, 1961); John A. Widtsoe, "The Missions of the Church," in *Priesthood and Church Government in the Church of Jesus Christ of Latter-day Saints* (Salt Lake City: Deseret Book, 1939), 336–349.

43. Reid L. Neilson, "The Nineteenth-Century Euro-American Mormon Missionary Model," in *Go Ye into All the World: The Growth and Development of Mormon Missionary Work*, ed. Reid L. Neilson and Fred E. Woods (Provo, UT: Religious Studies Center, 2012), 65–90.

44. David Golding, "Gender and Missionary Work," in *The Routledge Handbook on Mormonism and Gender*, ed. Amy Hoyt and Taylor G. Petrey (London: Routledge, 2020), 170–181.

45. See David J. Whittaker, "Mormon Missiology: An Introduction and Guide to the Sources," in *The Disciple as Witness: Essays on Latter-day Saint History and Doctrine in Honor of Richard Lloyd Anderson*, ed. Stephen D. Ricks, Donald W. Parry, and Andrew H. Hedges (Provo, UT: Foundation for Ancient Research and Mormon Studies, 2000), 459–538; Wilfried Decoo, "Expanding Research for the Expanding International Church," in *Directions for Mormon Studies in the Twenty-First Century*, ed. Patrick Q. Mason (Salt Lake City: University of Utah Press, 2016), 99–131.

46. Matthew McBride, "'Female Brethren': Gender Dynamics in a Newly Integrated Missionary Force, 1898–1915," *Journal of Mormon History* 44, no. 4 (2018): 40–67. See also Golding, "Gender and Missionary Work."

47. Gina Colvin and Joanna Brooks, eds., *Decolonizing Mormonism: Approaching a Postcolonial Zion* (Salt Lake City: University of Utah Press, 2018).

48. Christopher Cannon Jones, "'A Verry Poor Place for Our Doctrine': Religion and Race in the 1853 Mormon Mission to Jamaica," *Religion and American Culture* 31, no. 2 (Summer 2021): 262–295; Rachel Felt and Christopher Cannon Jones, "'The Religion Is Assailed by Most in the Country': A Letter from the First Mormon Converts in Jamaica, 1854," *Mormon Historical Studies* 20, no. 1 (Spring 2019): 111–127.

11. American Missionaries and the Struggle for Control of Christianity's Symbolic Capital

1. Peter Smith, "United Methodists Are Breaking Up in a Slow-Motion Schism," Associated Press (October 10, 2022); Mary-Jane Rubenstein, "An Anglican Crisis of Comparison: Intersections of Race, Gender, and Religious Authority, with Particular Reference to the Church of Nigeria," *Journal of the American Academy of Religion* 72, no. 2 (June 2004): 341–365; Michelle Boorstein, "Seventh-day Adventists Vote Against Female Ordination," *Washington Post* (July 8, 2015); 1 Corinthians 14:34–35.

2. This construction was popularized by the Scottish historian of missions, Andrew Walls, e.g., in his "Cross-Cultural Encounters and the Shift to World Christianity," *Journal of Presbyterian History* 81, no. 2 (Summer 2003): 112–116.

3. Galatians 3:28; E. Stanley Jones, *The Christ of the Indian Road* (New York: Abingdon Press, 1925), 18, 140.

4. For a study of multiculturalism as a movement similar to the classical liberal missionary project, see David A. Hollinger, *Postethnic America: Beyond Multiculturalism*, rev. ed. (New York: Basic Books, 2006).

5. For a study of the missionary project that highlights this liberalizing consequence of it, see David A. Hollinger, *Protestants Abroad: How Missionaries Tried to Change the World but Changed America* (Princeton, NJ: Princeton University Press, 2017).

6. Daniel J. Fleming, *Whither Bound in Missions* (New York: Association Press, 1925); for Frank Rawlinson's career, see Lian Xi, *The Conversion of Missionaries: Liberalism in American Protestant Missions in China, 1907–1932* (University Park: Pennsylvania State University Press, 1997), 59–94.

7. A capable overview of the development of the notion of "world religions" and the engagement of many Christians with Hinduism, Islam, and so on is Tomoko Masuzawa, *The Invention of World Religions: Or, How European Universalism Was Preserved in the Language of Pluralism* (Chicago: University of Chicago Press, 2005).

8. Elizabeth A. Clark, *The Fathers Refounded: Protestant Liberalism, Roman Catholic Modernism, and the Teaching of Ancient Christianity in Early Twentieth-Century America* (Philadelphia: University of Pennsylvania Press, 2019).

9. An excellent history of biblical scholarship from the earliest times through the early twentieth century, and extending even down to the most recent archaeological and philological discoveries, is John Barton, *A History of the Bible: The Story of the World's Most Influential Book* (New York: Viking, 2019).

10. Joel A. Carpenter, "Propagating the Faith," in *Earthen Vessels: American Evangelicals and Foreign Missions, 1880–1980*, ed. Joel A. Carpenter and Wilbert R. Shenk (Grand Rapids, MI: William B. Eerdmans, 1990), 126–127. For the exceptionally important case of John Leighton Stuart, see Yu-Ming Shaw, *An American Missionary in China: John Leighton Stuart and Chinese-American Relations* (Cambridge, MA: Harvard University Press, 1992), 71–72, 82–87.

11. The uncertainties about "indigenization" are a major theme of Hollinger, *Protestants Abroad*, esp. 72–75.

12. A pivotal work in enabling scholars to understand the ecumenical-evangelical divide as the "two-party system" of American Protestantism was Martin E. Marty, *Righteous Empire: The Protestant Experience in America* (New York: Harper and Row, 1970). A recent work documenting this divide in relation to the important oil industry of the United States and the varieties of political influence exercised by each side is Darren Dochuck, *Anointed with Oil: How Christianity and Crude Made Modern America* (New York: Basic Books, 2019).

13. Edmund Davison Soper, *The Philosophy of the Christian World Mission* (New York: Abingdon-Cokesbury Press, 1943); Harold Lindsell, *A Christian Philosophy of Missions* (Wheaton: Van Kampen Press, 1949).

14. David R. Swartz, *Moral Minority: The Evangelical Left in an Age of Conservatism* (Philadelphia: University of Pennsylvania Press, 2012), 80.

15. Cecil Northcott, "Renewal in Mission," *Christian Century*, August 21, 1968, 1042.

16. Rodger C. Bassham, *Mission Theology: 1948–1975, Years of Worldwide Creative Tension; Ecumenical, Evangelical, and Roman Catholic* (Eugene: Wipf and Stock, 1979), 240.

17. Grant Wacker, "Second Thoughts on the Great Commission: Liberal Protestants and Foreign Missions, 1890–1940," in Carpenter and Shenk, *Earthen Vessels*, esp. 298–300.

18. Molly Worthen, *Apostles of Reason: The Crisis of Authority in American Evangelicalism* (New York: Oxford University Press, 2014).

19. Philip Jenkins, *The New Christendom: The Coming of Global Christianity*, 3rd ed. (New York: Oxford University Press, 2011), 275. See also Richard Elphick, *The Equality of Believers: Protestant Missionaries and the Racial Politics of South Africa* (Charlottesville: University of Virginia Press, 2012), Brian Stanley, *Christianity in the Twentieth Century: A World History* (Princeton, NJ: Princeton University Press, 2018), and Robert Eric Frykenberg, *Christianity in India: From the Beginnings to the Present* (New York: Oxford University Press, 2008).

20. N. J. Demerath III, "Cultural Victory and Organizational Defeat in the Paradoxical Decline of Liberal Protestantism," *Journal for the Scientific Study of Religion* 34, no. 4 (December 1995): 458–469; Christian Smith and Patricia Snell, *Souls in Transition: The Religious and Spiritual Lives of Emerging Adults* (New York: Oxford University Press, 2009), 287; David A. Hollinger, "After Cloven Tongues of Fire: Ecumenical Protestantism and the Modern American Encounter with Diversity," *Journal of American History* 98, no. 1 (June 2011), esp. 46–49.

21. For an account of this incident and its public discussion, see Laurie Goodstein, "YouTube Videos Draw Attention to Palin's Faith," *New York Times*, October 24, 2008, https://www.nytimes.com/2008/10/25/us/politics/25faith.html.

22. Melani McAlister, *The Kingdom of God Has No Borders: A Global History of American Evangelicals* (New York: Oxford University Press, 2018).

23. I have developed this argument at greater length in David A. Hollinger, "Christianity and Its American Fate: Where History Interrogates Secularization Theory," in *The Worlds of American Intellectual History*, ed. Joel Isaac, James T. Kloppenberg, Michael O'Brien, and Jennifer Ratner-Rosenhagen (New York: Oxford University Press, 2016), 280–303.

24. Stanley, *Christianity in the Twentieth Century*, 366. Here I draw a critical review of Stanley's book: David A. Hollinger, "The Global South, Christianity, and Secularization: Insider and Outsider Perspectives," *Modern Intellectual History* 17, no. 3 (September 2020): 889–901.

25. For the Masowe, see Matthew Engelke, *A Problem of Presence: Beyond Scripture in an African Church* (Berkeley: University of California Press, 2007).

26. Mark A. Noll, David W. Babbington, and George M. Marsden, eds., *Evangelicals: Who They Have Been, Are Now, and Could Be* (Grand Rapids, MI: William B. Eerdmans, 2019); Pew Research Center, "Blacks: Religious Composition of Blacks," Religious Landscape Study (2014), https://www.pewresearch.org/religion/religious-landscape-study/racial-and-ethnic-composition/black.

27. Kristin Kobes Du Mez, *Jesus and John Wayne: How White Evangelicals Corrupted a Faith and Fractured a Nation* (New York: Liveright Publishing, 2020), 3.

28. For an interpretation of the history of Christianity in the United States showing that what counts as "Christian" always depends on who has the local franchise of the global Christian movement, see David A. Hollinger, *Christianity's American Fate: How Religion Became More Conservative and Society More Secular* (Princeton, NJ: Princeton University Press, 2022).

Index

Abbs, John, 28
Afrikaaners, 87
Aguilar, Antonio Alejo, 55
Alexander VI (pope), 10
American Board of Commissioners for Foreign Missions (ABCFM), 17–18, 23, 26, 30–31, 34–36, 38, 50; archives of, 26–27, 29–30, 32
Anderson, Rufus, 31
anticonversion laws, 41, 112–114
architecture, 76–78, 82, 85–86
Armenian-Ottoman conflict. *See* Ottoman Empire
Armenian relief, 35–44
Azarian, Stefano Pietro X., 39

Badger, Ralph, 86
Bannock, 54–55, 60
Bartholomew, Ronald E., 141
Bartlett, Shubael, 25
Barton, Clara, 39
Battelle, Louise, 21–22
Beardslee, Julius, 1–2
Bible reading, 127–128, 130–131
Bombay Guardian, 45, 51
Bombay Missionary Union, 50–51
"Branch of Love" (Cape Town), 80

caricatures, 70, 90–91
Catholic Armenians, 39
Christian Herald Armenian Relief Fund, 35–40
clothing, 74, 76
colonialism. *See* imperialism
Cook, Rachel, 60
cultural technologies, 124–130, 136
Cutler, Orville W., 69, 85

Daniels, William, 79–81
disaster relief, 95–96, 98–99, 102–103
discontinuity. *See* rupture

doctrine of discovery, 10, 12, 68–69
Dryden, John, 28–29
Duff, Alexander, 46
Dyer, Alvin R., 149

East India Company, 46
East India Mission (LDS), 46, 52
East India Mission (RLDS), 106, 111, 116, 121
ecumenical vs. evangelical views, 2–3, 96, 153, 158–161, 165
Edmo, Edward McCarey, 55, 60
education of missionaries, 23–24, 34, 118, 156–158, 160
Ellsworth, Miss, 22
Elwin, Verrier, 108
Endecott, John, 11
evangelical vs. ecumenical views. *See* ecumenical vs. evangelical views
Evarts, Jeremiah, 18

Farr, Aaron, 1–2, 7
Farrar, Cynthia, 24, 31
Findlay, Hugh, 45–49, 51–52
Fort Hall Indian Reservation, 54, 59–62
freedom of religion, 41–42, 112–113
Frost, Amelia J., 54, 59–60

Geddie, John, vii
Geller, Emmeline, 29
Global South, 96, 152–153, 161–163
governance, centralized vs. local, 117, 127, 132, 134, 137, 152, 158
Gowers, Alfred J. Jr., 88–89
Graffam, Lillian, 101–102
Graham, Annie Jane, 55
Graves, Mary, 31
Gregory, William, 27–28
Griffiths, David, 28
Grimké, Thomas Smith, 8
Guatemala earthquake (1976), 99–100

209

INDEX

Ham, assumed descent from, 72, 74
Harris, Paul, 79–80
Hawkins, Walter, 27–28
"heathen" lands and peoples, 8–14, 174–175n2
Hewlett, Emily Jones, 89
Hewlett, Franklin J., 85, 90
Hindu nationalism, 107, 111–112, 114–115
historiography, 145–147
"homecoming" vs. conversion, 115
Hübener, Helmuth, 123–126, 138
humanitarian service, 97–98, 100–101, 104

iconoclasm, 110
imperialism, 3, 14–15, 57, 68–69, 78–79, 82, 86, 96, 103–104, 112, 145–147, 154, 156, 158–159
India, 45–50, 52, 105–108, 154
indiginization, 107–108, 116–118

Jamaica, 1–2, 7
Jones, Alma T., 74–77, 79
Jones, E. Stanley, 154

Kimball, Abigail, 24–25
Kipper, Louisa S., 28–29

land and landscapes, 8–16, 81–82, 93, 112
language study, 47–48
literacy, 130–132, 137–138
Livingstone, David, 65, 69–70
Logan (Utah) Temple, 53–54
London Missionary Society (LMS), 127, 129–132; archives of, 27–29
Lyman, Francis M., 66

Mao Zedong, 130
Marathi, 46–47
marriage as factor in mission service, 21–22, 25, 28, 32–33
Mather, Cotton, 11
McMurray, W. Grant, 121
missiology, 107, 141–143, 147, 159; early absence of in Latter-day Saint practice, 141–144, 147–150; growing awareness of in Latter-day Saint practice, 149–151
Mitchell, John Murray, 46, 48
Mooneyham, W. Stanley, 101
Morse, Jedidiah, 13–16

Nash, Ermina, 17–18
Neff, Charles, 117–118
Nevado del Ruiz volcanic eruption (Columbia, 1985), 94–95

New Hebrides, vii
Nez Perce, 60
Niyogi Committee Report on Christian Missionary Activities, 113
nongovernmental organizations (NGOs) in quasi-ministry, 100–102, 191n57

orientalist missionaries, 46–50, 52
Ottoman Empire, 34–44, 103, 175n5

Padilla, C. René, 102–103
pagans. See "heathen" lands and peoples
photography, 67, 69, 74
pluralism, 145, 155
polygamy, 32–33, 51–52, 54–55, 118–120, 137–138, 149
Post, Flora, 24
Potter, William, 20–21
Price, Richard, 119–120

qualifications for mission work, 23–24, 144

race and racial hierarchies, 14–16, 57, 66, 71–72, 78–79, 81, 85, 135
Raika, Limpan, 105
railroad, 82, 85
Rhodes, Cecil, 86–88, 184–185n70
RLDS Reformation, 116–122
Robbins, James, 25
Robinson, Malcolm L., 91
Rogers, Orson M., 69–72
Root, Emily, 24
rupture, 106–107, 109–112, 116, 121–122

Sadler, Adeline, 24
Sangster, Margaret E., 37
Schnibbe, Karl-Heinz, 123
Scottish Enlightenment, 46
secularization, 138, 162
"sedentary" travel, 68, 79
self-governing congregations. See governance, centralized vs. local
sexuality, interracial, 28, 62
Sharp, June, 74, 79–81, 88
Sheehy, Howard "Bud," 121
Shoshone, 53, 55–56, 58–61
Simons, George W., 81
Smith, Judson, 38
Smith, Nicholas G., 79–80, 86
Smith, W. Wallace, 119, 121
Snow, Lorenzo, 45, 47
social service, 159–160, 191n57

Soras, 105–106, 108–111, 115, 118–120
South Africa, 66–67, 69–70, 72, 79, 81–82, 85–88
Stanley, Henry Morton, 70
Steed, Henry Lee, 82
Strong, Josiah, 82
Swan, William, 23–24

Tanner, Joseph M., 91–92
Thatcher, Hannah, 22–23
"third church," 163–164
Thrall, Cynthia, 25–26
transformation of center by mission periphery, 135, 142
travel narratives, 68

True Jesus Church, 127, 132–134
Turkey. *See* Ottoman Empire

Vitebsky, Piers, 108–109

Ware, Dr., 1
western imagination, 69
Widtsoe, John A., 149
Wilson, John, 46
women in mission work, 18–27, 29–33, 67, 89, 137, 146
world religions, 48–50, 156–157

Young, Levi Edgar, 91
Yun Daiying, 130

About the Authors

David Golding is a historian in the Church History Department of the Church of Jesus Christ of Latter-day Saints. He has contributed chapters on Mormon mission history to *World Religions and Their Missions* and *The Routledge Handbook of Mormonism and Gender*. He serves as a general editor of the Restoration Scripture Critical Editions Project.

Christopher Cannon Jones is Assistant Professor of History at Brigham Young University and editor of the *Journal of Mormon History*. His scholarship focuses on the intersections of race, religion, and slavery in early America and the Atlantic world and has been published in *Religion & American History*, the *Journal of Southern Religion*, and the *Journal of Mormon History*, as well as *A Companion to American Religious History* and *American Examples: New Conversations about Religion, Volume Two*.

Laurie F. Maffly-Kipp is the Archer Alexander Distinguished Professor of Religion and Politics at Washington University in St. Louis. Her scholarly works include studies of Mormonism in the American West and Pacific worlds and African American religious history.

Kathryn Gin Lum is Associate Professor of Religious Studies in collaboration with the Center for Comparative Studies in Race and Ethnicity and History (by courtesy) at Stanford University. She is the author of *Heathen: Religion and Race in American History* and *Damned Nation: Hell in America from the Revolution to Reconstruction* and the coeditor with Paul Harvey of *The Oxford Handbook of Religion and Race in American History*.

Emily Conroy-Krutz is the author of *Christian Imperialism: Converting the World in the Early American Republic* and *Missionary Diplomacy: Religion and Nineteenth-Century American Foreign Relations*. She teaches at Michigan State University.

Devrim Ümit is a transnational historian who specializes in American Protestant missionaries in the late Ottoman era. She holds an MA degree from the University of Nebraska–Lincoln and MPhil and PhD degrees from Columbia University. She was the founding chair of the Department of International

Relations at Karabuk University in 2011, a David M. Stone Fellow at Yale University in 2019, and a Katherine F. Pantzer Jr. Fellow at Harvard University in 2022 and 2023. She is preparing for book publication her dissertation titled "The American Protestant Missionary Network in Late Ottoman Turkey, 1876–1914: Political and Cultural Reflections of the Encounter."

Taunalyn Ford is a global women's history specialist in the Church History Department of the Church of Jesus Christ of Latter-day Saints. She received her BA and MA degrees at Brigham Young University and her PhD in the history of Christianity and religions of North America at Claremont Graduate University. She was a postdoctoral fellow at the Neal A. Maxwell Institute for Religious Scholarship at Brigham Young University, where she teaches as an adjunct professor of religion.

Amanda Hendrix-Komoto is an assistant professor at Montana State University, where she researches the intersections of religion, race, and colonialism in the American West. She is the author of *Imperial Zions: Religion, Race, and the Family in the American West*.

Jeffrey G. Cannon is a research associate at the Neal A. Maxwell Institute for Religious Scholarship at Brigham Young University, where his research focuses on local manifestations of Christianity and their relationship to the worldwide church. He has a PhD in world Christianity from the University of Edinburgh, an MA in church history and church polity from the University of Pretoria, and a BA in political science from Brigham Young University, where he also completed a minor in African studies.

Lauren F. Turek is Associate Professor of History at Trinity University. She is the author of *To Bring the Good News to All Nations: Evangelical Influence on Human Rights and U.S. Foreign Relations*. Her articles on religion in American politics and foreign relations have appeared in *Diplomatic History*, the *Journal of American Studies*, and *Religions*. She has contributed chapters to a number of edited volumes and is currently coediting with Cara Burnidge *The Routledge History of Religion and Politics in the United States since 1775*.

David J. Howlett is a visiting assistant professor of religion at Smith College. He is the author of the award-winning *Kirtland Temple: The Biography of a Shared Mormon Sacred Space* and coauthor with John Charles Duffy of *Mormonism: The Basics*.

Melissa Wei-Tsing Inouye is a senior lecturer in Asian studies at the University of Auckland and a historian in the Church History Department of the Church of Jesus Christ of Latter-day Saints. She specializes in the history of Christianity in China and is the author of *China and the True Jesus: Charisma and Organization in a Chinese Christian Church*.

ABOUT THE AUTHORS

David A. Hollinger is Preston Hotchkis Professor of History Emeritus at the University of California, Berkeley. His books include *Christianity's American Fate, Protestants Abroad*, and *After Cloven Tongues of Fire*. He is an elected member of the American Academy of Arts and Sciences and of the American Philosophical Society.

www.ingramcontent.com/pod-product-compliance
Lightning Source LLC
Chambersburg PA
CBHW020814230426
43666CB00007B/1006